ACCOUNTING
and
BUSINESS FLUCTUATIONS

ACCOUNTING and BUSINESS FLUCTUATIONS

DELMAS D. RAY

University of Florida Press
Gainesville - 1960

A University of Florida Press Book

Library of Congress Catalog Card Number 60-6718

Printed by The H. & W. B. Drew Company
Jacksonville, Florida

Preface

SOME OF THE BASIC IDEAS for this book occurred to the author when he was writing a term paper on a limited phase of the same subject while a graduate student at The University of Chicago. In later years, when accounting as an accentuating factor in business fluctuations was mentioned to any of his colleagues as a possible topic for investigation, however, the predominant reaction was: "Are there actually people who believe that accounting methods affect business fluctuations?" Because of this oft-expressed incredulousness the introductory chapter refers briefly to some of the writers who, in historical perspective, would presumably have answered the above question in the affirmative.

Throughout the discussion in the next three chapters also, much evidence is presented to show that over the years many writers have thought that accounting did affect business fluctuations via investment decisions and the points of contact with business cycle theory have been highlighted. Although no one of these writers has presented a comprehensive treatise, judged by modern standards, yet the cumulative writings, grubbed out of the literature, given certain inherent assumptions, do add up to a fairly sizable body of business cycle theory. In this earlier discussion much abstraction from the institutional framework has taken place.

In the fifth chapter the inherent assumptions on which the theoretical structure of the earlier chapters is built are examined. Certain alternative assumptions underlying investment behavior are considered and the remaining pieces of the present-day institutional framework have been replaced—especially changing technology and a consideration of the modifications necessary when the maximization of profits after income taxes is assumed to be the goal of economic behavior. A re-examination of some of the arguments presented in the earlier chapters is now made in the light of a more realistic treatment.

While chapters two to five deal primarily with the relationship of accounting methods to the investment function, chapters six and seven are chiefly concerned with the relation of accounting methodology to variations in consumption expenditures. These latter chapters are concerned principally with the maladjustment of the cost-price structure which was emphasized by earlier cycle theorists. Although investment and consumption expenditures have been artificially separated for individual consideration, they are interrelated.

There is a multiplicity of explanations of the causes of business fluctuations and, therefore, any explanation of *the* cause is suspect. It has become apparent in recent years that the economic system is so complex and that past business fluctuations have varied so widely in both amplitude and duration that no one theory nor one group of theories is capable of completely explaining their occurrence. The eclectic viewpoint adopted in the following chapters, while acknowledging the uniqueness of each cycle, also recognizes certain characteristics that are common to most: the relatively greater fluctuations in the production of durable goods, the "waves of optimism and pessimism," the expansion and contraction of bank credit, and the dissimilar movements of costs and prices.

The term "business fluctuations" used in the title was chosen over "cycles" for three reasons: (1) Each so-called cycle has unique features; (2) the different movements are so interrelated that it is impossible to isolate completely the Juglars and Kitchins from the other fluctuations in a time series; and (3) in the discussion of certain aspects of depreciation, the discussion will encompass a time span longer than that covered by the typical business "cycle" as defined by Wesley C. Mitchell in his *Business Cycles: The Problem and Its Setting* in 1927.

The author wishes to express his indebtedness to all those who have assisted in the preparation of this book in its various stages. The advice and criticism given by these individuals were invaluable in the preparation of the manuscript. He is especially indebted to the following faculty members of the College of Business Administration of the University of Florida who have offered helpful suggestions in the later stages of preparation of the manuscript: Dr. Ralph H. Blodgett, Dr. Allen M.

Sievers, and Dr. Roy L. Lassiter, Jr., all of the Department of Economics, and to Dr. Harvey T. Deinzer of the Department of Accounting. He is also grateful to Dr. Felix Muehlner of the Bureau of Economic and Business Research of the University of Florida for assistance in translating portions of Fritz Schmidt's "Die Industriekonjunktur—ein Rechenfehler!"

Extensive reference has been made to many sources in assembling the materials. Every attempt has been made to give credit to the various authors of this source material in the numerous footnotes and in the bibliography. Permission to quote copyrighted material is gratefully acknowledged to publishers as follows: Harvard University Press: "Profit Theory—Where Do We Go from Here?", *The Quarterly Journal of Economics,* by Peter L. Bernstein; "Monopoly Power and Price Rigidities," *The Quarterly Journal of Economics,* by J. K. Galbraith; *The Investment Decision: An Empirical Study,* by John R. Meyer and Edwin Kuh. The University of Chicago Press: *The Dynamics of Business Cycles,* by Jan Tinbergen and J. J. Polak; *Studies in the Economics of Overhead Costs,* by John Maurice Clark; "A Reconstruction of the Marginal Productivity Theory," *The Journal of Political Economy,* by M. W. Reder.

D. D. R.

Gainesville, Florida
July, 1960

Contents

List of Tables

Chapter I

Introduction

An analysis of a time series relating to economic activity, such as the gross national product or the number of people employed, reveals substantial fluctuations. While "crises" in the sense of serious trade disturbances are just as old as trade itself, business fluctuations, as we know them, had to await what has been referred to as a "business economy." Among the many theories which have been advanced as explanations of these fluctuations is a relatively obscure one which assigns to accounting methodology a rather prominent role.

In 1927, Dr. Fritz Schmidt, Professor of Business Administration, University of Frankfort, wrote a series of three articles published under the title of "Die Industriekonjunktur—ein Rechenfehler!" (The Business Cycle—An Error in Calculation). A large part of these articles was concerned with the causes of business fluctuations which Professor Schmidt attributed to a lack of stability in the monetary unit which must serve both as a store of value and as a medium of exchange. He puts the blame largely on accounting methods which do not reflect these changes in value separate from operating profits.[1] In periods of rising prices entrepreneurs, relying on accounting information, count rises in the prices of goods between the date of purchase and the date of sale as income rather than as being a part of national wealth. Since the entrepreneur thinks that his profits are greater than they actually are, an *excessive* demand for goods ensues on his part which causes further increases in prices, accompanied by an expansion in productive facili-

1. Fritz Schmidt, "Die Industriekonjunktur—ein Rechenfehler!" *Zeitschrift für Betriebswirtschaft*, 2. Sonderheft 1927, p. 72.

ties. In the period of falling prices which follows this period of expansion, historical costs are mistakenly used for the lower replacement costs and the *apparent* income of the businessman is reduced, which in turn, causes a further reduction in his demand for goods. In a later article Schmidt[2] came even closer to assigning the principal cause of business cycles to wrong methods of accounting: "It is certain that the development of business cycles, as far as general economic conditions are their causes, would be practically obviated if wrong accounting methods, basing depreciation on original costs, could be eliminated." Although he says that recovery is sure to follow hard times, "between the sharp crisis and this recovery lies one or several years of economic misery and this largely, and perhaps, only, as a result of wrong calculation."

Furthermore, Schmidt thought that accounting methods tended to perpetuate fluctuations in business activity. Speaking of the practice of charging past costs to production during the downswing, Schmidt said:

> Production is stagnating, trade is dull, although accounting at present-day cost prices would show that it is possible to make profits on each sale above the cost value of the selling day. The consequences furthermore are unemployment, and failures and liquidations, which could often be avoided by right accounting. . . . Each newly occurring price fluctuation leads by way of the accounting of apparent profits and apparent losses to new frictions in the economic equilibrium.[3]

It was not by accident that a German writer on business cycles gave a central role to the method of calculating business profits. In the years following World War I, Germany experienced the most devastating inflation of any modern industrial nation. From January, 1914, to November, 1923, the German mark depreciated to the point where a 1923 mark was worth only one-trillionth of a 1914 mark,[4] and in November, 1923, the paper mark exchanged at the rate of 4,200,000,000,000 to the dollar.[5] This extreme inflation made accounting information obtained by orthodox methods all but useless. That Schmidt believed, however, that accounting methodology was distorting even in a more moderate inflation is shown by these words:

2. "The Basis of Depreciation Charges," *Harvard Business Review,* April, 1930, pp. 262 and 263.
3. "The Valuation of Fixed Assets in Financial Statements," *Proceedings of the International Congress on Accounting,* 1929, p. 17.
4. Henry W. Sweeney, "Effects of Inflation on German Accounting," *The Journal of Accountancy,* March, 1927, p. 180.
5. Carl T. Schmidt, *German Business Cycles 1914-1933,* p. 11.

Even in the United States where the gold standard has been upheld, there was between the years 1914 and 1920, a strong rise of selling and cost prices. It seems certain that most of the showing of these was a false prosperity and nothing but the result of wrong accounting.[6]

While Schmidt appears to be the first writer to attempt to incorporate the effects of accounting techniques into business cycle theory, it had already been recognized that the assumption of a stable monetary unit caused distortion in accounting statements during periods of shifting price levels. In the United States before World War I, arguments over changing price levels and their effect upon profit determination were largely academic due to the stability of the prewar price level. As a result of these price changes, in the years immediately following this war, traditional accounting methods came under fire by businessmen, economists, and even some accountants.[7]

Wesley C. Mitchell, in an address in January, 1923, placed a certain amount of responsibility for controlling business fluctuations on accountants.[8] "But your profession has an especially important part to play in guiding business men, because you are especially concerned with ascertaining the facts that are of crucial importance in guiding their decisions—the facts relative to profits." In the same speech Mitchell pointed out the need for "men of trained minds conversant with actual business experience [to study business cycles]. Need I say that accountants constitute such a group and that the possession of these qualities confers upon them an obligation to take an active share in the effort to control the business cycle?"

A. C. Littleton, in an address before the American Association of University Instructors in Accounting in December, 1924, also discussed the relation of accounting to the business cycle. His plea was for accountants to learn about the business cycle in order to advise their clients how to adapt themselves to it. He mentioned "normal burden" and "normal inventory" as adaptations to the cycle. He spoke hopefully: "Perhaps they [accountants] may eventually acquire some degree of

6. Fritz Schmidt, "Is Appreciation Profit?" *The Accounting Review,* December, 1931, p. 290.

7. See Livingston Middleditch, Jr., "Should Accounts Reflect the Changing Value of the Dollar?" *The Journal of Accountancy,* February, 1918, pp. 114-120; John Bauer, "Renewal Costs and Business Profits in Relation to Rising Prices," *The Journal of Accountancy,* December, 1919, pp. 413-419; W. A. Paton, "Depreciation, Appreciation and Productive Capacity," *The Journal of Accountancy,* July, 1920, pp. 1-11.

8. "Accountants and Economics with Reference to the Business Cycle," *The Journal of Accountancy,* March, 1923, pp. 161-171.

skill in anticipating coming changes; and when that time comes for any considerable number, the time will be at hand when a material stabilization of the courses of business may be expected as a result."[9]

While no writer since Schmidt has written as complete a treatise on the subject,[10] the idea that accounting methodology accentuates business fluctuations has persisted in accounting and economic literature down to the present time.[11] There are, to be sure, some protests against the viewpoint that accounting methods accentuate business fluctuations.[12] The writers[13] on the subject, with the exception of Schmidt, did not insist that accounting methodology *caused* fluctuations, but held that it did accentuate them. Walter Froehlich, for example, states:

> The analysis of different income concepts held by enterprisers and the influence on reinvestment must not and does not imply that cycles are caused by employing certain concepts. . . . In fact, such a theory must presuppose that, for reasons other than the influence of 'false accounting', prices rise and, therefore, accounting might be misleading.

John B. Canning expresses a similar viewpoint: "Erratic accounting

9. "The Relation of Accounting to the Business Cycle," *Papers and Proceedings of the Ninth Annual Meeting of the American Association of University Instructors in Accounting,* pp. 115 f.

10. K. Lacey, *Profit Measurement and Price Changes,* might be considered a possible exception to this statement. However, only the first 40 pages (out of a total of 125) of Lacey's book deal with the possible effects of accounting on business fluctuations. The remainder of the book deals with suggested reforms, both for improving the reporting of profits and for income taxation.

11. See, for example: John B. Canning, "A Certain Erratic Tendency in Accountants' Income Procedure," *Econometrica,* I (1933), 52-62; Norman S. Buchanan, *The Economics of Corporate Enterprise,* pp. 225-230; Norman S. Buchanan, "Toward a Theory of Fluctuations in Business Profits," *The American Economic Review,* December, 1941, pp. 731-753; Edwin G. Nourse, *Price Making in a Democracy,* especially pp. 328 ff., 372, 383; K. Lacey, "Profit Measurement and the Trade Cycle," *The Economic Journal,* December, 1947, pp. 456-474; R. A. Gordon, "Short-Period Price Determination in Theory and Practice," *The American Economic Review,* June, 1948, pp. 265-288; Kenneth Boulding, *Economic Analysis,* p. 803; Walter Adams, "Accounting Practices and the Business Cycle," *The Journal of Business,* April, 1949, pp. 119-133; and W. T. Baxter, "The Accountant's Contribution to the Trade Cycle," *Economica,* May, 1955, pp. 99-112.

12. Two of the best that have come to the author's attention are: H. W. Singer, "Profit Measurement and the Trade Cycle," *The Economic Journal,* December, 1948, pp. 594-596; and A. R. Prest, "Replacement Cost Depreciation," *Accounting Research,* I (November, 1948 - July, 1950) 385-402.

13. See Walter Froehlich, "The Role of Income Determination in Reinvestment and Investment," *The American Economic Review,* March, 1948, p. 84; and Canning, *op. cit.,* p. 61.

does not generate business cycles, but, given an external generating impetus, belief in the accountants' figures leads to action that must increase the amplitude of the business cycle swings."

It is believed by the writer that the discussion of the relationship of accounting methods to business fluctuations as found in the literature is very naive as to assumptions, and that the treatment of the subject is inadequate. The reasoning is mainly a priori and practically no effort has been made to test the theories in the "real world." Scarcely any of the proponents of the theories have taken into consideration the institutional framework within which present-day business operates. Little attention has been given, for example, to the question of whether the market structure, in which businesses large enough to affect the cycle operate, would make a difference in evaluating the effect of accounting methodology on the business cycle. Likewise, little attention has been given to the relative importance of the two determinants of net profit (sales and expenses) with respect to investment decisions and, in turn, the influence of the accountant in determining the magnitude of these two determinants.[14]

The writers have made practically no effort to state the inherent assumptions underlying their theories, much less to ask if these assumptions are realistic within the present institutional framework of the economy. Fact and fancy are so interwoven as to be indistinguishable. As a result, later writers have taken for granted that accounting methods do accentuate the cycle instead of merely accepting it as an hypothesis. This is well illustrated by the following quotation: "The first-in first-out method of charging operations for the cost of short-term inventories and for the allocations of longer term plant and equipment has greatly added to the height of the 'booms' and to the depth of the 'busts.' "[15]

In the following chapters, an inquiry into this theory that accounting accentuates business fluctuations will be made. It will be demonstrated how accounting *could* theoretically affect business fluctuations by determining how its methodology fits into present-day business cycle theory. The assumptions inherent in the theory will be ascertained and the modern institutional framework in which business operates will be examined in an effort to judge whether the assumptions appear to be in accord with the facts. More specifically, the object will be to determine

14. For a notable exception to the last two statements, see Norman S. Buchanan, "Anticipations and Industrial Investment Decisions," *The American Economic Review, Supplement No. 1*, March, 1942, pp. 141-155.

15. Paul Grady, "Accounting for Fixed Assets and Their Amortization," *The Accounting Review*, January, 1950, p. 17.

whether accounting, as generally practiced, is capable—given certain assumptions—of affecting business decisions relative to investment, dividend policy, wages, and prices in such a way as to accentuate business fluctuations on both the upswing and the downswing, as is rather frequently alleged, and to determine whether the underlying assumptions seem realistic, given the institutional framework within which modern business operates. In addition, an attempt will be made to determine whether there have been changes since Schmidt's day in the institutional arrangement or in accounting techniques that would tend to modify accounting methodology as an accentuating factor in business fluctuations. Schmidt's writings were completed prior to the development of national income accounting and, hence, before the better knowledge of the economy and the interrelationships of its various parts.

It may be well to state what is not to be examined. No attempt will be made to determine the causes of business fluctuations, and, therefore, the turning points per se will not be considered. On the cumulative processes of expansion and contraction there is remarkable accord. As one writer has stated: "However much economists may quarrel about the forces determining the 'turning points' of the cycle, i.e., crisis and recovery, there exists today fairly wide agreement that the intermediate periods of the cycle, i.e., prosperity and depression, are characterized by self-reënforcing processes of expansion and contraction of employment and output."[16] Furthermore, it should be understood that the writer is neither advocating nor condemning conventional accounting methods. No reforms of accounting practices are to be suggested. Neither is he attempting to state whether economic stability is itself a worthy goal since "economic stability is but one among a number of widely accepted objectives for social policy."[17]

Since accounting methodology is dealt with as a reinforcing factor, endogenous rather than exogenous theories of business fluctuations will receive primary emphasis. Although the incentives of businessmen in making investment decisions will be dealt with at some length, and even though these incentives are, in part, noneconomic (psychological), no psychological theory of the cycle will be adopted. Those who suggest that accounting methodology accentuates the cycle, however, do put

16. L. M. Lachmann, "Investment and Costs of Production," *The American Economic Review,* September, 1938, p. 469.

17. American Economic Association, "The Problem of Economic Instability," A Report Prepared by a Subcommittee of the Committee on Public Issues, *The American Economic Review,* XL (1950), 506. The Committee mentions three other objectives, viz., "peace, progress, and freedom," *ibid.*

emphasis on the psychological factors, as is shown by the following words: "It would seem that the maintenance of a relatively stable level of periodic income might do much to reduce the effect of 'waves of optimism and pessimism' on the level of business activity."[18] The present author, however, believes that psychological factors alone are not sufficient to explain business fluctuations.

Since business accounting is in monetary terms, the discussion must perforce be largely in these terms, but this is not to say that the writer believes that the cycle is only a monetary phenomenon. The concept of the cycle which is adopted is an eclectic one. It would be consistent with this school of thought to assume, for example, that prospects for profit were a result of new inventions and improved production techniques put into use by swarms of innovators, that they were a result of the credit policies of the commercial banking system, or to assume that at different times they were the result of a combination of these and other forces.

Since the central purpose is to evaluate an accentuating factor in business fluctuations, we need to know what is alleged to be accentuated. What measures, or what set of indicators, will be studied? Is it to be physical production, prices, or employment? Prior to the recession of 1957-1958, all these indicators, in general, have tended to move up and down together as indicated by Alvin H. Hansen:

> The fluctuations of cyclical movements may be characterized in terms of either money income, real income (the output of material and services), or employment. . . . Cyclically . . . the three move more or less in consonance, though the trend movement is likely to differ considerably under varying circumstances . . . frequently in discussing economic fluctuations or cyclical movements all three may be regarded without serious error as moving together, whether in the upswing or in the downswing.[19]

Therefore, reference may be made to any or all of the usual indicators in characterizing business fluctuations.

Since, at a given time, the level of income and employment depends upon the total amount spent upon new goods and services, any discussion of an accentuating factor in business fluctuations must be in terms of its effect on aggregate demand. Fortunately, we now have the national income statistics to quantify many of the relationships with which

18. Samuel R. Hepworth, "Smoothing Periodic Income," *The Accounting Review,* January, 1953, p. 34.

19. *Fiscal Policy and Business Cycles,* pp. 14 f.

TABLE 1
GROSS NATIONAL PRODUCT AND THE PERCENTAGE DISTRIBUTION OF ITS COMPONENTS
1929-1957

Year	Gross National Product		Personal Consumption Expenditures		Gross Private Domestic Investment		Net Foreign Investment		Government Expenditures	
	Amount Millions of Dollars	Per Cent	Amount Millions of Dollars	Per Cent	Amount Millions of Dollars	Per Cent	Amount Millions of Dollars	Per Cent	Millions of Amount Dollars	Per Cent
1929	104,436	100	78,952	75.6	16,231	15.5	771	.7	8,482	8.1
1930	91,105	100	70,968	77.9	10,265	11.3	690	.8	9,182	10.1
1931	76,271	100	61,333	80.4	5,523	7.2	197	.3	9,218	12.1
1932	58,466	100	49,306	84.3	913	1.6	169	.3	8,078	13.8
1933	55,964	100	46,392	82.9	1,391	2.5	150	.3	8,031	14.3
1934	64,975	100	51,894	79.9	2,888	4.4	429	.7	9,764	15.0
1935	72,502	100	56,289	77.6	6,277	8.7	—54	—.1	9,990	13.8
1936	82,743	100	62,616	75.7	8,404	10.2	—93	—.1	11,816	14.3
1937	90,780	100	67,259	74.1	11,747	12.9	62	.1	11,712	12.9
1938	85,227	100	64,641	75.8	6,661	7.8	1,109	1.3	12,816	15.0
1939	91,095	100	67,578	74.2	9,309	10.2	888	1.0	13,320	14.6
1940	100,618	100	71,881	71.4	13,155	13.1	1,509	1.5	14,073	14.0
1941	125,822	100	81,875	65.1	18,072	14.4	1,124	.9	24,751	19.7
1942	159,133	100	89,748	56.4	9,875	6.2	—207	—.1	59,717	37.5
1943	192,513	100	100,541	52.2	5,600	2.9	—2,245	—1.2	88,617	46.0
1944	211,393	100	109,833	52.0	7,130	3.4	—2,099	—1.0	96,529	45.7
1945	213,558	100	121,699	57.0	10,430	4.9	—1,438	—.7	82,867	38.8
1946	210,663	100	147,109	69.8	28,140	13.4	4,595	2.2	30,819	14.6
1947	234,289	100	165,409	70.6	31,459	13.4	8,917	3.8	28,504	12.2
1948	259,426	100	178,313	68.7	43,087	16.6	1,929	.7	36,097	13.9
1949	258,054	100	181,158	70.2	32,977	12.7	522	.2	43,397	16.8
1950	284,599	100	195,013	68.5	49,970	17.6	—2,204	—.8	41,820	14.7
1951	328,975	100	209,805	63.8	56,334	17.1	229	.1	62,607	19.0
1952	346,999	100	219,774	63.3	49,863	14.4	—160	*	77,522	22.3
1953	365,385	100	232,649	63.7	50,340	13.8	—2,017	—.6	84,413	23.1
1954	363,112	100	238,025	65.6	48,872	13.5	—401	—.1	76,616	21.1
1955	397,469	100	256,940	64.6	63,843	16.1	—420	—.1	77,106	19.4
1956	419,214	100	269,400	64.3	68,180	16.3	1,376	.3	80,258	19.1
1957	440,328	100	284,442	64.6	65,292	14.8	3,462	.8	87,132	19.8

Source: Dollar figures from U.S. Department of Commerce, Office of Business Economics, *Survey of Current Business*, July, 1958, pp. 4 f.

*Less than .1 per cent.

this study is concerned. Of the four components of gross national product—gross private domestic investment, personal consumption expenditures, government purchases of goods and services, and net foreign investment—the effect of accounting on the first two only is considered. Net foreign investment is ignored because of its small size ($3.5 billion in 1957 out of a gross national product of $440.3 billion). (See Table 1.) Government expenditures are largely ignored, not because of their size ($87.1 billion in 1957), but because it is felt that these expenditures are not materially influenced by the accounting policies of business firms. It may be argued, however, that accounting influences the amount of income which business firms report, which in turn influences the amount of income taxes collected by governments, which influences government spending. However, our experience over the last twenty-five years, especially, has demonstrated that the spending of the national government, at least, is not dependent in any great degree upon currently collected taxes.

While the effect of accounting methodology on business fluctuations must often run in macroeconomic terms, much of the discussion will also be in microeconomic terms since considerable attention will be directed to investment behavior and its motivation at the individual firm level. In studying business behavior at the firm level, the emphasis will be on the large corporation for two reasons: (1) better information is available for the large corporation, and (2) the large corporation does the lion's share of the business of the country. One-half of the free world's industrial output is produced by the United States, and one-half of the United States output, in turn, is produced by the five hundred largest corporations (in terms of sales) in the United States.[20] These five hundred corporations account for two-thirds of the net earnings of all United States industrial firms and employ 44 per cent of the industrial work force.

Much of the material presented will be qualitative in nature, the evidence presented will many times be indirect, and the propositions will, therefore, not be subject to direct "proof." Opinions of economic specialists who have spent a considerable part of their lives studying specific points must be relied on rather heavily. However, whenever possible the relationships will be expressed quantitatively.

Very frequently the lack of knowledge of how investment decisions are really made has been pointed out as the principal gaping hole in the empirical backdrop against which the theories of the cycle may be

20. "Box Score of Business Bigness," *Fortune,* July, 1955, p. 96.

tested. The Temporary National Economic Committee in 1941 stated that "little is known of the criteria that in day-to-day business operations govern investment decisions."[21] While some of the gaps have been filled in since, the picture is far from complete as a later publication has emphasized: "Many economic and political factors, general and specific, tend to affect investment decisions. Theories abound: Classical, Keynesian, anti-Keynesian, etc. Basically, there is an inadequacy of complete statistical evidence for most of them."[22]

While the author is cognizant of the fact that the methods used and the conclusions drawn may not be as clear-cut as the scientist would wish, he feels, however, that "it is better to be vaguely right than precisely wrong."[23]

21. Oscar L. Altman, *Saving, Investment, and National Income,* Temporary National Economic Committee Monograph No. 37, p. 2.

22. U.S. Congress, Staff of the Subcommittee on Investment, Joint Committee on the Economic Report, *Factors Affecting Volume and Stability of Private Investment,* Senate Document No. 232, 81st Cong., 2d Sess., pp. 3 ff.

23. Professor Wildon Carr, quoted by G. F. Shove in "The Place of Marshall's Principles in the Development of Economic Theory," *The Economic Journal,* December, 1942, p. 323.

Chapter II

Accountants' Misstatement of Profits as a Reinforcing Factor

ANY INQUIRY into the relationship of accounting methodology to business fluctuations is essentially a study of its relationship to changes in the level of gross national product (or of national income). In modern business cycle theory, discussion of the causes of these changes in the level of gross national product runs largely in terms of the relationship between savings and investment. Whenever planned savings exceed planned investment, then gross national product will tend to fall below its present level and whenever planned investment exceeds planned savings, gross national product will tend to rise above its present level. Thus an attempt by any sector of the economy to change either current savings or current investment will tend to change the level of the gross national product. This viewpoint seems to have been generally accepted, as is exemplified by these words: "*From the point of view of income determination,* the principle that at any given level of aggregate income investors collectively may want and attempt to invest more (or less) than savers collectively want to save, with a stimulating (or retarding) effect on the economy, is generally accepted and is an important part of many theories of economic fluctuations."[1]

Business Investment as the Key Factor

Domestic investment expenditures have been the most volatile of the

1. Irwin Friend and Vito Natrella, *Individuals' Saving,* pp. 7 f.

four types of expenditures. (See Table 1.) Domestic investment fell from 15.5 per cent of gross national product in 1929 to 1.6 per cent in 1932. Consumption expenditures, on the other hand, increased from 75.6 per cent in 1929 to 84.3 per cent in 1932. In absolute terms consumption expenditures and investment expenditures tend, in general, to rise and fall together. Both consumption and investment expenditures were at a high point in 1929. Expenditures for investment fell to a low in 1932, whereas consumption expenditures fell to a low in 1933. In post-World War II years, although investment expenditures dropped in 1949, 1952, 1954, and 1957, consumption expenditures have risen steadily. Frederick C. Mills, in a study using 1927 as a base year, showed that the physical production of capital goods climbed to an index of 119 in 1929 and dropped to a low of 36 three years later. Consumption goods, on the other hand, climbed to 111 in 1929 but dropped only to 69 in 1932.[2] Thus it can be seen that consumer spending, when compared to investment expenditure, is much more stable.

A good many writers on business fluctuations take the position that consumer spending is passive, being tied to the level and distribution of income, while investment, on the other hand, is the active component of national income. There is not complete agreement, however, on the passivity of consumer spending, or of its complement, savings. Raymond W. Goldsmith thinks the thesis that savings is tied strictly to income is not borne out statistically:

> The doubts concerning the stability of the saving function, particularly in the short-run, which are suggested by an analysis of time series of saving are reinforced by the investigation into the behavior of samples of households. These investigations seem to have led to the conclusion that there is a considerable degree of autonomy, i.e., independence from close adaptations to changes in income or other economic variables, in saving decisions and in actual saving, not only for individual households, but also for all households together.[3]

H. G. Moulton likewise does not accept wholeheartedly the thesis that capital expenditures "are the pivot around which the economic system revolves."[4]

The Alleged Role of Accounting Profits in Investment

The emphasis on business investment as the active factor in busi-

2. *Changes in Physical Production, Industrial Productivity and Manufacturing Costs, 1927-1932,* National Bureau of Economic Research Bulletin No. 45, p. 3.
3. *A Study of Saving in the United States,* I, 21 f.
4. *Controlling Factors in Economic Development,* p. 375, n. 114.

ness fluctuations throws the spotlight on the businessman. With the exception of government investment and the bulk of private housing, it is the businessman who makes investment decisions. The fact that the businessman occupies the center of the economic stage, has been acknowledged for some time.[5] Veblen was one of the first to give recognition to the fact that prosperity and depression arise from certain technical exigencies of profit-making itself. Mitchell also pointed out that the active role of allocating the resources of the country is played by the businessman.

What motivates the businessman in allocating the firm's resources to alternative forms of investment? A generally accepted axiom underlying economic behavior has been that of profit maximization. It is assumed that the businessman will invest in such a way as to maximize his future expected returns. Some writers even state that profit prospects are the most important, if not the sole, guide to business investment. Others, however, are not quite so positive as to the role of profits in the investment process. While admitting that investment decisions are generally related to prospects of profit, they believe that the relationship is very rough, inexact, and is tempered by feelings of optimism and pessimism.[6]

If prospective profits are accepted as the principal motivation underlying investment decisions, how are these prospective profits to be measured? It is felt by many students of business fluctuations that prospective profits are judged largely on the basis of current realized profits, or at least those profits that have been earned in the recent past. Tinbergen and Polak are among the leading exponents of this school of thought:

> There is always a strong and well-understandable tendency to extrapolate the recent past and current events into the future. . . . There is, therefore, very much to be said for the proposition that the volume of investment depends to a considerable extent on the level of profits at the time when investment plans are made.[7]

Furthermore, in an uncertain world this tendency to base future prospects on past performance is rational according to some writers. The

5. Thorstein Veblen, *The Theory of Business Enterprise,* pp. 4, 19, 241; Wesley C. Mitchell, *Business Cycles: The Problem and Its Setting,* p. 157.

6. For an expression of the first viewpoint, see U.S. Congress, Staff of the Subcommittee on Investment, Joint Committee on the Economic Report, *op. cit.,* p. 38; for an expression of the second viewpoint, see Altman, *op. cit.,* p. 109.

7. Jan Tinbergen and J. J. Polak, *The Dynamics of Business Cycles,* pp. 166 f.

fact that the company has past earnings indicates that those in control were able to cope with changing conditions in the past, and even though conditions will probably change in the future, it may be assumed that management will be able to handle these situations with equal facility.[8] Fabricant states that while "there is little agreement on the full theory, most economists would allot some weight to calculated business income, current and past, as a factor operating directly or indirectly on current investment decisions."[9] Moreover, this point of view is sometimes expressed by businessmen themselves:

> Profits, when they become large, signal the need for expansion in those lines of production in which demand is increasing. Contrariwise, a lack of profits indicates the necessity of contraction in those industries which have been overexpanded or whose products are in diminishing demand.[10]

The measurement of this business income has emerged as the principal function of accounting. Well-known writers in the accounting field have emphasized this point in recent years.[11] Paton calls the determination of the periodic income of the business enterprise "the most significant and crucial phase of the accountant's task." This point of view was also adopted by the Committee on Accounting Procedure of the American Institute of Accountants in 1938: "A fair determination of income for successive accounting periods is the most important single purpose of the general accounting reports of a corporation."

Writers other than accountants have also recognized this function of accounting.[12] Veblen has said that "the all-dominating issue in business is the question of gain and loss. Gain and loss is a question of accounting." Other writers have pointed out that "the actual cost data available to management and to the economist are limited to accounting and statistical records." Buchanan has stated that while most people would doubtless agree that in a capitalistic economy the aim and ob-

8. Buchanan, *The Economics of Corporate Enterprise,* p. 228.

9. Based on a memorandum by Solomon Fabricant in American Institute of Accountants, *Changing Concepts of Business Income,* Report of Study Group on Business Income, p. 76.

10. Testimony of Robert Dunlop, President, Sun Oil Company, found in U.S. Congress, *Profits,* A Report of a Subcommittee of the Joint Committee on the Economic Report on Profit Hearings, 80th Cong. 2d Sess., p. 8.

11. William A. Paton, *Advanced Accounting,* p. 438; Quotation by American Institute of Accountants, *op. cit.,* p. 19.

12. Veblen, *op. cit.,* pp. 84 f.; "other writers," Committee on Price Determination, National Bureau of Economic Research, *Cost Behavior and Price Policy,* p. 8; Buchanan, *op. cit.,* p. 225.

jective of business enterprises are to secure maximum profits "it is not so generally recognized and appreciated that about the only way of measuring the achievements of individual concerns in this mutual pursuit is by the use of accounting methods."

Furthermore, it is *accounting* income by which the businessman is said to be guided. George D. Bailey, past president of the American Institute of Accountants, at the hearings on corporate profits before the Joint Committee on the Economic Report held in December, 1947, identified the businessman's concept of income with that of the accountant:[13]

Senator O'Mahoney. We have three kinds of profit now, if I understand you, the economists' definition of profit, the businessman's definition of profit, and the accountants' definition.
Mr. Bailey. I meant to take the last two pretty much together, businessmen and accountants.
Senator O'Mahoney. Do they agree?
Mr. Bailey. Yes; by and large they do, and I will give you some figures.

In addition to accounting profits offering the principal incentive for the businessman to invest, they are also considered to be a factor in the ease with which this investment can be financed. Under modern conditions the process of capital allocation is achieved largely through two media: the market for new issues and the reinvestment of earnings by already established concerns. Accounting is avowed to influence both of these media.

Individuals with liquid resources to invest will place these funds in such a way as to secure the greatest return. These returns tend to be judged by the earnings reports of the corporations. The increased demand for the stock in the profitable companies tends to bid up the price of their stock. Garfield V. Cox summed up the influence of reported profits on the price of securities in these words:

It is a commonplace that corporate earnings are a major factor in determining the prices of common stocks. . . . Granting that official financial statements do not always reflect the true earnings, they constitute, nevertheless, the principal earnings data upon which the investing public and the business analyst must rely.[14]

13. U.S. Congress, *Corporate Profits,* Hearings Before the Joint Committee on the Economic Report, 80th Cong., 2d Sess., p. 87.

14. "The Relation of Stock Prices to Earnings," *The Journal of Business,* October, 1929, p. 383.

The resulting increase in the prices of shares facilitates the raising of outside equity capital. J. Tinbergen thinks that share prices exerted a considerable influence on the course of the American cycle beginning in 1924 and having its boom year in 1929. He states that "share prices have an influence on the ease with which capital issues may be floated and therefore on investment in general."[15]

Although the question of dividends versus earnings as a factor in stock prices has been debated in business and economic literature for some time, one authority concluded: "It appears, as would be expected, that earnings have more influence than dividend payments in the determination of stock prices."[16] While Tinbergen and Polak state that share prices are largely determined by dividends, they think that dividend policy is, in turn, largely determined by profits.[17]

In summary, the chain of causation from accounting profits to investment via security prices is thought to run as follows: The reported profits affect the price of shares, the price of shares affects the ease with which monetary capital can be raised, which in turn, affects the rate of investment. In fact, Norman S. Buchanan considers this relationship between recorded profits and stock prices as the most important link between accounting practices and the business cycle.[18]

In addition to the influence of accounting profits on investment via the price of shares, it is stated that it has a more direct influence on businesses which cannot, or do not wish to, make use of the capital market.[19] Since these businesses regard reported profits as one of the main sources of investment funds, any accounting bias in the computation of profits will have an immediate effect on investment decisions.

It is further argued that accounting profits are not only influential in the raising of equity capital, but also tend to influence the ability to raise borrowed capital. This is exemplified in the practice of expressing the relation of earnings to interest requirements and is often stated in such terms as "times interest earned" and "earnings coverage." As to what is meant by "earnings" in these expressions one writer has stated: "In all cases the inference one draws is that the word 'earnings' means past and perhaps present earnings."[20]

15. "The Dynamics of Share-Price Formation," *The Review of Economic Statistics,* November, 1939, p. 153.

16. Alfred Cowles 3rd and Associates, *Common Stock Indexes 1871-1937,* pp. 44-46.

17. *Op. cit.,* p. 167.

18. "Toward a Theory of Fluctuations. . . ," p. 751.

19. See Tinbergen and Polak, *op. cit.,* p. 167.

20. Gilbert Harold, *Bond Ratings as an Investment Guide,* p. 62.

The demonstration of some sort of relationship between accounting profits and business fluctuations via investment decisions, however, is not the same as establishing that accounting methodology is a factor in accentuating these fluctuations. Before this possible link can be forged, it must be shown how accounting methods are thought to misstate profits and, moreover, that they tend to overstate profits on the upswing and to understate them on the downswing, thereby influencing the entrepreneur to invest more during the upswing and less during the downswing than would be the case if profits were measured in some other fashion. Furthermore, when one speaks of an overstatement or an understatement of profit, this misstatement must be relative to some standard. This standard is usually referred to as "economic profit." Before proceeding with an examination into how the misstatement of profits by accountants, as judged by this standard, is said to cause businessmen to overinvest during prosperity and underinvest during depression, it is pertinent to inquire into the nature of accounting profit and "economic profit."

Postulates Underlying the Measurement of Accounting Profits

Revenue arises at the moment when realization is deemed to take place. One of the most widely enunciated accounting postulates underlying business income determination is that revenue is recognized in the accounts only when it is realized; that is, evidenced and supported by a genuine asset, preferably in liquid form. Of the many possible bases which have been suggested for recognizing revenue, the sale has emerged as the step in the productive process at which revenue is generally recognized. It has been stated that desirable characteristics of revenue are:[21] (1) It should be considered definitely ascertainable, (2) the certainty of receipt should be high, (3) a cause of action against outsiders should be present, and (4) it should be possible to include the amount in liquid funds which will be available shortly for expenditures or distribution.

Of the possible bases of recognition of revenue, the sale comes nearest to meeting these criteria. The sale is considered the end-product of operating activity, and, as a rule, transfer of product to the customer is coupled with passage of title. The "sale" is not restricted to physical merchandise; rather a broader view of business activity is adopted.

21. E. A. Heilman, "Realized Income," *The Accounting Review,* June, 1929, p. 81.

"Revenue is a generic term for (a) the amount of assets received or liabilities liquidated in the sale of the products or services of the enterprise, (b) the gain from the sales or exchanges of assets other than stock in trade, and (c) the gain from advantageous settlements of liabilities."[22]

The sale as the final step in revenue recognition has been criticized as being both too conservative and not conservative enough. The sale is said to be too conservative since income is earned through the productive process rather than the exchange process. Here the accountant stresses realization as distinct from earning as a criterion. Exception is made to the sale where there is definite assurance of collections, such as in the case of cost-plus contracts and construction projects, or in other cases where the product has a ready market and accretion has taken place, so that recognition of all the revenue at any one time would cause distortion. Those who think that the sale is not conservative enough have in mind the "after costs" of the sale; for example, returns, collections, expenses, and bad debts. The accountant may allow for these through the deduction of estimates based on past experience.

Fluctuations in the value of the monetary unit, which is the accounting symbol, may be ignored. This postulate is among the oldest in accounting theory. It has become axiomatic that financial accounting is based on the "cost principle." The cost of any factor of production as established in the market place represents, at the date of acquisition, the economic significance of the factor.

Costs to be acceptable to the accountant must be objective. Thus accountants frown on imputed costs. Consequently, hypothetical interest on invested capital and imputed costs covering the services of owners are not usually recognized as costs. Costs to the accountant must be verifiable. One critic of accounting methods has said: "The accounting apparatus grips most firmly those figures that are based on original cost, figures that are as comfortable as old friends and as unchanging, tried as they are by the acid test of the paid voucher."[23] Once a cost has been incurred, it remains unaltered except as it expires in the earning of revenue or its usefulness to the business is deemed to have disappeared. Cost is, therefore, not synonymous with value except to the extent that cost and value are presumed to coincide at the date of acquisition of the asset.

22. American Accounting Association, Executive Committee, "Accounting Concepts and Standards Underlying Corporate Financial Statements," *The Accounting Review,* October, 1948, p. 341.

23. Solomon Fabricant, *Revaluations of Fixed Assets, 1925-1934,* National Bureau of Economic Research Bulletin No. 62, p. 9.

Accountants have recognized that in periods of major price movements the assumption of a stable measuring unit is invalid for certain purposes. In general, they have taken the position, however, that significant changes in the price level, when needed to interpret the financial statements correctly, should be disclosed parenthetically, by footnote, or in a supplementary schedule.[24] Even though original cost may lose much of its economic significance in periods of rapid price changes, it is still objective and verifiable.

The business entity is considered a going concern. This postulate is an assumption that must not be lost sight of in any discussion of profit. It is the only sound foundation upon which a system of periodic income measurement could be built, and is justified, on the whole, by experience, especially among the larger businesses. This postulate helps to explain the reluctance of accountants to recognize the change in values of the assets of the concern due to changing price levels.[25] Since the assets were bought for use in the business and not for sale, accountants generally take the position that the effect on profit of changes in the value of the assets should be recognized gradually in the profit and loss statement via the depreciation charges as the assets are used in operations.

From a going concern angle, the fiscal period is one of the important conventions of accounting. This convention is subject to limitations especially in a dynamic economy characterized by business fluctuations. The income for a period is regarded as a "test reading" since no one can know the income of a business, with any exactness, except in retrospect after it has closed its doors in liquidation. The American Institute of Accountants has formally recognized that the annual income statement is "a tentative instalment in the long-time financial results"[26] of an enterprise.

The difference between revenue and the costs deemed to have expired during the accounting period is profit. Considering revenues as positive and assigned costs as negative, accounting profit is the algebraic sum of the two. Hence, the accountant's principal task in measuring profit is generally considered to be the determination of the amount of origi-

24. American Accounting Association, *op. cit.,* p. 343.

25. The amortization of historical cost and the going concern concept are seen as incompatible by some writers; see, e.g., Carl Thomas Devine, "Depreciation and Income Measurement," *The Accounting Review,* January, 1944, p. 43.

26. American Institute of Accountants, Committee on Accounting Procedure, "Combined Statement of Income and Surplus," *Accounting Research Bulletin No. 8,* February, 1941, p. 64.

nal cost which should be written off to reflect consumed, expired, or lost usefulness, and the amount which should be carried forward to be written off over future periods.

The Difficulty of Defining "Economic Profit"

Traditionally, accountants have taken very little interest in the origin of profits. They have been interested primarily in measuring the amount of profits, in dollars for given periods of time. They have taken for granted that profits, as they define them, are present and along with the businessman have viewed profits as a measure of accomplishment. Historically, economists, on the other hand, have not been interested in the problem of the measurement of profits. They have been more interested in explaining why profits exist and why they are tolerated. Profit is considered a social phenomenon associated with the distribution of the proceeds of society's productive activities among the factors responsible for that production.[27] In recent years, however, there is evidence that many economists are abandoning this viewpoint. In measuring the national income and in acting in an advisory capacity to business firms they have had to meet the problem of profit measurement. Economists have come to realize that a concept of profit, to have significance, must be measurable. Likewise, accountants are coming to realize that they cannot intelligently measure what they do not understand conceptually. Hence, the traditional differentiation in viewpoint of the two disciplines relative to profits is tending to break down.

Although there are frequent allusions to accountants' misstatement of "economic profit," an exact definition of this concept is not easy to find. J. R. Hicks' definition of income has been adopted by many economists.[28] He has defined a man's income as "the maximum value which he can consume during a week, and still expect to be as well off at the end of the week as he was at the beginning." While Hicks is referring here to a person, he later uses "profit" and "income" as interchangeable when discussing a business firm. Some writers have, however, tended to make a distinction between the terms "income" and "profit." Frank A. Fetter has stated this difference as follows:

In economic usage the term income is still, in greater part, applied broadly to things accruing to individuals and available for consumption; whereas profits are peculiarly the impersonal yield of any busi-

27. A. C. Littleton, "What is Profit?" *The Accounting Review,* September, 1928, p. 278.

28. *Value and Capital,* pp. 172 and 196.

ness no matter what the type of ownership. In conformity with earlier and long established usage it would not be permissible to speak of the "income" of a corporation.[29]

Although Hicks has given economists a widely quoted definition of business income, or profit, he does not think much of it as a tool of analysis. In speaking of Income, Saving, Depreciation, and Investment, he says: "At bottom, they are not logical categories at all; they are rough approximations, used by the business man to steer himself through the bewildering changes of situations which confront him."[30]

Many accountants also accept Hicks' concept of income as an ideal. Speaking of Hicks' income concept, Devine says: "With few exceptions, the accountant probably accepts as an ideal the function of income figures as measures of the amounts which a man can consume or a corporation can distribute without impairing future earning possibilities."[31]

Inherent in Hicks' definition of profit is the idea that capital must be kept intact. The problem of measuring income is thus inseparable from measuring changes in the value of capital. A. C. Pigou highlights the capital intact requirement of net income by stating that in a *stationary state* "net income consists of the whole of the annual output minus what is needed to maintain the stock of capital intact." [32] According to him, the idea of "maintaining capital intact" is clear-cut in a stationary state and means that the physical stock of capital is to be kept intact; that is, "its physical state is held constant." The concept of the "maintenance of capital intact" in a dynamic economy is, however, not so simple. Fabricant says: "It is extremely difficult to compose an unambiguous definition of capital consumption—of what is meant by keeping capital intact—for an economy characterized by cyclical movements and secular trends in its every element."[33]

Henry W. Sweeney[34] discusses four different concepts of maintaining capital intact: (1) the maintenance of relative capital, (2) the maintenance of absolute material capital, (3) the maintenance of absolute

29. "Reformulation of the Concepts of Capital and Income in Economics and Accounting," *The Accounting Review,* March, 1937, p. 10.

30. *Op. cit.,* p. 171.

31. *Op. cit.,* p. 40.

32. "Net Income and Capital Depletion," *The Economic Journal,* June, 1935, p. 235.

33. "On the Treatment of Corporate Savings in the Measurement of National Income," *Studies in Income and Wealth,* I, 141.

34. "Maintenance of Capital," *The Accounting Review,* December, 1930, pp. 277-287.

nominal capital, and (4) the maintenance of real capital based on price indices. According to Sweeney, the object of the maintenance of relative capital is to preserve for the business entity the same proportion of the total social capital that was possessed at the time the capital was originally invested. Very few accountants or economists would accept this view. Men do not usually enter business to compete with one another for the relative share of whatever general economic goods the community may have. According to the second view, maintenance of capital means preservation of the same amount of material physical objects. A person or a business is assumed to have kept capital intact if, for example, at the end of a given time period the same kind of machine is possessed in as good condition as that in which the original investment was made. The third viewpoint, the maintenance of absolute nominal capital, is that postulated by traditional accounting theory. The fourth concept, the maintenance of real capital based on price indices, Sweeney subdivides into two categories: (1) maintenance of individual real capital—the original absolute command exercised by the capital over the goods and services of most importance to the particular concern—and (2) maintenance of general real capital or the preservation of general purchasing power.

Thus it can be seen that although maintaining capital intact may be conceptually simple in a stationary economy, it is exceedingly complex in a dynamic one. While net income in a dynamic economy is still the balance of the gross income over what is needed to keep capital intact, the keeping of capital intact is no longer a clear-cut concept and, therefore, the concept of net income is not clear-cut.

In 1895 Professor F. W. Taussig referred to profit as a "mixed and vexed income."[35] Many years after this article was written there was still evidence that profit has remained a "mixed and vexed" income. Frank H. Knight said in 1933: "Perhaps no term or concept in economic discussion is used with a more bewildering variety of well established meanings than profit."[36] Intervening writers on the subject have commented upon this same difficulty of finding an unambiguous and workable theory of profit.[37] More recently, Hicks has cautioned: "We

35. "The Employer's Place in Distribution," *The Quarterly Journal of Economics,* October, 1895, p. 86.

36. "Profit," *Encyclopaedia of the Social Sciences,* XII (1933), 480.

37. E.g., Maurice Dobb, *Capitalist Enterprise and Social Progress,* p. 62, "We discover, instead, that the theory of profits is still, perhaps, the darkest part of the whole subject of economic distribution"; and S. H. Nerlove, "Recent Writings on Profits," *The Journal of Business,* October, 1929, p. 382, "Both the

shall be well advised to eschew *income* and *saving* in economic dynamics. They are bad tools, which break in our hands."[38]

Thus the conclusion must inevitably be reached that in an economy characterized by innovations and by fluctuations in prices and in the level of business activity, the term "economic profit" does not have a clear-cut conceptual boundary, nor has any economist been able to devise a satisfactory measurement of profit under these conditions. In other words, the standard against which accounting profits are said to be measured is itself a will-o'-the-wisp. When one speaks of "economic profit" in a dynamic economy, therefore, the term itself is meaningless unless defined explicitly or by context. Since the statement has been reiterated so frequently, however, that accounting profits are a misstatement of "economic profits," the next task will be to inquire more specifically into a more exact meaning of this misstatement.

The Accountants' "Misstatement" of Profit

Since accounting profits are misstated according to many writers, they must disagree with some or all of the basic accounting postulates as enumerated above. Which of the accounting postulates of profit determination do these critics reject? Let us consider the first postulate; that is, that the sale is the basis for recognizing revenue. Fritz Schmidt himself says:

> A further question arises as to how an increase over the initial assets can be produced. It can result only from the activity of the enterprise, and that activity is called *umsatz* (sale or exchange). Only through a sale or exchange transaction can the assets of an enterprise be increased.[39]

Thus critics of accounting methods of profit determination would seem to have no particular quarrel with the sale as the test of gross revenue. It is true that economists hold out for a production theory of revenue for the economy as a whole, but at the firm level this seems to represent a minority viewpoint.

Neither do those critical of accounting methods object to the going concern concept interpreted narrowly. Joel Dean has said: "For corporations, life is eternal, and net income can be measured as the maxi-

---

businessman and the professional economist are in great need of a workable profit theory at the present time."

38. *Op. cit.*, p. 177.

39. "The Importance of Replacement Value," *The Accounting Review*, September, 1930, p. 235.

mum amount that can be distributed in dividends (theoretically from now into the indefinite future) without impairing the company's earning power."[40] Likewise, when the value of a business is assumed to be the present value of a perpetuity determined by dividing its annual income by an interest rate, the going concern concept is, in effect, being adopted. When the accountant uses going concern as the basis for refusal to recognize change in value, however, the harmony of viewpoint ceases.

Many critics of accounting methods will even go along with accountants' acceptance of cost at the time of acquisition as a satisfactory measure of value. This acceptance is illustrated in the words of one writer as follows: "In the overwhelming majority of cases, of course, cost is a practically satisfactory measure of the value of assets at the time of acquisition, and this fact, added to its obvious availability and convenience, has made it almost universally the depreciation base for purchased assets."[41] It does not follow, however, that those who object to accounting methods of profit determination accept *original* costs as relevant beyond the time of acquisition. Schmidt says:

> Replacement costs as of the day of sale must be the fundamental values for profit and loss calculation. Only this can show the manager of the business whether or not his production or trading is profitable at a given time, whether or not a business entanglement is necessary, due to good profits, or whether, in consequence of a decrease in the selling margin, curtailment is necessary.[42]

In other words, in terms of Sweeney's maintenance-of-capital arguments, it would seem that most critics object to accountants' traditional emphasis upon the maintenance of nominal capital in determining net profit.

Many modern economists reject the idea that maintenance of capital means the preservation of the same amount of material physical objects. They insist that it is the investment in the asset that should be kept intact. Terborgh, for example, states: "I do not believe the function of depreciation is to maintain the physical capacity of the incumbent asset. Instead it is to recover the capital committed to the asset."[43] This concept of the "maintenance of capital" is in harmony with Sweeney's fourth concept and, if accepted, the argument over the measurement

40. *Managerial Economics,* p. 14.
41. George Terborgh, *Realistic Depreciation Policy,* p. 24.
42. "The Importance of Replacement Value," p. 240.
43. "Economic Aspects of Underdepreciation," *Replacement Costs and Depreciation,* Studies in Business Policy No. 27, p. 6.

of profit largely simmers down to what constitutes the relevant costs to be deducted from revenue in arriving at net profit. In other words, the ignoring of the fluctuations in the value of the monetary unit in the computation of costs constitutes one of the main objections of those who insist that accountants misstate profits. Moreover, this objection to the computation of cost in profit measurement is shared by many accountants. William A. Paton, an accountant-economist, says:

> All accountants give their allegiance to the view that in case of purchased items cost is the best measure of initial value and hence is the proper point from which to start the accounting record. This is the sense in which accounting is based on cost. But it doesn't at all follow that recorded cost continues to represent the original economic quantum when a change has taken place in the significance of the measuring unit itself.[44]

While the critics of accounting methods of profit measurement are in substantial agreement that the maintenance of the investment in the asset—that is, the maintenance of purchasing power—is to be kept intact, they are not in accord as to how the maintenance of purchasing power should be determined. The argument still continues as to whether this purchasing power should be measured in terms of specific assets or in terms of generalized purchasing power. The generalized purchasing power viewpoint was adopted by the Committee on Concepts and Standards Underlying Corporate Financial Statements of the American Accounting Association:

> The effects of price fluctuations upon financial reports should be measured in terms of the over-all purchasing power of the dollar—that is, changes in the general price level as measured by a GENERAL price index. For this purpose, adjustments should not be based on either the current value or the replacement costs of specific types of capital consumed.[45]

44. "Measuring Profits Under Inflation Conditions: A Serious Problem for Accountants," *The Journal of Accountancy,* January, 1950, p. 20. Willard J. Graham has made a similar statement: "I have firm personal convictions that *current costs, and only current costs, should enter into the determination of income.*" "The Effect of Changing Price Levels upon the Determination, Reporting, and Interpretation of Income," *The Accounting Review,* January, 1949, p. 15.

45. American Accounting Association, Committee on Concepts and Standards Underlying Corporate Financial Statements, "Price Level Changes and Financial Statements," *The Accounting Review,* October, 1951, p. 471. For the viewpoint that the purchasing power that is to be kept intact applies to specific assets, see William Blackie, "What is Accounting Accounting For - Now?" *National Association of Cost Accountants Conference Proceedings,* 1948, p. 37.

Under the above concept of the maintenance of capital, if prices did not change, and if the cost of an asset should generally be equal to the present value of an associated future stream of receipts, the differences between economists' and accountants' concepts of income and capital would be narrowed considerably. As Dean says: "Even though accountants and economists start from widely different viewpoints in measuring income, they could conceivably come up with the same estimates, but this could occur only in a stationary economy, where prices were frozen and where competition insured that cost was a good measure of value."[46]

Although the difference between accounting profit and so-called economic profit is narrowed under a stable price level, not all the differences are eliminated. The majority of American economists hold to a concept of "pure profit." This difference in viewpoint is primarily due to the reluctance of the accountant to recognize implicit costs. If the business is a sole proprietorship or a partnership, the residual income as computed by the accountant will contain elements of both wages and interest. If the firm is a corporation, accountants' profit figures still include interest on the stockholders' investment. Even in case of the corporation, however, the wage deduction is not clear-cut since "management" may receive more or less than the competitive rate of return. In the sense of "pure profits," therefore, we could always say that accounting profits were misstated and, more specifically, "overstated." It could be argued that the overstatement of profits in this sense is an accentuating factor in the upswing and a stabilizing factor in the downswing. This unilateral argument, however, has not been utilized by those who think that accounting methods accentuate business fluctuations and will not be considered further in the discussion of the misstatement of profits by accountants.

In an economic world characterized by business fluctuations as has been shown, economists are not willing to accept accountants' customary measurement of business profit. Since a private enterprise economy is essentially a dynamic one, in this type of economy accountants' measurement of profit is usually unsatisfactory to economists. Sales are recorded at current prices while the costs matched against these sales are based on historical prices which, if prices are fluctuating, means a different price level. Business income as customarily computed is thus a hodgepodge and is partially a reflection of the stage of the business

46. "Measurement of Profits for Executive Decisions," *The Accounting Review,* April, 1951, p. 187.

cycle at the time of reporting. Schmidt points out the effect of accountants' adherence to historical cost on the measurement of profit with a fluctuating price level as follows:

> We have to remember that in the case of a balance sheet at purchasing day cost price, which very often contains hidden reserves, the profit and loss account itself is falsified. It shows apparent profit in periods of general increase in prices and apparent losses in periods of decreases in prices, so that the estimates of the earning value are liable to be wrong.[47]

An excellent summary of the exaggeration in profits with rising price levels caused by accounting methods was given by an accountant in the hearings before the Joint Committee on the Economic Report in December, 1948:

> A consequence of this practice [ignoring fluctuations in the value of the domestic currency] is that in periods of significantly rising prices, reported profits, like other incomes, tend to show extraordinary dollar gains. At such times, costs, calculated on the book value of yesterday, fall short of the amounts needed to provide the physical replacement of inventory and plant used up in current production. Conversely, in periods of rapidly falling prices, as in the early 1930's, profits expressed in dollars tend to be understated, and operating losses, not uncommon at such times, tend to be magnified.[48]

Thus it may be contended that accountants have chosen a concept of net profit which can be more easily measured than that of economists but which yields misleading results under conditions of fluctuating price levels. Economists, on the other hand, have attempted to construct a profit concept which would stand up under these fluctuating conditions but which is not so easily applied to a business firm.

In discussions of the misstatement of profits by accounting techniques with fluctuating price levels practically all the criticism is directed at asset valuation and the effect of expense calculations based on the historical cost of these assets. Much is made of the "overstatement" of profits during periods of rising price levels and the "understatement" of profits during periods of falling price levels as a result of accounting techniques. The impact of changing price levels on the valuation of long-term liabilities and the effect of this valuation upon profit meas-

47. "The Valuation of Fixed Assets in Financial Statements," *Proceedings of the International Congress on Accounting*, 1929, p. 16.

48. Testimony of George D. Bailey, Partner, Touche, Niven, Bailey and Smart, in U.S. Congress, *Profits*, p. 37.

urement is very seldom mentioned in these discussions. Corporate bonds require the repayment of a fixed number of dollars regardless of the purchasing power of the dollars at the time of repayment. If price levels have risen subsequent to the incurrence of the obligation, the settlement of the debt in dollars of decreased purchasing power gives rise to an "economic" profit during the time the obligation is outstanding which is not recorded in the accounting records of the issuing corporation. If bonds make up a portion of the capital structure during a period of rising prices, the accounting assumption that a "dollar is a dollar" in the valuation of these liabilities can be said to result in an "understatement" of profit which should be offset against any "overstatement" resulting from cost expirations based on accounting asset valuations, before the amount of the "misstatement" of profit is determined. If, at the time the bonds are repaid, price levels are lower than the date of issuance—that is, the purchasing power of money has risen—the result is an unrecorded loss and, hence, reported profits can be said to be "overstated" as a result of accounting techniques. Thus, if substantial amounts of long-term bonds are outstanding, the net "misstatement" of profits by accounting methods may not be as large as is sometimes assumed. The predilection for bond financing in recent years, largely a result of corporate income tax regulations, gives added significance to a consideration of this opposing tendency.

A number of studies have been made in an attempt to quantify the misstatement of profits by conventional accounting methods. Joel Dean, for example, has compared the book profits of General Electric Company, Westinghouse Electric Corporation, and Radio Corporation of America with their "real economic earnings" for the period of 1935 to 1948. Each major group of assets was deflated by means of an appropriate price index and all assets were stated in terms of their 1935 price levels. Profits were determined by changes in the companies' total net assets from year-end to year-end, plus dividends, and minus new capital funds added which were also stated in 1935 dollars. Total profits per books of the three companies during the fourteen years were $1,375,292,000 while in constant 1935 dollars they were $580,330,000.[49] In only one year, 1938, did profits in constant dollars exceed the profits per books.

Ralph C. Jones made a similar study of nine steel companies from 1941 to 1947. Jones converted every item on every financial statement into 1935-1939 dollars by dividing each item by the index number for the relevant date or period, and the results were combined into a composite

49. "Measurement of Profits. . . ," p. 195.

picture of the industry in terms of purchasing power. Among other things, Jones found that for 1946, the companies' statements showed total profits of $200,000,000 before transfers from reserves compared to a real loss before transfers from reserves of $88,000,000.[50] For 1947, the reported net income available to investors was $356,000,000 compared to $91,000,000 when converted to 1935-1939 dollars.

Turning from the firm level to corporate business as a whole, Sumner Slichter estimated that total corporate earnings were overstated from 1946 to 1948 by $16.4 billion.[51] As to the reason for this overstatement Slichter said: "The principal reason probably is that accounting is a conservative and conventional art, and accountants are slow to adapt their methods to new conditions and new problems. Accountants are not used to taking account of permanent changes in the price level."[52]

According to Column 3 of Table 2, accounting methods have overstated profits every year from 1929 to 1949 except for the years 1930-1932, and the year 1938, with the largest overstatement being in 1947. A comparison of column one and column two of this table also brings out the greater volatility of profits as compared with sales during business fluctuations. This greater volatility means that expenses do not vary proportionately with sales since profit is the difference between sales and expenses. The rigidity of expenses arises partly from the fact that costs are based on historical data and partly from the fact that certain expenses are treated as being independent of sales and production. Thus, the fact that accountants use historical costs which do not "roll with the cycle" tends to exaggerate the volatility of profit.

The Effect of Accountants' "Misstatement" of Profits

This alleged misstatement of profit due to accounting methodology is said to influence businessmen in a good many ways. Buchanan says it is like looking at a thermometer: "One is inclined to feel much hotter or colder after reading the temperature than he was before, even though he was previously conscious of being warm or chilled. So a business man is likely to be more elated or depressed after reading the accountant's statement of net income than he was before."[53] Schmidt

50. "Effect of Inflation on Capital and Profits: The Record of Nine Steel Companies," *The Journal of Accountancy,* January, 1949, p. 13.
51. U.S. Congress, *Profits,* Table XVI, p. 175.
52. U.S. Congress, *Corporate Profits,* p. 8.
53. *The Economics of Corporate Enterprise,* p. 279.

TABLE 2
CORPORATE SALES, PROFITS, AND ESTIMATED MISSTATEMENT OF PROFITS DUE TO ACCOUNTING METHODS
1929-1949
(Millions of Dollars)

Year	Sales	Profits Before Tax	Misstatement of Profits§
	(1)*	(2)†	(3)‡
1929	$138,640	$ 9,628	$ 389
1930	118,294	3,322	(2,716)
1931	92,365	—780	(2,158)
1932	69,185	—3,017	(1,162)
1933	73,027	151	2,041
1934	89,553	1,716	824
1935	101,953	3,145	452
1936	119,462	5,740	963
1937	128,884	6,235	508
1938	108,551	3,300	(515)
1939	120,789	6,403	1,166
1940	135,248	9,320	717
1941	176,181	16,982	3,193
1942	202,777	20,882	2,158
1943	233,435	24,554	1,770
1944	246,737	23,320	1,275
1945	239,512	18,977	1,590
1946	270,898	22,551	6,793
1947	347,801	29,525	8,576
1948	388,744	33,000	5,420
1949	370,079	26,370	1,162

*U.S. Department of Commerce, *National Income—A Supplement to the Survey of Current Business,* 1954 ed., pp. 204 f.

†*Survey of Current Business,* July, 1958, pp. 4 f.

‡Computed by adding algebraically amounts in Col. 1, Table 7, and amounts in Col. 3, Table 13.

§Parentheses indicate understatement.

compares accounting to a compass which points to magnetic north instead of geographical north but insists that the skippers believe the needle points toward the geographic pole.[54] In other words, the businessman tends to think in monetary terms rather than in real terms.

This mistaken notion of his profits is said to affect a businessman's behavior on both the upswing and the downswing.[55] Putnam describes the effect of the overstatement of profit on the upswing in these words:

The head of the firm, unmindful of the danger that lurks in his profit

54. "Die Industriekonjunktur—ein Rechenfehler!" p. 94.

55. George E. Putnam, "The Role of Paper Profits in Industry," *Harvard Business Review,* January, 1926, p. 134; Schmidt, "The Valuation of Fixed Assets in Financial Statements," p. 17.

and loss account, notes with satisfaction the large "profit" in his business. . . . Sooner or later he will be prompted by business instinct or by the tactics of competitors to do one or all of three things on the strength of phenomenal earnings, namely, pay out more in dividends, increase the fixed investment, or carry larger inventories.

Schmidt describes the effect of the misstatement of profits on the downswing as follows:

The exaggerated expansion of plants creates overproduction and not until the new factories are finished will the price of the products be stabilized or deflated. Then, the apparent profits disappear and the general decrease of prices during the period of depression leads to apparent losses . . . if the purchasing-day cost prices are applied to the accounting.

Thus, the overstatement of profit during prosperity and the understatement during depression are said to cause the businessman to expand further during prosperity and contract further during depression than he would if profits were stated on an "economic basis."

So far, the discussion has been in terms of the effect of the misstatement of profit on the individual businessman. In so far as errors of judgment based on this misstatement tend to cancel out—that is, while some businessmen are optimistic, others are pessimistic—the economy as a whole may be unaffected. However, it is thought that there is a tendency for the errors to be in one direction. Pigou mentions three influences at work which tend to "generalize errors of forecast."[56] First, among businessmen, even when engaged in different occupations, there often exists a certain measure of psychological interdependence. A change in tone in one part of the business world diffuses itself in quite unreasoning manner over other and wholly disconnected parts. Secondly, an error of optimism on the part of one group creates a justification for some improved expectations on the part of other groups. Thirdly, a connection among businessmen is set up by the debtor-creditor relationship. If because of an excess of enthusiasm on the part of the producers from whom a concern buys its material, it is able to get longer and larger credits, then it is more inclined to pass on the same concessions to its customers, to whom it in turn grants longer and larger credit. According to Pigou these three links among businessmen "act as conducting rods along which an error of optimism or pessimism, once generated, propagates itself about the business world."

56. *Industrial Fluctuations,* pp. 86 ff.; second quotation, p. 89.

Lavington[57] has likened businessmen to skaters on a pond who infect one another with confidence and optimism. Thus, net errors of forecast tend to occur more frequently than if these links were nonexistent and these large errors are thought to carry with them sizable fluctuations in the aggregate volume of business activity. Furthermore, errors of optimism and pessimism are not independent of each other. A. C. Pigou[58] speaks of "mutual generation of errors" and the tendency of an "error of pessimism" to be followed by a "new wave of optimism." If the businessman *believes* his profits to be larger during the upswing and smaller during the downswing than they actually are, this *could* lead to the chain reaction described above.

According to some writers, the businessman does have this tendency. One writer [59] has expressed his belief as follows:

> Here we have reflected one factor making for the stimulation of business enterprise when the secular movement of prices is upward, and the depression of business enterprise when the secular movement of prices is downward. The reason for this phenomenon is found, in part, in the tendency of business men to look to the money counters in which business is transacted as the final criterion and purpose of their activities. . . . In the complex changing situation business men cannot see far enough, or clearly enough. It is partly for this reason that they tend to hold fast to the unchanging reality of cost prices, and it may be partly for this reason that waves of optimism and pessimism tend periodically to sweep over business enterprise.

Consequently, accounting methods by "misstating" business profits are said to accentuate the oscillation in the expectations of businessmen between optimism and pessimism.

Schmidt points out in the following words that, although accounting techniques are logically constructed, *all* entrepreneurs alternatively report fictitious profits and fictitious losses: "This basic principle is the miscalculation of the entrepreneurs which per se, though it contains also a severe mistake in construction, is nevertheless constructed logically and necessarily so that under certain conditions of the economy all entrepreneurs must simultaneously count fictitious profits and under other circumstances fictitious losses."[60]

57. L. Lavington, *The Trade Cycle,* p. 32 f.
58. Pigou, *Industrial Fluctuations,* Chapter VII; and p. 94.
59. Solomon Fabricant, *Measures of Capital Consumption, 1919-1933,* National Bureau of Economic Research Bulletin No. 60, pp. 12 and 13.
60. Translated from *Zeitschrift für Betriebswirtschaft,* p. 94.

This misstatement of profits and its simultaneous concomitant effect on businessmen's optimism and pessimism is thought to widen the gap between planned saving and planned investment on both the upswing and downswing. In this connection K. Lacey says: "Briefly, I maintain that the present system of profit measurement tends to widen the excess of investment over planned saving in the boom and similarly to widen the excess of planned saving over investment in the early stages of the slump."[61]

Thus the links between the misstatement of profits at the firm level by accounting methods and business fluctuations via investment decisions are said to be forged. These links are thought to be the mistaking of reported profits for "economic" profit and the consequent errors made in investment decisions. Simon Kuznets has said: "It is perhaps not an overstatement to say that the disparity between real and apparent net income constitutes an important factor in business cycles."[62]

Summary

Abstracting away the heavy hand of government and ignoring foreign investment, the gross national product is composed of consumers' expenditures and investment expenditures. The thesis of most modern writers on business fluctuations that in a private enterprise economy it is business spending that is the more active of the two in affecting the level of employment and income has been accepted. In any study of a factor that is believed to accentuate the fluctuations of business, therefore, attention should be directed primarily to the determinants of private investment expenditures.

Since it is the entrepreneur who makes the investment decisions, an evaluation of any factor that is presumed to accentuate business fluctuations boils down primarily to the question as to how this factor motivates businessmen relative to their investment decisions. They are assumed to invest in such a way as to maximize their expected future profits. They are further assumed to judge future profit prospects by present and past profits. The measurement of these past business profits, however, is the special function of the accountant and it is on the accountant's figures that businessmen tend to rely. Furthermore, accounting profits are considered to be a factor in the raising of monetary capital with which to implement these investment decisions.

It has been demonstrated that there is no single criterion of "eco-

61. *Profit Measurement and Price Changes,* p. 2.

62. "Changing Inventory Valuations and Their Effect on Business Savings and on National Income Produced," *Studies in Income and Wealth,* I, 155, n. 4.

nomic profit" against which accounting profits are said to be "misstated," since, in a dynamic economy, economists themselves are not agreed on profits conceptually nor on their measurement. In a stationary economy, on the other hand, accountants and economists, in general, have a common meeting ground in Hicks' idealized concept of income, and the two disciplines thus come closer to an agreement on the concept of profit and its measurement.

Since the statement has been so often reiterated, however, that accountants misstate "economic profit" even in the real world characterized by business fluctuations, a further search into the exact meaning of this statement was conducted. Of the basic accounting postulates underlying the measurement of profits, it was found that the ignoring of the fluctuations in the value of the dollar—that is, the reliance of accounting methods on the maintenance of dollar, or nominal, capital intact rather than "real" capital—was the one most often under attack by those who claim that accountants misstate "economic profit." In other words, critics of the methods of computing accounting profit insist that the costs to be deducted from revenue before net profit is determined should be current costs instead of historical costs. In practical application, the adherents of the current cost doctrine tend to rely upon index numbers to convert the historical cost of the accountant to current costs. There is still disagreement among the advocates of current cost, however, as to whether the index number to be used should be one based on the general price level, or one based on the price level of the specific asset to be replaced.

If the misstatement of profits by accountants affects the cycle, then it must be because of action taken by individual businessmen who have made mistakes of judgment based on the misstatement of profits; that is, they have mistaken accounting profits for "economic profits." Furthermore, it is alleged that accountants' overstatement of profits on the upswing and their understatement of them on the downswing furnish such a factor on which mistakes of judgment are made, thereby causing overinvestment on the upswing and underinvestment on the downswing. Lastly, through certain psychological links which businessmen have with one another, this mistaken judgment at the firm level is translated into a generalized mistake for the economy.

The specific accounting practices most frequently criticized as misstating profit with fluctuating price levels are inventory valuation techniques and depreciation methods. In the next two chapters attention will be focused on these two subjects of criticism.

Chapter III

Accounting Inventory Valuation and Profit Fluctuation

STUDENTS OF BUSINESS FLUCTUATIONS have tended to neglect the role of inventories. Most of their attention has been directed to fluctuations in durable capital goods, while inventories have been relegated to a relatively insignificant role. More recently, writers have begun to pay much more attention to the relationship of inventories to business fluctuations.[1] In these writings a distinction is made between planned and unplanned investment in inventories. The desire on the part of the businessman to add to stocks (planned investment) stimulates the producing and purchasing of more goods. On the other hand, goods added to stock may not have been in response to a desire to invest. The quantity of goods sold during the period may not be identical with the amount that businessmen *planned* to sell. The difference represents unplanned investment and disinvestment in inventories. This distinction between unplanned and planned investment is important because of the effect which it produces on the future action of the businessman. If there is unplanned investment, in the future the holders of excess stocks will curtail output, or purchases, and business will be depressed. Similarly, if stocks are reduced below the planned investment, then in the subsequent period the results will be expansionary.

1. See, for example, Moses Abramovitz, *Inventories and Business Cycles,* and Lloyd A. Metzler, "Factors Governing the Length of Inventory Cycles," *The Review of Economic Statistics,* February, 1947, pp. 1-15.

It is to be noted that in theorizing about cyclical investment in inventories, writers, such as Abramovitz and Metzler, have been concerned primarily with changes in real investment; that is, changes in physical stocks. The principal concern in this chapter, however, is with changes in the valuation of a fixed physical volume of inventory as well as with a combination of changes in physical stocks and in valuation.

Inventory Valuation and Profit Measurement

If the determination of profit for the fiscal period is accepted as the principal function of accounting, the primary emphasis with respect to the valuation of inventories should be the effect of this valuation upon the reported profit. The cost of goods sold, and hence accounting profit as usually calculated, is affected by the change in valuation between the beginning and ending inventory. The standard formula (omitting such relatively minor details as freight-in, allowances and discounts on purchases, and purchase returns) is: Beginning inventory plus purchases less ending inventory equals cost of goods sold. With emphasis placed on the end result of this formula, that is, the merchandise costs for the period, the dollar amount of inventory at any given time becomes merely the residual after the matching of these absorbed costs against revenue.

The pricing of the items in the ending inventory would present no special problem if prices remained the same throughout the accounting period. Since the prices of many of the individual items carried in the inventory typically fluctuate, however, some assumption must be made as to the prices to be assigned to those items remaining unsold at the end of the period. Many "acceptable" methods have been devised for handling this problem. If prices are changing, the different methods give a different valuation for the ending inventory. These different valuations, in turn, affect the profit for the period by way of the cost of goods sold. Other things being equal, the larger the value placed on the ending inventory, the smaller the cost of goods sold and thus the greater the profit for the period. This is inherent in the basic formula: Beginning inventory plus purchases less ending inventory equals cost of goods sold. Inventories may be valued at the "lower of cost or market," market referring, in general, to the replacement cost of the inventory on the balance sheet date. If the replacement cost is lower than historical cost, the inventory is valued at replacement cost; if historical cost is lower than replacement cost, the inventory is valued at cost. This rule has been defended primarily on the basis of conservatism.

Many accountants object to the lower of "cost or market" and prefer to stick strictly to cost. Valuation of inventories at cost is thought by this group to conform to the postulate that the sale is the basis for the recognition of revenue. It is contended that the use of any other basis than cost results in the recognition of unrealized gains or losses; that is, gains or losses prior to the period of sale.

When goods are purchased at varying prices during the accounting period, some method of estimating cost must be used in order to apply either the cost, or the lower of cost or market procedure. Three possibilities suggest themselves: The ending inventory can be priced at the latest invoice prices at which the goods were purchased—first-in, first-out (Fifo); at the prices prevailing in the beginning inventory, with any additions to inventory during the year priced on the basis of the earliest purchases during the period—last-in, first-out (Lifo); or at some sort of average price prevailing during the period.

Let us assume that the first-in, first-out procedure is used and that the physical stock of goods is the same at the beginning and at the end of the accounting period; that is, the inventory investment during the period is zero. If prices rise during the period, then the ending inventory will be valued at the cost of the higher prices prevailing at the end of the period, and will thus be larger than if some alternative procedure were used. This will give a lower cost of goods sold and, therefore, a larger reported profit than with other methods. This may be seen by consulting Table 3 and comparing the cost of goods sold (inventory investment zero) during the first two periods under Fifo and Lifo. With rising prices, the cost of goods sold for the first period under Fifo is $26,450 and under Lifo, $27,050; for the second period, $41,600 under Fifo and $42,600 under Lifo. Thus with rising prices and inventory investment equal to zero, more profit would be reported using Fifo than using Lifo.

If prices decline during the period, then under Fifo the ending inventory will be priced at the lower prices prevailing at the end of the period causing the valuation of the ending inventory to be smaller, the cost of goods sold larger, and the reported profit smaller, than if alternative procedures were used. This is illustrated in Table 3 where, with inventory investment equal to zero, and prices falling, cost of goods sold at the end of the third period is $33,300 under Fifo and $33,100 under Lifo; at the end of the fourth period, the corresponding figures are $21,100 and $20,250.

If physical inventories remain constant, reported profit will be smaller

TABLE 3
BEHAVIOR OF COST OF GOODS SOLD WITH FLUCTUATING PRICES UNDER LIFO AND FIFO*

INVENTORY INVESTMENT ZERO	FIFO		LIFO	
	Units	Dollars	Units	Dollars
First Period-Prices Rising:				
Beginning inventory	1,000	4,000	1,000	4,000
Purchases	6,000	27,050	6,000	27,050
Total	7,000	31,050	7,000	31,050
Less ending inventory	1,000	4,600	1,000	4,000
Goods sold	6,000	26,450	6,000	27,050
Unit Cost of Goods Sold	....	4.408	....	4.508
Second Period-Prices Rising:				
Beginning inventory	1,000	4,600	1,000	4,000
Purchases	8,000	42,600	8,000	42,600
Total	9,000	47,200	9,000	46,600
Less ending inventory	1,000	5,600	1,000	4,000
Goods sold	8,000	41,600	8,000	42,600
Unit Cost of Goods Sold	....	5.200	....	5.325
Third Period-Prices Falling:				
Beginning inventory	1,000	5,600	1,000	4,000
Purchases	6,000	33,100	6,000	33,100
Total	7,000	38,700	7,000	37,100
Less ending inventory	1,000	5,400	1,000	4,000
Goods sold	6,000	33,300	6,000	33,100
Unit Cost of Goods Sold	....	5.550	....	5.516
Fourth Period-Prices Falling:				
Beginning inventory	1,000	5,400	1,000	4,000
Purchases	4,000	20,250	4,000	20,250
Total	5,000	25,650	5,000	24,250
Less ending inventory	1,000	4,550	1,000	4,000
Goods sold	4,000	21,100	4,000	20,250
Unit Cost of Goods Sold	....	5.275	....	5.063

*The detailed calculations on which this table is based are given in the appendix to Chapter III.

TABLE 3—*Continued*

INVENTORY INVESTMENT INCREASING	FIFO Units	FIFO Dollars	LIFO Units	LIFO Dollars
First Period-Prices Rising:				
Beginning inventory	1,000	4,000	1,000	4,000
Purchases	6,500	29,300	6,500	29,300
Total	7,500	33,300	7,500	33,300
Less ending inventory	1,200	5,520	1,200	4,850
Goods sold	6,300	27,780	6,300	28,450
Unit Cost of Goods Sold	....	4.410	....	4.516
Second Period-Prices Rising:				
Beginning Inventories	1,200	5,520	1,200	4,850
Purchases	9,000	48,200	9,000	48,200
Total	10,200	53,720	10,200	53,050
Less ending inventory	1,600	8,960	1,600	6,770
Goods sold	8,600	44,760	8,600	46,280
Unit Cost of Goods Sold	....	5.204	....	5.381
INVENTORY INVESTMENT DECREASING				
Third Period-Prices Falling:				
Beginning inventory	1,600	8,960	1,600	6,770
Purchases	5,000	27,620	5,000	27,620
Total	6,600	36,580	6,600	34,390
Less ending inventory	1,200	6,520	1,200	4,850
Goods sold	5,400	30,060	5,400	29,540
Unit Cost of Goods Sold	....	5.567	....	5.470
Fourth Period-Prices Falling:				
Beginning inventory	1,200	6,520	1,200	4,850
Purchases	3,500	17,690	3,500	17,690
Total	4,700	24,210	4,700	22,540
Less ending inventory	1,100	5,050	1,100	4,425
Goods sold	3,600	19,160	3,600	18,115
Unit Cost of Goods Sold	....	5.322	....	5.032

under Lifo than under alternative procedures when prices rise, and larger when prices fall. Lifo thus tends to iron out the fluctuations in reported profits over the cycle. If prices eventually return to their former level after a rise, the average profit for a series of years will be the same under either Fifo or Lifo. The use of an average cost procedure gives results in between Fifo and Lifo.

Thus, even though the physical inventory remains constant, if prices rise and if Fifo is used, reported profit will be larger than if prices remained constant even though no more goods are actually sold during the period. This is due to the higher-priced goods remaining in the ending inventory, causing the cost of goods sold to be less and the profit to be more than would have been the case if prices had remained constant. This extra profit has been labeled "inventory profits" or "paper profits." One writer has even referred to them as "Fool's Profits."[2] J. Keith Butters and Powell Niland[3] define "paper profits" or "inventory profits" as "profits measured by the increase in value placed on a constant volume of physical inventories," but point out that the term "inventory profits" has been used by other writers to label at least two other concepts.

When prices are falling the valuing of the same physical inventory using Fifo will give rise to "inventory losses." As long as prices continue to fall, the constant inventory will be valued at lower and lower figures, and the cost of goods sold will be charged with the higher-priced goods bought earlier. As a result of this procedure, the opposite of inventory profits, that is, inventory losses, will be reported. If Lifo is used, as long as the physical inventory remains the same, the ending inventory will be reported at the same figure. An illustration of these phenomena is given in Table 3 where the physical inventory remains at 1,000 units throughout the four periods. Under Fifo, the five inventories in dollars are: \$4,000, \$4,600, \$5,600, \$5,400, and \$4,550; with the use of Lifo, each of the five inventories would have been \$4,000. The valuing of ending inventory at cost or market, with cost determined on a Fifo basis may aggravate the "error" still further at the start of the downgrade. With prices falling, the ending inventory is valued at market which is even lower than cost. In addition to the usual "error," this period's cost of goods sold account is loaded with a bit of what would have been next period's cost if inventories had been valued on a cost basis. In subsequent years, since both the beginning and ending inventory are valued at

2. Arundel Cotter, *Fool's Profits.*
3. *Effects of Taxation—Inventory Accounting and Policies,* pp. 2 and 142.

market, the double "error" tends to be smaller even though prices tend to fall at the same rate.

All the foregoing remarks have been predicated on the assumption that the volume of inventories remains constant; that is, inventory investment equals zero. What is the case over the cycle when, as Abramovitz[4] has shown, there is a concomitant increase in inventory investment during the upswing and a decrease during the downswing? From Table 3 it can be seen that in this model the tendency for inventory investment to increase during the upswing and to decrease during the downswing accentuates the fluctuation in the cost of goods sold as between Fifo and Lifo. With rising prices, the difference between the unit costs of Lifo and Fifo is greater with rising stocks than with constant stocks. Likewise, with falling prices the difference between the unit costs is greater with falling stocks than with constant stocks. Therefore, other things being equal, the difference between the profit reported under Fifo and that reported under Lifo will be greater if stocks are rising on the upswing and falling on the downswing than if inventory investment remained at zero throughout the cycle. In interpreting these results, it must be kept in mind that this simplified model assumes that sales, inventory investment, and prices are all moving with the cycle—which has tended to be the typical situation; also that prices never reach their former level and that inventories are not liquidated down to their former level.

In discussing the effect on profit of different methods of inventory valuations there are two special methods that are important enough to consider. With the retail inventory method, widely used by many department stores, the inventory is taken at retail and reduced to approximate cost by applying the average percentage of markup during the year and subtracting the resulting figure from the inventory at retail. Under the conventional retail method, the procedure used causes the inventory to approach the lower of cost or market valuation. This is accomplished by ignoring the markdowns in the computation of the percentage. If it is desired that the method approximate a cost procedure, then both markups and markdowns are included in computing the percentage. Hence the foregoing remarks on the effect of inventory valuation on profit apply to the retail method depending on the variation of the procedure which is used.

The "base stock" or "normal stock" method, used largely in the smelting industry, is a forerunner of the Lifo method. This method is

4. *Op. cit.*, pp. 345 f.

based on the assumption that a supply of raw materials sufficient in volume to maintain operations during the average turnover period must be maintained. This assumption is combined with the theory that replacement costs are the only pertinent costs to use when this material is issued for use in production. A fixed amount of inventory is designated as the minimum amount needed for the operations of the firm and, this "normal stock" once chosen, is not changed frequently. Usually the price on this stock is as low or below any level of costs which has been experienced by the industry to date. Units issued are priced at the most recent cost. If the inventories are deficient at the end of the accounting period, that is, below the normal stock, the deficiency is usually valued at current cost and deducted from the normal stock for statement purposes. Inventories in excess of the normal stock are usually priced at the most recent cost and added to normal stock to arrive at the total inventory valuation.

Thus both the Lifo and base stock method tend to price the goods at current costs. However, under Lifo there is no fixed "reservoir inventory" and hence no "excess" or "deficiency" to be added to, or subtracted from, normal stocks at current costs. The remarks made relative to the effect on profit fluctuations with Lifo are, in general, applicable to the base stock method.

In choosing among so many alternatives, what criteria have been used for deciding which of the various inventory valuation methods to use? At least four criteria have been used:[5] (1) the flow-of-goods criterion, (2) the relationship which cost and selling price bear to each other, (3) the disposable cash criterion, and (4) the current cost criterion.

The flow-of-goods criterion has traditionally influenced the thinking of accountants. Accountants who argue for this criterion put great emphasis on the notion that costs "attach" to the goods as they pass through the concern. Much is made of the good business practice of using or selling the oldest goods first. W. A. Paton and A. C. Littleton, for example, state: "In the development of a policy or procedure designed to divide the stream of production costs into inventory on the one hand and cost of sales on the other, a basic requirement is the adoption of a clear conception of the manner in which the component elements move through the enterprise."[6] The first-in, first-out method has been defended as being in harmony with this concept. As an example consider this statement: "A paper mill . . . using pulp wood in manufacture consumes the oldest wood first so that it will not rot away. The first-in,

5. Butters and Niland, *op. cit.*, pp. 11 f.
6. *An Introduction to Corporate Accounting Standards,* p. 78.

first-out rule seems to be in line with the physical conditions of that industry."[7]

It should be noted that their penchant for historical costs has also influenced accountants in their preference for Fifo. In more recent years, first-in, first-out has been defended on the basis of a flow of costs separate and apart from the order in which goods are sold, or used physically in manufacturing. The flow of goods criterion is no longer emphasized so strongly as shown by a statement of Carman G. Blough, Director of Research of the American Institute of Accountants: "In considering the relative merits of each of these assumptions, it is essential to recognize that, despite the implications of some of the terminology used, the matter of the flow of *goods* is of relatively little significance."[8]

The American Institute of Accountants[9] sanctions the second criterion of inventory valuation—the relationship of costs to selling price. Methods are favored which

> recognize the variations which exist in the relationships of costs to sales prices under different economic conditions. Thus, where sales prices are promptly influenced by changes in reproductive costs, an assumption of the "last-in first-out" flow of cost factors may be the more appropriate. Where no such cost-price relationship exists, the "first-in first-out" or an "average" method may be more properly utilized.

Carman Blough also uses as a justification for Lifo the possible relationship between costs and selling prices:

> Lifo and base-stock, on the other hand, might be said to assume that there is a close correlation between current sales prices and current purchase or production costs; that, while the specific goods delivered may come from stock on hand, the cost of current purchases or production are incurred to cover current sales. This line of reasoning might be appropriate—for instance, where a company bases its prices on current costs.

This line of reasoning is also partly responsible for the "lower of cost or market" procedure. The assumption seems to be that, if the cost of the

7. Homer N. Sweet, "The Case for a 'Cost or Market' Basis," *N. A. C. A. Bulletin,* December 1, 1937, pp. 402 f.

8. "Changing Accounting and Economic Concepts Affect Methods of Inventory Pricing," *The Journal of Accountancy,* September, 1948, p. 205.

9. American Institute of Accountants, Committee on Accounting Procedure, "Inventory Pricing," *Accounting Research Bulletin No. 29,* July, 1947, pp. 237 f.; Blough, *op. cit.,* p. 206.

merchandise has fallen since the date of the purchase, the selling price of the goods must be reduced to conform to this lower purchase price. Therefore, the ending inventory should be valued at market, thus taking the "loss" this period, and thereby maintaining the margin of markup next period.

The third criterion, the disposable cash criterion, is the one stressed most strongly by management and writers on management. According to this viewpoint any method of inventory valuation that gives a profit that is nonexpendable should be shunned. This is well illustrated by a statement made by a president of Swift and Company: "What we need and are seeking most of all is cash profits, profits that can be paid out in dividends or reinvested in the business as occasion requires."[10] Another writer on inventory profits, George E. Putnam, advocates the use of this criterion: "What the business community obviously needs is a new definition of profits and an accounting technique which will keep fictitious and unexpendable gains out of the profits statement."[11]

Many advocates of the disposable cash criterion use the "base stock" argument, emphasizing that a certain amount of inventories is of the nature of a fixed asset since a certain amount of stock must be kept on hand at all times. F. Sewell Bray, for example, has advocated showing "standard inventories" on the balance sheet as fixed assets.[12] The proponents of the disposable cash criterion recognize that the composition of the stock of merchandise is constantly changing but still insist that it represents a fixed investment. It is insisted that under Fifo part of the reported profit represents only the increased cost of carrying inventories and cannot be realized if physical stocks are to be maintained without liquidating other assets or increasing the indebtedness of the company. It is clear, of course, that business as a whole does not move out from under its inventories when prices are high and restock when prices are low. As Henry B. Arthur says: "The typical business cycle shows the smallest inventories during the early recovery phase (when they are cheap) then rising inventories as business improves, and peak inventories at some time during the period of general price collapse."[13] This statement has been confirmed, in general, by Abramovitz's study. Therefore, according to a disposable cash criterion, inventory profits are not

10. Swift and Company, *50th Anniversary Yearbook,* 1935, p. 4.

11. "What Shall We Do About Depressions?" *The Journal of Business,* April, 1938, p. 145.

12. "Accounting Dynamics—III," *Accounting Research,* July, 1955, pp. 271 f.

13. "Inventory Profits in the Business Cycle," *The American Economic Review,* March, 1938, p. 30.

only unrealized but they are also unrealizable if the concern is to continue in business. This criterion has found favor among companies where there are large investments in raw materials that fluctuate widely in price.

The current cost criterion can be regarded either as a fourth criterion or as a variant of the disposable cash criterion. Many economists have long insisted that replacement cost should be used in computing the cost of goods sold. J. Maurice Clark, for example, has said:

> What the concern expends now is materials which it now has, not the money which it paid out for them some months ago, and the sacrifice now involved in putting these materials into a given order is really represented by what the concern could realize on these materials if it did not make them up and sell them to this particular customer. This sacrifice is measured by the market price of the materials and not by the original cost.[14]

Economists, businessmen, and many accountants who believe that current costs are the pertinent costs for computing cost of goods sold view Lifo and Fifo as alternative historical cost methods. William Blackie, a vice president of Caterpillar Tractor Company, says: "The real justification for 'Lifo' would be that it *approaches* a current cost basis, and thus produces the approximation of a coordinated relationship between sale and acquisition *on one common price level.*"[15] They thus accept Lifo only because it normally gives figures approaching replacement costs. In a period of rapidly rising prices the spread between replacement cost and Lifo may still be sizable.

Factors Determining the Size of Inventory Profits, or Losses

It has already been demonstrated that the size of inventory profits, or losses, of a business firm depends upon the particular accounting technique, selected according to certain criteria, for the valuation of the ending inventory. In the last twenty years, a number of studies of the inventory valuation methods used by business firms have been made.

A survey was made by the Research Department of the American Institute of Accountants of 500 published reports of companies which were listed on the New York Stock Exchange for the year 1939. Of these 500 reports, 442 contained one or more inventory items. A total of 1,333

14. *Studies in the Economics of Overhead Costs,* p. 197.
15. *Op. cit.,* p. 34.

TABLE 4
INVENTORIES
METHODS OF DETERMINING COST
1946-1956

Method of Determining Cost	1956	1954	1952	1950	1948	1946
1. Last-in, first-out	200	198	187	161	91	79
2. First-in, first-out	141	143	133	128	87	102
3. First-in, first-out, retail stores	......	......	4	4	......	......
4. Average cost	145	146	127	119	110	100
5. Standard cost	27	29	30	29	26	23
6. Approximate cost	11	11	16	19	......	......
7. Production cost	5	2	12	7	......	......
8. "Actual" cost	4	8	7	10	8	......
9. Replacement cost	5	1	3	2	......	......
10. "Estimated" cost	5	4	2	2	5	......
11. Retail method	16	10	8	6	6	......
12. Base or normal stock method	4	7	7	6	6	6
13. Job-order method	3	1	4	4	......	......
14. Various other methods	12	2	5	5	......	......
15. Invoice cost	1	......	......	......	......	......
Total	768	562	545	502	......	......
16. Not indicated	......	......	......	......	295	289
17. Lifo—retail method	......	......	......	......	6	12
18. Fifo—retail method	......	......	......	......	6	......
19. Specific invoice cost	......	......	......	......	10	......
20. Inventories negligible	......	......	......	......	4	2
21. Relative value method	......	......	......	......	1	......
22. Market prices of ingredients plus manufacturing	......	......	......	......	1	1
Total	......	......	......	......	662	614

Source: American Institute of Certified Public Accountants, *Accounting Trends and Techniques*. 1946 and 1948, 4th Annual Cumulative Survey, 1950, p. 37. 1950 and 1952, Seventh Edition, 1953, p. 67. 1954 and 1956, Eleventh Edition, 1957, p. 53.

inventory items was contained in the 500 reports. Given below is a tabulation of the results of the analysis made by the American Institute:[16]

(1) Cost or market, whichever is lower, or variations thereof . . . 747
(2) Cost, standard cost, estimated cost, or other cost bases . . . 267
(3) Market, selling price, realizable amounts, and the like . . . 47
(4) Basic or fixed prices . . . 21
(5) Less than cost, less than market, cost less unspecified reserve, and other "less than" or "not in excess of" bases . . . 180
(6) Other bases specified . . . 7
(7) Total of above items for which basis specified . . . 1,269
(8) Basis not given . . . 64

Later surveys by the American Institute have also revealed that cost or market whichever is lower is by far the most prevalent method of inventory valuation in use, with cost as a poor second.[17] It should be recalled that the lower of cost or market tends to accentuate inventory losses during an accounting period when prices are falling.

Of particular interest is the technique used in the determination of cost since most of the criticism of inventory valuation techniques from the standpoint of the determination of profit has been leveled at a particular method, Fifo. Table 4 shows the methods used by companies to determine cost. It is worthy of note that in the years 1948, 1954, and 1956, average cost was more common in the companies surveyed than was Fifo. In the years shown, Lifo has been the most prevalent method of determining cost since 1948.

Furthermore, there has been a definite trend toward a wider use of Lifo. (See Table 5.) It is especially worthy of note that a large number of companies adopted Lifo in 1950 and 1951, which were years of large reported profits.

Another study showing the trend to Lifo was made by the Office of Business Economics of the U.S. Department of Commerce. This survey covered over 2,300 corporations of all sizes and in every phase of manufacturing. The companies were asked to report the book value of their Lifo inventories. Replies to this survey were supplemented by Lifo data from the published financial statements of large firms not covered by the survey. The results of this study are summarized in Table 6.

16. "Inventories," *The Journal of Accountancy,* October, 1940, p. 335.
17. American Institute of Accountants, *Accounting Trends and Techniques,* 4th Annual Cumulative Survey, 1950, p. 35; Seventh Edition, 1953, p. 67; and Eleventh Edition, 1957, p. 53.

TABLE 5
LIFO INVENTORY COST METHOD
CHANGES DURING THE YEAR
1949-1952

Number of Companies	1952	1951	1950	1949
1. Using Lifo at beginning of year	185	161	117	117
2. Adopting Lifo during year	3	26	43	1
3. Readopting Lifo during 1950	......	......	1	......
4. Abandoning Lifo during year	(1)*	(2)	......	(1)
5. Using Lifo at end of year	187	185	161	117
6. Not referring to use of Lifo as of year end	413	415	439	483
Total	600	600	600	600
7. Extending Lifo to additional inventory classes during year	3	6	15	1
8. Partially abandoning Lifo during year	1	1	1	......

Source: American Institute of Accountants, *Accounting Trends and Techniques,* Seventh Edition, 1953, p. 74.
*Parentheses indicate deduction.

TABLE 6
ESTIMATES OF LIFO INVENTORIES FOR MANUFACTURING INDUSTRIES, YEAR-END, 1951 AND YEAR-END, 1947
(Millions of Dollars)

	1951			1947
	Total Book Value	Lifo Book Value	Lifo Per Cent	Lifo Per Cent
Total manufacturing	$43,056	$6,375	15	12
Durable-goods industries	22,650	2,999	13	10
Nondurable-goods industries	20,406	3,376	17	14

Source: U.S. Department of Commerce, *Survey of Current Business,* May, 1953, p. 17.

In addition to revealing a trend to Lifo, Table 6 also shows the per cent of manufacturers' inventories estimated to have been on a Lifo basis for the years 1947 and 1951. Another pair of researchers, Butters and Niland, estimated that for 1947 at least 13 per cent of total manufacturers' inventories were on Lifo with the possibility that the figure may have been as high as 17 per cent and conclude that "Lifo inventories no longer can be brushed aside as of negligible importance."[18]

As far as the individual firm is concerned, in addition to the method of inventory valuation used, the size of the inventory profits and losses

18. *Op. cit.,* p. 55 and p. 7.

is dependent on several other factors. The first of these additional factors is the violence of the price change. The more rapid the change in prices, the greater will be the inventory profits, or losses. A second factor is the length of the inventory turnover period. If the turnover is rapid, the stock is sold out before any substantial changes occur in the value of the stock on hand. In the case of manufacturers with long periods of production this factor becomes very important. A third factor is the ratio of inventories to total assets. In companies where this ratio is large, inventory profits and losses are of more importance than in companies where the ratio is negligible. A fourth factor mentioned by one writer[19] is the "volatility" of demand. The demand for some types of goods, for example, luxury goods, can almost disappear during depressions; hence, the possibility of inventory losses is greater. A fifth factor is the relation of sales prices to the cost of goods sold. Inventories could be large relative to total assets or to net worth without being large in relation to net income. The smaller the rate of gross profit, other things being equal, the more important the method of inventory valuation becomes. Some writers mention the degree of integration of the business unit as being a factor in the size of inventory profits and losses. The integrated producer is thought less likely to be affected by fluctuations in inventory valuation than his nonintegrated competitors.[20]

An inventory profit, or loss, during a fiscal period for a business firm is a measure of the combined effect of price level changes and the particular inventory valuation method used. This profit, or loss, being a component of accounting profit, is one of the alleged factors in the misstatement of reported profit.

Inventory Profits and Losses in the Economy

The inventory valuation techniques chosen by individual business firms will determine the amount of inventory profits, or losses, for the economy as a whole since this amount is a summation of the inventory profits, or losses, of the various firms. In other words, inventory profits, or losses, for the economy may be viewed as the total "misstatement" of profits due to the failure of accounting methodology to adjust the valuation of inventories for changes in the price level. Assuming the amount of reported profits is a determinant of the size of investment expenditures, the magnitude of these aggregate inventory profits, or losses, may be regarded as indicative of the degree to which the business sector of the

19. Cotter, *op. cit.*, p. 87.

20. *Ibid.*

TABLE 7
INVENTORY VALUATION ADJUSTMENT
1929-1957
(Millions of Dollars)

YEAR	CORPORATE	NONCORPORATE	TOTAL
	(1)	(2)	(3)
1929	$ (472)*	$ (142)	$ (614)
1930	(3,260)	(755)	(4,015)
1931	(2,414)	(611)	(3,025)
1932	(1,047)	(295)	(1,342)
1933	2,143	525	2,668
1934	625	54	679
1935	227	50	277
1936	738	120	858
1937	31	29	60
1938	(963)	(221)	(1,184)
1939	714	166	880
1940	200	45	245
1941	2,471	615	3,086
1942	1,204	367	1,571
1943	773	156	929
1944	287	69	356
1945	564	106	670
1946	5,263	1,705	6,968
1947	5,899	1,471	7,370
1948	2,152	410	2,562
1949	(1,856)	(463)	(2,319)
1950	4,965	1,094	6,059
1951	1,199	327	1,526
1952	(981)	(201)	(1,182)
1953	997	168	1,165
1954	318	49	367
1955	1,749	198	1,947
1956	2,560	497	3,057
1957	1,548	297	1,845

Source: U.S. Department of Commerce, *Survey of Current Business,* July, 1958, pp. 4 f.

*Parentheses indicate understatement of profit.

economy is "misled" by conventional inventory valuation methods in making these decisions.

The "inventory valuation adjustment" of the U.S. Department of Commerce (see Table 7) is considered adequate by some writers to indicate the general magnitude of aggregate inventory profits and losses.[21] The year of largest inventory losses was 1930, and the year of

21. Butters and Niland, *op. cit.,* p. 16; for an estimate of the inventory valuation adjustment from 1897-1928, see Raymond W. Goldsmith, *op. cit.,* I, 903.

largest inventory profits was 1947. For 1930, if the inventory valuation adjustment is made for corporate profits, reported profits will increase from $3,322 million (before income taxes) to $6,582 million, an increase of 98.1 per cent.[22] For the same year, the reported profits of nonfarm unincorporated enterprises is increased from $6,655 million to $7,410 million, or 11.3 per cent, if the inventory valuation adjustment is applied. For 1947, corporate profits are reduced from a reported $29,525 million to $23,626 million, or approximately 20 per cent, by applying the inventory valuation adjustment. For this same year profits of nonfarm unincorporated enterprises decrease from reported profits of $21,419 million to $19,948 million, or approximately 7 per cent.

TABLE 8
USE OF LIFO METHOD OF INVENTORY VALUATION IN DIFFERENT SIZED COMPANIES

Assets (Millions of Dollars)	Companies Reporting	Companies Using Lifo	
		Number	Per Cent of Total
0 - 4.9	175	33	18
5 - 24.9	221	37	17
25 - 99.9	115	33	28
100 and over	48	21	44
Total	559	124	22

Source: James A. Finley, *Handling Higher Replacement Costs,* Studies in Business Policy No. 47, p. 14.

Since 1952 inventory profits have been small relative to reported profits before taxes. This decrease in relative size may be attributed largely to the more stable price level that has prevailed since this date. Another factor is probably a trend toward the use of Lifo by more companies, as well as the tendency for the Lifo procedure to be concentrated in the large companies. (See Table 8.) Butters and Niland believe that the concentration of Lifo in a limited range of industries, and in the large companies within these industries, makes its importance greater than may be realized.[23]

Thus business firms have traditionally used accounting methods,

22. The dollar figures used in this paragraph are from the U.S. Department of Commerce, *Survey of Current Business,* July, 1958, pp. 4 f.

23. *Op. cit.,* p. 7. The authors mention these industries as being Lifo industries: Meat packing, textiles and apparel, leather and its products, lumber and basic timber products, petroleum, iron and steel companies, and nonferrous metals. *Ibid.,* p. 51.

which with fluctuating price levels have caused aggregate inventory profits, or losses, to appear. It has been shown that these inventory profits and losses are sizable during periods of rapid price changes. Even though inventory profits relative to total reported profits before adjustment have been small since 1952, they continue to exist. The tendency for aggregate inventory profits to appear during the upswing and for aggregate losses to appear during the downswing has been one of the factors that is said to lead to "waves of optimism and pessimism," which, in turn, is thought to contribute to mistakes in investment decisions.

Summary

The accounting methods of inventory valuation have come under attack by many students of business fluctuations. This is due to the fact that the method of computing the value of ending inventories affects the profit for the period through the cost of goods sold; the higher the value placed on the ending inventory, the lower the cost of goods sold and hence, the greater the reported profits. Different "acceptable" accounting methods of valuing the same inventory, as far as physical quantities are concerned, will give different dollar figures, which in turn, will be reflected in the net profit for the period.

Traditionally, inventories have been valued at the lower of cost or market, with cost being computed on a Fifo or average cost basis. With a rising price level this method is said to overstate the ending inventory, and thus to overstate profits for the period. When prices are falling, the situation is reversed. This technique produces "paper profits" or "inventory profits," which are due to an increase in value placed on a constant volume of physical inventories. The size of these inventory profits depends upon many factors and is, therefore, not of the same degree of significance in all businesses or industries. In periods of rapidly changing prices this problem is especially acute with respect to industries having large investments in inventories relative to total assets—or to net worth—a slow rate of inventory turnover, and a low rate of gross profit based on sales; for example, the meat packing industry. For the economy, the inventory valuation adjustment of the U.S. Department of Commerce is a rough measure of the "misstatement" of profits due to accounting methods of inventory valuation.

The inclusion of these inventory profits and losses in financial reports is one of the principal means by which accounting methodology is said to misstate "economic profits," thereby accentuating business fluctuations by influencing investment decisions.

Appendix

Assumption: A beginning inventory of 1,000 units at $4.00 per unit.

I. Physical units constant on each inventory date.

A. First Period-Prices Rising

Purchases:

Units		Price	Amount
1,000	at	$4.25	$4,250
2,000	at	4.50	9,000
3,000	at	4.60	13,800
6,000			$27,050

Ending Inventory (1,000 units):

	Units		Price	Amount
FIFO:	1,000	at	$4.60	$4,600
LIFO:	1,000	at	4.00	$4,000

B. Second Period-Prices Rising

Purchases:

Units		Price	Amount
1,000	at	$4.80	$4,800
1,500	at	4.90	7,350
3,500	at	5.50	19,250
2,000	at	5.60	11,200
8,000			$42,600

Ending Inventory (1,000 Units):

	Units		Price	Amount
FIFO:	1,000	at	$5.60	$5,600
LIFO:	1,000	at	4.00	$4,000

C. Third Period-Prices Falling

Purchases:

Units		Price	Amount
2,000	at	$5.60	$11,200
1,500	at	5.50	8,250
1,500	at	5.50	8,250
1,000	at	5.40	5,400
6,000			$33,100

Ending Inventory (1,000 Units):

	Units		Price	Amount
FIFO:	1,000	at	$5.40	$5,400
LIFO:	1,000	at	4.00	$4,000

D. Fourth Period-Prices Falling

Purchases:

Units		Price	Amount
1,000	at	$5.40	$5,400
1,000	at	5.30	5,300
1,000	at	5.00	5,000
500	at	4.60	2,300
500	at	4.50	2,250
4,000			$20,250

Ending Inventory (1,000 Units):

	Units		Price	Amount
FIFO:	500	at	$4.60	$2,300
	500	at	5.50	2,250
	1,000			$4,550
LIFO:	1,000	at	$4.00	$4,000

II. Inventory Investment Increasing

A. First Period-Prices Rising

Purchases:

Units		Price	Amount
1,000	at	$4.25	$4,250
2,500	at	4.50	11,250
3,000	at	4.60	13,800
6,500			$29,300

Ending Inventory (1,200 Units):

	Units		Price	Amount
FIFO:	1,200	at	$4.60	$5,520
LIFO:	1,000	at	$4.00	$4,000
	200	at	4.25	850
	1,200			$4,850

B. Second Period-Prices Rising

Purchases:

Units		Price	Amount
1,000	at	$4.80	$4,800
1,500	at	4.90	7,350
3,500	at	5.50	19,250
3,000	at	5.60	16,800
9,000			$48,200

Ending Inventory (1,600 Units):

	Units		Price	Amount
FIFO:	1,600	at	$5.60	$8,960
LIFO:	1,000	at	$4.00	$4,000
	200	at	4.25	850
	400	at	4.80	1,920
	1,600			$6,770

III. Inventory Investment Decreasing

A. Third Period-Prices Falling

Purchases:

Units		Price	Amount
2,000	at	$5.60	$11,200
1,200	at	5.50	6,600
1,000	at	5.50	5,500
800	at	5.40	4,320
5,000			$27,620

Ending Inventory (1,200 Units):

	Units		Price	Amount
FIFO:	800	at	$5.40	$4,320
	400	at	5.50	2,200
	1,200			$6,520
LIFO:	1,000	at	$4.00	$4,000
	200	at	4.25	850
	1,200			$4,850

B. Fourth Period-Prices Falling

Purchases:

Units		Price	Amount
1,000	at	$5.40	$5,400
800	at	5.30	4,240

700	at	5.00	3,500
500	at	4.60	2,300
500	at	4.50	2,250
3,500			$17,690

Ending Inventory (1,100 Units):

FIFO:	500	at $4.50		$2,250
	500	at	4.60	2,300
	100	at	5.00	500
	1,100			$5,050
LIFO:	1,000	at $4.00		$4,000
	100	at	4.25	425
	1,100			$4,425

Behavior of Average Unit Costs with Fluctuating Prices under FIFO and LIFO

I. Prices Rising

	Constant Stocks		*Increasing Stocks*	
1st year	LIFO	$4.508	LIFO	$4.516
	FIFO	4.408	FIFO	4.410
		$ .100		$ .106
2nd year	LIFO	$5.325	LIFO	$5.418
	FIFO	5.200	FIFO	5.204
		$ .125		$ .214

II. Prices Falling

	Constant Stocks		*Falling Stocks*	
3rd year	FIFO	$5.550	FIFO	$5.567
	LIFO	5.516	LIFO	5.429
		$ .034		$ .138
4th year	FIFO	$5.275	FIFO	$5.322
	LIFO	5.063	LIFO	5.032
		$ .212		$ .290

Chapter IV

Depreciation Policy and Investment Decisions

A SECOND TARGET of those who think that accounting methodology accentuates business fluctuations by influencing investment decisions is the accounting methods of computing the depreciation of fixed assets. Inherent in any concept of net profit, or its complement, maintaining capital intact, is a related depreciation policy. Since there is no one definition of net profit on which there is general agreement, it is not surprising that there are as many concepts of depreciation as there are concepts of profit. Before dealing with any "misstatement" of net profit as a result of depreciation accounting, the various concepts of depreciation, as well as the purposes of depreciation accounting, should be considered. Although this discussion will include the historical cost versus the replacement cost argument already encountered with respect to inventory accounting, the allocation of the depreciation expense between accounting periods is thought by many to have additional implications for long-term growth as well as cyclical ramifications.

Concepts of Depreciation

Professor James C. Bonbright[1] has pointed out that substantially all technical meanings of depreciation are variants of four basic concepts: (1) the fall in value of an asset between two points of time; (2) the difference between the present value of an asset and the present value of a hypothetical new asset; (3) impaired serviceableness; and (4) amortization of cost.

1. *The Valuation of Property,* I, 183.

The fall in the value of an asset between two points of time accords with the popular usage of the term depreciation. According to Bonbright, value as used in this sense may be either "market value" or "value to the owner." This usage of the term does not emphasize the *causes* of the decrease in value between the two points of time. The fall in value might be due to a fall in the price level, or impaired usefulness, or to any combination of these two causes. This view of depreciation is adopted by some economists. Joel Dean mentions the opportunity cost of using the equipment for a year and states: "The opportunity cost could then be measured by the fall in value of the equipment during the year."[2] In case of certain assets having no alternative use the opportunity cost would be zero.

The second concept of depreciation is frequently referred to as the "appraisal concept of depreciation."[3] Depreciation is thought of as the difference between the present worth of an old asset and the present worth of a new and modern asset for performing the same kind of service. According to those holding this concept of depreciation, the ultimate object is to contrast the values of two properties as of the same date. The new asset will have advantages due to longer life expectancy, lower operation and maintenance costs, and increased receipts from sales of product or service.

Impaired serviceableness has been described as the "engineering concept of depreciation."[4] An asset may be "just as good as new" in the sense that it will produce as many units of product as ever within a time period but this ignores higher operating costs, the shortened service life, and the fact that more economical means of producing the same output may be available. This concept of depreciation is not a value concept, and hence, the assumption that "just as good as new" means "just as valuable as ever" is a serious error, even though a popular one.

The amortization of cost is the accepted accounting meaning of depreciation. This concept is set forth in Accounting Research Bulletin No. 22 in these words:

Depreciation accounting is a system of accounting which aims to distribute the cost or other basic value of tangible capital assets, less salvage (if any), over the estimated useful life of the unit (which may be a group of assets) in a systematic and rational manner. It is a process of allocation, not of valuation. *Depreciation for the year* is the portion of

2. "Measurement of Profits. . . ," p. 187.
3. Eugene L. Grant and Paul T. Norton, Jr., *Depreciation,* p. 13.
4. *Ibid.*

the total charge under such a system that is allocated to the year. Although the allocation may properly take into account occurrences during the year, it is not intended to be a measurement of the effect of all such occurrences.[5]

Much has been written concerning the *causes* of depreciation. These causes are, in general, of two kinds: (1) the wear and tear from physical operations, commonly referred to as "physical causes"; (2) "functional causes" consisting of such things as obsolesence induced by technical developments and loss of demand for the product. Accountants in recent years have broadened the concept of depreciation to include both causes. This is taken care of by the rough and ready formula of writing off the asset over the estimated physical use life or the estimated economic life, whichever is shorter. No effort is typically made by the accountant to separate the two expenses into depreciation and obsolescence.

Purposes of Depreciation Accounting

Another controversy related to the nature of depreciation is that of the purpose of the periodic deduction for depreciation in the determination of net income. This controversy is by no means a new one.[6] Furthermore, not all economists, all businessmen, nor all accountants are on one side or the other of this debate. Many accountants agree with economists and with businessmen up to a point. What are the different views on the purpose of depreciation accounting?

There is a rather widespread feeling that the primary purpose of depreciation accounting is to provide for the replacement of the related asset when its utility to the business concern has been exhausted. Turgot in his *Reflections on the Formation and the Distribution of Riches* in 1770 emphasized this replacement aspect of depreciation: "In the case of enterprises in agriculture before there is any *net produce* there must be deducted that wherewith to replace annually the wear and tear of the property employed in their undertaking, the cattle that die, the tools that wear out, etc."[7]

5. American Institute of Accountants, Committee on Accounting Procedure, "Depreciation," *Accounting Research Bulletin No. 22,* May, 1944, p. 179.

6. See Bauer, *op. cit.,* pp. 413 f.; H. C. Hasbrouck, "Cost vs. Value in Depreciation Accounting for Public Utilities," *The Journal of Accountancy,* October, 1923, p. 280; and N. D. Farmer, "The Argument in Favor of Depreciation on Replacement Values," *National Association of Cost Accountants Year Book,* 1923, p. 193.

7. Anne Robert Jacques Turgot, *Reflections on the Formation and the Distribution of Riches,* p. 55.

In the past the emphasis has been on maintaining the productive capacity of the plant. Farmer stated this position as follows:

> What is to be gained by charging depreciation? This answer is, to insure the continued productive capacity of a going business. It goes a step beyond protecting the capital investment based on cost. The point I wish to emphasize is that depreciation is designed to insure the continuation of this productive capacity.[8]

Implied in this idea of depreciation is Sweeney's second concept of maintaining capital intact; that is, the maintenance of capital means the preservation of the same amount of material physical objects. (See Chapter II.) More recently, it has been recognized by some writers that even though assets may not be replaced in kind, nevertheless depreciation is said to be measured by replacement value of equipment that will produce comparable earnings. From this point of view, replacement costs are important not because the asset will in fact be replaced but because they are the best measure of current costs, and it is current costs that are considered important in business decisions. William Blackie, vice president of Caterpillar Tractor Company, exemplified this viewpoint in these words: ". . . replacement cost is here indicated, not at all because the assets will be replaced at these or at any other costs, but only because replacement cost is generally to be expected to offer a reasonably acceptable measurement of appropriate current costs—as well as a reasonably available means of measuring it."[9]

In the postwar years, especially, the replacement cost concept of depreciation has been widely advocated by businessmen.[10] Frank M. Hesse, vice president of National Steel Corporation, in speaking of three sources of funds for replacement says: "The third source is depreciation reserves out of which we can replace our properties from year to year at whatever rate is made necessary by competitive conditions." Enders McC. Voorhes, chairman of the Finance Committee of U.S. Steel Corporation, also stressed the replacement concept of depreciation: "In my opinion the replacement of facilities should be part of the cost, and that turnover or that cash should be recovered in the selling price for the people who obtain the product and therefore the service."

The second point of view as to the purpose of depreciation accounting is that the original dollars invested in the depreciable asset should be

8. *Op. cit.*, p. 193.

9. *Op. cit.*, pp. 37 f.

10. See Frank M. Hesse, "Management's Viewpoint," *Replacement Costs and Depreciation Policy*, Studies in Business Policy No. 27, p. 13; and Enders McC. Voorhes in U.S. Congress, *Profits*, p. 54.

recovered before any profit is reported. According to this point of view, the depreciation expense should be measured in the same dollars as originally invested even though the purchasing power of those dollars has changed. This insures that the dollar value of the capital will remain intact. As pointed out in Chapter II, this maintenance of the nominal capital is the orthodox, traditional accounting viewpoint. The American Institute has stated that "accounting for fixed assets should normally be based on cost, and any attempt to make property accounts in general reflect current values is both impracticable and inexpedient."[11] Depreciation is regarded as the accounting for a past expenditure and as only indirectly related to the replacement of an asset. The loose relationship between depreciation accounting and the replacement of the assets is emphasized by the Committee on Accounting Procedure of the American Institute of Accountants: "It may be desirable to point out that depreciation is only indirectly related to replacement. It contemplates the amortization of the cost of existing property—not anticipation of the cost of replacing it as a replacement reserve might do."[12] The committee recognizes that when prices have risen substantially since the original investment in plant and facilities was made, a substantial portion of reported net income must be reinvested in the business in order to maintain assets at the same level of productivity at the end of a year as at the beginning. However, the stand is taken that stockholders, employees, and the public should be informed of this fact by the use of supplementary schedules, explanations, and footnotes.

A third viewpoint is that the purpose of depreciation accounting is the recovery of the original investment in terms of equivalent purchasing power but is not to be confused with replacement policy. George Terborgh, one of the leading advocates of this proposition, states:

We should stop confusing depreciation policy with replacement policy. The two have nothing to do with each other. The function of depreciation is to recover the capital investment, not to replace the asset. If the recovery is good, if it is equal to the investment in real purchasing power

11. American Institute of Accountants, Committee on Accounting Procedure, "Depreciation on Appreciation," *Accounting Research Bulletin No. 5,* April, 1940, p. 37.

12. American Institute of Accountants, Committee on Accounting Procedure, "Report of Committee on Terminology," *Accounting Research Bulletin No. 16,* October, 1942, p. 142; and American Institute of Accountants, Committee on Accounting Procedure, "Depreciation and High Costs," *Accounting Research Bulletin No. 33,* December, 1947, p. 270 B.

at the time it was made, it makes no difference whatsoever what is subsequently done with the funds recovered.[13]

The adherents of this doctrine agree that the purpose of depreciation should be the amortization of cost but do not go along with the accounting concept of original cost. This group thinks that the approach to the problem of changing price levels via replacement cost is wrong in theory as well as being fraught with practical difficulties. They believe that capital assets are rarely replaced in kind but are replaced because better assets are available.

The question of the purpose of depreciation thus revolves around the concept of net income chosen. In other words, every method of depreciation presupposes a definition of net income and of capital. If "real" capital is to be kept intact, or if the stream of "real" earnings is to be maintained, then the primary consideration is replacement cost, or the purchasing power equivalent of historical cost. If, on the other hand, money capital is to be kept intact, historical cost is the proper depreciation base.

In order to clarify the third viewpoint as to the purpose of depreciation accounting it will be helpful to see what has been proposed to convert depreciation from historical cost to "dollars of equivalent purchasing power." Terborgh has divided the various proposals into "one-shot" adjustments and continuous adjustments. He is an advocate of the one-shot adjustment. He prescribes it primarily on the basis of expediency and not on the basis of principle. He admits that the one-shot adjustment is "less accurate and flexible but much simpler" than continuous adjustment since "the continuous adjustment of temporally heterogeneous accounts is a rather fussy business."[14] He advocates supplementing depreciation on prewar assets (those bought prior to 1942) by a flat 50 per cent surcharge. Depreciation on assets bought since the war would be adjusted accordingly. When the one-shot adjustment gets out of line with the current price level, there would be another "one-shot adjustment." In using continuous adjustment, the depreciation on original cost is multiplied by the ratio of the price level in the current year to the price level of the year in which each asset was acquired.

A second question which must be faced is the purchasing power that is to be preserved—generalized or specific. Terborgh advocates the pres-

13. "Economic Aspects of Underdepreciation," *Replacement Costs and Depreciation Policy,* p. 6.

14. *Depreciation Policy and the Postwar Price Level,* p. 13.

TABLE 9
COMPANIES RECOGNIZING HIGHER REPLACEMENT COSTS IN 1947 FINANCIAL STATEMENTS BY ASSET SIZE

Assets (Millions of Dollars)	Companies Reporting	Companies Making Provision in Financial Statements	
		Number	Per Cent of Total
0 - 4.9	175	26	15
5 - 24.9	221	22	10
25 - 99.9	115	9	8
100 and over	48	11	23
Total	559	68	12

Source: James A. Finley, *Handling Higher Replacement Costs,* Studies in Business Policy No. 47, p. 15.

ervation of generalized purchasing power. Blackie, on the other hand, recommends a specific purchasing power index: "As both a theoretical and a practical, usable concept, therefore, the 'appropriateness' of indexes to be used for the contemplated purposes would have to rest on their construction as measurements of purchasing power in terms of only whatever it is that is purchased—inventories, machinery, buildings—all reflecting both material and labor."[15] Terborgh states that from a practical angle if we used a generalized purchasing power concept, we would get roughly the same index for both consumers' and producers' goods.[16]

What accounting practices have actually been used by firms to adjust historical cost depreciation? In 1948 the National Industrial Conference Board reported on the 1947 practices of a sample of 572 companies relative to the recognition of higher replacement costs in their 1947 financial statements. As a result of this survey, the statement was made that "accounting-wise there is evidence that many managements have weighed the advantages of departing from traditional accounting practices and gearing their depreciation charge to current costs," but that few "have taken this step."[17] Table 9 shows that 68, or 12 per cent of the companies, gave accounting recognition to higher replacement costs. Of the 68 companies giving accounting recognition to higher replacement costs, 28 supplied information as to the relationship of the special

15. *Op. cit.,* p. 37.
16. *Depreciation Policy and the Postwar Price Level,* p. 11.
17. James A. Finley, *Handling Higher Replacement Costs,* Studies in Business Policy No. 47, p. 15.

charge to normal depreciation. The results are given in Table 10. Of these 68 companies, reports of 32 were available for review by those making the study. Six had established special reserves out of accumulated earnings, 21 deducted the special provision from current net profit, and only 5 included the item as a cost before determining net profit. No clear-cut pattern emerged as to the basis of determining the amount to be set aside, the methods being rather arbitrary in most cases.

TABLE 10
RELATION OF SPECIAL CHARGE FOR HIGHER REPLACEMENT COSTS TO NORMAL DEPRECIATION CHARGE

Relation of Special Charge to Normal Depreciation Charge	Number of Companies
26% - 50%	8
51 - 75	10
76 - 100	4
101 - 125	2
Over 125	4
Total	28

Source: Finley, *op. cit.*, p. 16.

The purposes and motives behind depreciation adjustments are also revealing. In field interviews with 22 companies which constituted about one-half or more of the large companies with a highly developed depreciation adjustment for price changes, E. Cary Brown found the following purposes underlying the adjustments:[18] (1) to accumulate funds for the future replacement of assets; (2) to match current revenues by costs stated in terms of current purchasing power; (3) to amortize excess costs against present revenues since they believed that currently purchased high-cost plant could not compete with lower-cost plant purchased in some future period. As to the motives behind the adjustments, Brown mentions: the justification of small dividends to stockholders, the justification of prices, the reduction of wage demands, and the reduction of overoptimism within the firm. The National Industrial Conference Board study, cited above, gives as reasons for failure of more firms to make accounting adjustments:[19] (1) They are not allowed for tax reporting purposes; (2) they are frowned upon by the

18. *Depreciation Adjustments for Price Changes,* p. 11.
19. Finley, *op. cit.,* p. 15.

SEC; and (3) they are officially disapproved of by the society of professional accountants.

Depreciation Accounting Contrasted with Inventory Accounting

One of the problems encountered in computing depreciation expense by business firms involves the same basic argument over the use of historical costs and current costs which has already been encountered in inventory accounting. The cyclical implications of basing depreciation expense on historical cost are, in general, the same as those of the use of Fifo in inventory valuation. Depreciation expense will generally be lower during the upswing and higher during the downswing if based on historical cost rather than on current costs. The same misstatement of profit is alleged to occur with its concomitant effect on investment decisions. There are, however, some special controversies which are encountered with respect to depreciation based on the Lifo principle that were not encountered in the case of inventory accounting.

As far as orthodox accounting is concerned, the Lifo method of inventory valuation is, at least, regarded as an actual *cost* method. Depreciation on the basis of replacement cost, or based on historical cost converted to current cost by means of an index number, is often regarded as charging depreciation on a hypothetical cost. While discussions in Chapter II and Chapter III have shown that these techniques would be in accordance with most economists' concept of income, it is still anathema to the majority of the accounting fraternity. This attitude is summed up in the words of Carman G. Blough, director of research of the American Institute of Accountants:

> Under the theory of LIFO goods sold are charged out at a cost that has actually been incurred for some that were acquired during the year. The procedures that have been advocated for charging costs of fixed assets cannot be related to any actual costs. They are not designed to charge the latest costs of facilities into expense. Instead they contemplate a charge based on the cost of facilities not yet acquired. Someone has appropriately dubbed this the NIFO method—next in, first out. Its effect may have some of the same effects that LIFO has for inventories, but it seems to be highly unrealistic as a possible procedure to meet this problem.[20]

Some accountants do not regard the use of index numbers in the com-

20. "The Accountant's View," *Replacement Costs and Depreciation Policy*, p. 11.

putation of depreciation expense as a departure from the cost basis, but they believe the use of index numbers gives a measurement in current dollars of the actual dollars spent at a time when the purchasing power of the dollars was different. One of this group has stated: "It is the dollars themselves that have changed, not the costs."[21]

Another, and more basic, difference is that fixed assets last for relatively long periods of time, whereas inventories frequently turn over many times within an accounting period. According to J. Frank Gaston, fixed assets are turned over on an average of once each twenty-five years.[22] Solomon Fabricant in a study of the expected life of business capital goods manufactured in 1929 estimated that approximately 29 per cent of the value of the output of the capital goods industry had an expected life of more than twenty-five years.[23] When the change in the price level comes to an end, inventory profits and losses disappear. However, depreciation expense will continue to be computed for many years on the basis of a price level that has long ceased to exist.

In addition to the controversy over historical and current costs as the proper base for computing depreciation together with the associated cyclical implications, the fact that fixed assets last for long periods of time creates another problem—how the cost, or other basis is to be spread over the use life of the asset. The way in which this is done is said to have cyclical and long-range effects both on investment and on consumption. The effects of accounting depreciation methods on consumption will be discussed in Chapter VI.

Implications of Time Shape of Periodic Depreciation Charge

If one of the "value concepts" of depreciation is adopted, there is inherent in the method used a process of allocation of depreciation expense to the accounting period. On the other hand, if cost is accepted as a satisfactory measure of the *total amount* of depreciation to be allocated over the service life of assets, the problem of the amount of depreciation to be assigned to each accounting period must be considered. On this question of the method of spreading the cost of the asset over its estimated use life, accounting literature has much less to say concerning the criteria to be used than is the case relative to the de-

21. Samuel J. Broad, "The Effects of Price Level Changes on Financial Statements," *National Association of Cost Accountants Conference Proceedings,* 1948, p. 20.

22. *Effects of Depreciation Policy,* Studies in Business Economics No. 22, p. 8.

23. *Measures of Capital Consumption, 1919-1933,* National Bureau of Economic Research Bulletin 60, June 30, 1936, Table 4, p. 7.

preciation base. The Committee on Accounting Procedure of the American Institute of Accountants states: "All that the various methods have in common (which is all that could be embodied in a definition) is that they are designed to distribute the estimated total depreciation incurred or to be incurred during the useful life . . . in a systematic and equitable manner.[24]

This "systematic and equitable" distribution is said to maintain the accountant's independence, especially from management. Blough states: "Business as a whole will suffer if there should be any widespread feeling among the users of financial statements that charges to income are based on the whim of management, are not in accordance with generally accepted accounting procedures, and cannot be tested for fairness within reasonable limits."[25] There is not so much stress in accounting literature on the effect on profit measurement of the various methods of distributing the depreciation expense through time.

Historically, the accounting profession and the Internal Revenue Service have tended to favor the straight-line method of depreciation.[26] Its main advantages are simplicity and the large amount of experience behind its use. This method considers depreciation as solely a linear function of time and hence the depreciation expense does not vary with output. Depreciation expense as computed by this method tends to be a larger proportion of the sales dollar during slack times than during times of large sales. The penchant of the accountant for the straight-line method has been the target for most of the criticism of those who insist that the accountants' method of spreading depreciation over time tends to overstate profits during the upswing and to understate them during the downswing. This is especially true when this method is coupled with historical cost since on the upswing, for example, the base is also alleged to be understated and depreciation is a smaller per cent of the sales dollar than on the downswing.

The critics of this method fall into two groups. One group argues that from a cyclical point of view depreciation should vary with use or production. The second group stresses that, due to rapid technological changes and to the impaired usefulness of assets as they become older, the straight-line method typically understates depreciation ex-

24. *Accounting Research Bulletin No. 16,* p. 142.

25. "The Accountant's View," p. 11.

26. A detailed discussion of the various methods may be found in H. A. Finney and Herbert E. Miller, *Principles of Accounting—Intermediate,* pp. 352-372; and in Paton, *Advanced Accounting,* Chapter 12.

pense in the early years and overstates it during the latter years of the life of the asset.

Critics of the straight-line method do not accept the function-of-time argument as a justification for its use. Although depreciation is conceded to be a function of time, it is not necessarily a linear function. Fabricant, a pioneer in the study of capital consumption and various adjustments thereto, says that "the mere fact that physical deterioration in capital goods is a function of time and not of output does not mean that the only logical method is to distribute the concomitant costs evenly over time."[27] Kenneth E. Boulding, who advocates an exponential allocation of profit through time, that is, an allocation at a constant rate based on invested capital at the end of the preceding accounting period, points out that the annuity method of depreciation is in harmony with this concept of profit, provided the interest rate chosen for the depreciation formula is equal to the internal profit rate, and the revenues assigned to the asset each period are equal.[28]

The advocates of the working hours method and the production method stress the fact that these methods, or their variants, would tend to stabilize net profit over the cycle. Sumner H. Slichter, a severe critic of the straight-line method, says that

> In good years the depreciation charge per unit of output is too small and in bad years too large. As a result, profits are overstated in good years and understated in bad. If each unit of output were charged a uniform amount for depreciation, the profits of business enterprises in the long run would not be affected, but they would fluctuate less from year to year.[29]

According to Fabricant,[30] if depreciation charges had been computed on a unit of output basis at the bottom of the depression of the thirties, they would have been about 60 per cent of the charges as computed by the usual method (both expressed in 1929 dollars). He states that would have made a two billion dollar difference.

Many accountants also agree, in principle, that a method of depreciation that varies with production would give a better matching of costs and revenues. Paton, for example, says: "There is considerable force in the proposition that plant assets should be written off in proportion to

27. *Capital Consumption and Adjustment,* p. 194.
28. *Op. cit.,* pp. 789 and 810.
29. "Must We Have Another Boom?" *The Atlantic Monthly,* May, 1937, p. 604.
30. *Capital Consumption and Adjustment,* p. 199.

actual use and results accomplished rather than by periods of time as such."[31] The difficulty of estimating the use life in terms of working hours or units of product and the fear that management may arbitrarily choose a method of writeoff that is not "systematic" appear to be the two greatest deterrents to its wider adoption. William J. Vatter has said that "the accounting profession must take positive steps toward securing uniformity and consistency in depreciation computations, lest through looseness of method and abandonment of principles the science of accounting becomes a mere manipulation of figures to produce desired or predetermined results."[32]

In recent years much has been written concerning the economic effects of "accelerated depreciation." Brown[33] has defined accelerated depreciation "broadly viewed" as: "An increase in the speed with which the historic cost of an asset is written off through depreciation deductions." While accounting literature has emphasized a relatively few methods for accomplishing this speed-up in the writeoff of fixed assets—such as the sum of years' digits method and the fixed-percentage-of-diminishing-balance method—Brown states concerning his field study that "we have limited our scrutiny to fifteen plans," thus implying a multitude of plans actually encountered.

Although much of the discussion of accelerated depreciation has been in connection with the rewriting of the tax laws in order to encourage the replacement of obsolete equipment, there are those who advocate accelerated depreciation separate and apart from tax considerations. Brown[34] mentions two reasons that have been proposed for accelerated depreciation, namely, to adjust to price level changes, and to encourage the replacement of fixed assets or to stimulate the purchase of new plant. Since accelerated depreciation is still a *cost* method, it has escaped much of the criticism from the accounting profession which has been leveled at other means of adjusting to price level changes. For this reason it has been advocated in lieu of computing depreciation on the basis of higher replacement costs.

In so far as the cyclical effects are concerned, the reasons advanced for a more widespread adoption of accelerated depreciation are those already encountered in the above discussion of varying depreciation with output. The longer range problem with respect to the effect of ac-

31. *Advanced Accounting,* p. 291.

32. "Depreciation Methods of American Industrial Corporations, 1927-1935," *The Journal of Business,* April, 1937, p. 146.

33. *Op. cit.,* pp. 115 and 50.

34. *Ibid.,* p. 116.

celerated depreciation on replacement, or on the investment in new assets, will be discussed later in this chapter.

"Misstatement" of Profits Due to Accounting Depreciation

Although accounting depreciation methods have been criticized from other angles, most of the criticism has been directed at accountants' use of historical cost as the depreciation base and at their use of the straight-line method of spreading depreciation through time. These two faults of accounting methodology are said to contribute to the overstatement of profits during the upswing and to the understatement of them during the downswing. To what extent are the accusations that accountants use historical cost as the depreciation base, and the straight-line method of allocating depreciation expense to accounting periods, true?

In a 1936 survey of depreciation methods of a representative company in 39 industries, R. P. Marple[35] received 28 replies to his questionnaires. Twenty-four of the 28 used cost as the basis for depreciation. As to methods of spreading the depreciation cost through time, 24 of the 28 used straight-line, 2 used a reducing balance method, and 2 used other methods. Marple also gives the results of a study made by MAPI of 150 companies engaged in the manufacture of machinery. Of the 150, 12 did not answer, 126 used the straight-line method, 9 used a reducing balance method, one used a unit of product method, and 2 used a productive hour basis. On the basis of a survey made by the National Industrial Conference Board of 572 cooperating companies, it was stated that over 90 per cent of the concerns surveyed employed the straight-line method while 5 per cent used a unit of product method.[36]

Despite accounting conventions plant and equipment may be written up or down, thus causing depreciation expense based on these new valuations to vary although the straight-line method is used. Since the price level, sales, and production tend to vary together, this result may accomplish in a roundabout way what the units of product method or the working hours method accomplish directly. A study made by Fabricant of 208 large industrial concerns (mining and manufacturing chiefly, with a few from trade, construction and service) covering the years 1925-1934, inclusive, throws some light on the prevalence of the practice

35. "Depreciation Policy in Manufacturing Industries," *N.A.C.A. Bulletin,* May 1, 1936, pp. 1054 and 1059.

36. Finley, *op. cit.,* p. 9.

of writeups and writedowns. The companies were chosen at random from the file of SEC reports of the New York Stock Exchange. A summary of the results is given in Table 11. That the writeups and writedowns tend to follow a cyclical pattern may been seen by reference to Table 12.

TABLE 11
NUMBER OF CORPORATIONS REPORTING REVALUATIONS OF FIXED ASSETS
1925-1934

Period During Which Incorporated	Number of Corporations in Sample	Corporations Reporting Revaluations	
		Number	Per Cent of Total
Before 1901	33	24	73
1901-1914	47	30	64
1915-1920	57	49	86
1921-1924	16	13	81
1925-1934	55	41	75
Totals	208	157	75

Source: Solomon Fabricant, "Revaluation of Fixed Assets, 1925-1934," *National Bureau of Economic Research Bulletin No. 62,* p. 2.

TABLE 12
AMOUNT OF WRITEUPS AND WRITEDOWNS PROPERTY, PLANT, AND EQUIPMENT
1925-1934
(Thousands of Dollars)

Year	Writeups	Writedowns	Net Writeups*
1925	10,254	12,495	(2,241)
1926	6,614	24,008	(17,394)
1927	15,980	10,471	5,509
1928	24,086	21,474	2,612
1929	11,426	10,171	1,255
1930	12,315	7,630	4,685
1931	5,343	96,698	(91,355)
1932	. . .	236,263	(236,263)
1933	. . .	60,984	(60,984)
1934	77	59,730	(59,653)

Source: Fabricant, *op. cit.*, p. 6.
*Parentheses indicate net writedowns.

Do writeups and writedowns typically affect the amount of the depreciation expense? A study by Vatter in 1937 of 184 corporations covering approximately the same period (1927-1935) as the study of Fabricant partially answers this question. Data for this study were taken from *Poor's, Moody's,* or *Standard's Corporation Reports.* Concerning the effect of revaluation on depreciation charges, Vatter says: "One item of special interest is the effect of revaluations upon depreciation charges. Wherever downward revaluations of considerable amount were actually reported by the management, they were accompanied by reductions in depreciation charges."[37] Furthermore, Vatter found that "strict straight-line cost methods of depreciation computation, if they ever were used by a substantial majority of industrial corporations, seem, in spite of published statements of policy indicating the use of such methods, to have been largely abandoned." Thus, it would seem that while firms have largely used historical cost as the depreciation base and the straight-line method of allocating depreciation expense, in actuality some rough cyclical adjustment for depreciation expense has been made during periods of drastic price changes.

To what extent are total profits affected by using original cost as the depreciation base rather than some form of replacement cost? The Department of Commerce in computing national income does not make an adjustment for depreciation comparable to the inventory valuation adjustment.

A number of approximations of the difference between historical cost depreciation and depreciation on replacement costs have been made, however. A pioneering study by Solomon Fabricant covering the years from 1919 to 1935 was published in 1937. According to his estimates, depreciation on a current cost basis exceeded that on an original cost basis in all the years covered with the exception of 1931 to 1935.[38] The most comprehensive depreciation estimates are those of Raymond W. Goldsmith covering the period from 1897 to 1949. The estimates from 1929 to 1949 are presented in Table 13.

In addition to the estimates of Fabricant and Goldsmith a number of more limited estimates of the difference in historical and current cost depreciation have been made. Slichter estimated that profits were overstated due to inadequate depreciation by \$1.3 billion for 1946 and \$1 billion for each of the years 1947 and 1948.[39] Brown estimated that historic cost depreciation would have had to be increased from \$2 to 2.5 billion per year for the years 1948 to 1951 to bring it up to replacement cost depreciation.[40]

37. *Op. cit.,* pp. 134 and 145.

38. "On the Treatment of Corporate Savings in the Measurement of National Income," *Studies in Income and Wealth,* I, 129.

39. U.S. Congress, *Profits,* Table XVI, p. 175.

40. *Op. cit.,* p. 28.

TABLE 13
CORPORATE DEPRECIATION ADJUSTMENT 1929 TO 1949
EXCLUSIVE OF TRANSPORTATION AND PUBLIC UTILITIES
(Millions of Dollars)

Year	Estimated Depreciation Original Cost	Estimated Depreciation Current Cost	Excess of Current Over Original Cost Depreciation
	(1)	(2)	(3)
1929	3871	4732	861
1930	3986	4530	544
1931	4003	4259	256
1932	3693	3578	–115
1933	3496	3394	–102
1934	3362	3561	199
1935	3352	3577	225
1936	3286	3511	225
1937	3342	3819	477
1938	3352	3800	448
1939	3443	3895	452
1940	3520	4037	517
1941	3765	4487	722
1942	3914	4868	954
1943	3916	4913	997
1944	3950	4938	988
1945	3977	5003	1026
1946	4199	5729	1530
1947	5220	7897	2677
1948	6150	9418	3268
1949	6750	9768	3018

Source: Raymond W. Goldsmith, *A Study of Saving in the United States,* I, 955.

A number of summary statements comparing totals of historic cost and replacement cost for a number of years may be found. Raymond W. Goldsmith estimates that over the period studied (1897-1949) capital consumption allowances were $89 billion, or 15 per cent, higher on a replacement cost basis than on an original cost basis.[41] Terborgh says that in only two of the years from 1910 to 1953 was replacement cost less than original cost.[42] Goldsmith shows this to be true also for 1913 and 1914. Gaston's statement, "If replacement-cost depreciation were used, profits would have been reduced in every year from 1937 to the present,"[43] is thus in harmony with the findings of both Terborgh and Goldsmith. Goldsmith found that the average yearly adjustment for depreciation, ignoring signs, is about $600 million compared to the inventory adjustment of $1,000 million.[44]

41. *Op. cit.,* I, 31.
42. *Op. cit.,* p. 142.
43. *Op. cit.,* p. 15.
44. *Op. cit.,* II, 543.

Direct Effects of Depreciation on the Inducement to Invest

So far, the discussion has been confined to the effect of depreciation accounting on the inducement to invest through its effects on the amount of profit reported. The inducement to invest is thus affected indirectly: Depreciation affects the amount of reported profit which is considered *an* important factor, if not *the* important factor in investment decisions. Aside from this indirect effect, depreciation accounting is also presumed by some writers to affect investment decisons more directly. In this connection, straight-line depreciation has come in for severe criticism.

Adopting an "impaired serviceableness" concept of depreciation, it is stressed by some writers that the value of the services furnished by fixed assets becomes less as the assets get older. Terborgh states that "rising operating costs, impaired service quality or adequacy, and improved alternatives—combine to reduce the value of the service as the assets age."[45] Straight-line depreciation, therefore, from this point of view tends to undercharge depreciation in the early years of an asset and overcharge it in the later years compared with the "ideal" method. Furthermore, the adherents of this viewpoint believe that the empirical evidence is sufficient to charge depreciation on the basis of this decreased serviceableness and thus they attempt to undermine one of the reasons given for the preference for straight-line depreciation accounting; that is, the experience in estimating use life in time periods. Terborgh believes that a "realistic allocation procedure should get rid of at least one-half of the initial value over the first third of the service life and at least two-thirds over the first half."[46]

Grant and Norton advocate a declining balance method using a rate 2.5 times the appropriate rate under the straight-line group method as corresponding "to the objective that the authors have suggested as appropriate for many economy studies" and state that this method "will write off about half of the cost of a group of assets in the first quarter of the average service life and about three-fourths of the cost in the first half of the average life."[47]

As contrasted with the arguments that depreciation charges should be based on replacement cost, or that depreciation expense should vary with output, thereby stabilizing reported profits before tax, and hence, investment expenditures, these accelerated methods would speed up the process of depreciation accrual. Furthermore, some writers believe it is possible that the use of accelerated depreciation causes firms to replace

45. *Op. cit.*, p. 33. 46. *Ibid.*, p. 47. 47. *Op. cit.*, p. 312.

their old equipment sooner than they would otherwise. Thus accelerated depreciation is thought to affect investment decisions directly.

While it is admitted that, from the viewpoint of economic analysis, the fact that past investment has not been fully depreciated is irrelevant to replacement decisions, it is nevertheless alleged by the advocates of accelerated depreciation methods that depreciation accounting does actually affect investment decisions. As can be seen by the following typical statement, the argument is one pertaining to long-term growth more than to cyclical fluctuations:

> Only through the rapid replacement of equipment is it possible for industry to take advantage of scientific and technological progress. If improvements in industrial equipment were not put into place until the old equipment were fully depreciated, there would be a sizable lag between technological progress and the general benefits to be derived from that progress.[48]

One reason given for accelerated depreciation being a stimulant to investment is that depreciation is normally the major source of business investment funds. Depreciation accounting, furthermore, seems to be used in some companies as a partial substitute for financial budgeting. Grant and Norton point out this tendency as follows: "In many manufacturing businesses, both large and small, budget policies operate so that under ordinary circumstances the funds made available for acquisition of new fixed assets for all purposes (replacement, plant modernization, plant expansion) are limited to an amount of money equal to the current depreciation charge on the books of account."[49]

The second reason given by those who argue that depreciation accounting directly affects investment decisions is the reluctance of the businessman to "take a loss" by writing off an undepreciated asset. George Katona speaks of this reluctance as follows: "It appears that replacing a machine that is not yet written off is an especially difficult decision, that is, one that requires compelling reasons."[50] Grant and Norton also emphasize that "there is no doubt that the high book value of old assets often operates as a deterrent to economical retirement."[51]

At least one accountant concurs in this belief:

> When the question arises as to the advisability of discarding an old, but still usable, machine, and substituting a newer model, one faces the

48. Gaston, *op. cit.*, pp. 31 and 33.
49. *Op. cit.*, p. 328.
50. *Psychological Analysis of Economic Behavior,* pp. 244 f.
51. *Op. cit.*, p. 311.
52. Henry Rand Hatfield, "Replacement and Book Value," *The Accounting Review,* January, 1944, p. 66.

necessity of writing off the book value of the obsolete machine. It is always disagreeable to write off an asset.[52]

Summary

The nature of depreciation and the purpose of depreciation accounting have been subjects of controversy for decades. Although there are many facets to these controversies, most of the argument has been over the question as to whether depreciation accounting should be concerned with the provision for the replacement of the asset when its utility to the business has been exhausted, or with the amortization of a past cost. Over the years, replacement cost advocates have at times used two arguments, or variants of them, for the first point of view: (1) depreciation on the basis of replacement cost tends to maintain the physical productive capacity of the business; (2) provision should be made to replace old equipment with equipment that will enable earning power to be maintained, and since replacement costs are current, they are the correct costs to match against current dollars of revenue in determining whether earning power has been maintained.

The amortization-of-cost adherents are divided into two schools of thought. Depreciation should be measured in the same dollars as those originally invested. This has been the traditional accounting point of view. The advocates of the second school of thought agree that the purpose of depreciation accounting is the writing off of the past cost of the old equipment but insist that the historic cost should be converted into dollars equivalent in purchasing power to those originally invested before deducting it from revenue in order to determine net income. There is further disagreement as to the index to be used in converting the historical cost dollars to dollars of equivalent purchasing power. Should the index be one of generalized purchasing power, or a specific index computed on the basis of the changes in the price of the asset that is to be replaced?

While the controversy over the depreciation base is similar to the Lifo versus Fifo argument with respect to inventories, there are also differences. These differences revolve around the fact that fixed assets last for relatively long periods of time and the allocation of depreciation expense through time is thought to have cyclical and long range ramifications. The critics of accounting methods single out especially the straight-line method of allocation and insist that depreciation should vary with income or with production in order to level out reported income, and hence, to stabilize investment expenditures.

While studies have revealed that the straight-line method is the predominant method in use, other studies have cast doubt on its rigid application throughout all phases of the business cycle. Although the U.S. Department of Commerce does not make use of an adjustment for depreciation as it does for inventories, other estimates of the "misstatement" of depreciation expense have been made. These estimates have shown that the "historic cost error" due to depreciation, while smaller on an average than in the case of inventories, is still sizable.

In addition to the effect on investment decisions through the computation of net income, depreciation accounting—especially straight-line depreciation accounting—is thought to affect investment more directly. Relying on the impaired serviceableness concept of depreciation, these critics insist that depreciation accounting should be accelerated. The failure to do so is thought to retard the investment in improved facilities and is thus thought to impede long-term economic growth. While it is admitted by many of these critics that depreciation accounting *should* not influence investment in improved assets, it is *thought* to do so. The reluctance of the businessman to write off assets not fully depreciated on the books and the tendency to limit investment expenditures to the amount of the current depreciation charges are the two chief reasons given for this belief.

Thus, (1) *accepting* the thesis that business fluctuations are tied primarily to private business investment expenditures; (2) *abstracting away*: (a) technological change as a factor in investment decisions, and (b) the income tax structure; and (3) *assuming*: (a) that businessmen attempt to invest in such a way as to maximize expected business profits, (b) that prospective business profits are judged by past profits as measured by accounting techniques, and (c) that, since accounting techniques—largely, inventory and depreciation accounting—overstate these profits on the upswing and understate them on the downswing, thus leading the businessman to invest more on the upswing and less on the downswing than if these profits were stated on an "economic" basis, the result would seem to follow that accounting techniques accentuate business fluctuations. Certainly the theoretical framework is imposing.

Before it can be said with any degree of certainty, however, that accounting methodology does accentuate business fluctuations, via investment decisions, it is necessary to examine the assumptions and to replace the economy within the institutional framework from which it has been abstracted.

Chapter V

Some Further Considerations of Business Investment Decisions

IN THE PRECEDING CHAPTERS the following assumptions as to businessmen's behavior in making investment decisions have been inherent in the discussion: (1) Businessmen attempt to invest in such a way as to maximize expected profits; (2) prospective profits are judged by past profits as measured by accounting techniques; and (3) businessmen are "misled" by these accounting profits into investing in such a way as to accentuate the swings in business fluctuations. In the present chapter it is proposed to examine these assumptions carefully. In so far as it can be shown that these assumptions are not in conformity with reality, or that there are alternative assumptions that appear to fit the facts equally well, the superstructure built up in the earlier chapters is weakened. Furthermore, in the discussion to date, changing technology as a factor in investment decisions has been largely neglected. The fact that a large share of reported profits is siphoned away in the form of income taxes has been entirely ignored. The dropping of these limiting conditions may strengthen or weaken accounting profits as a factor in business investment decisions.

In Chapter IV the argument was presented that accelerated depreciation tends to encourage a high level of investment but no evidence was presented to substantiate this argument nor was any attempt made to see if there were counterarguments, or offsetting tendencies. In the present chapter an evaluation of this argument will be made. In the light of the more realistic environment presented in the current chapter, a further evaluation of accounting profits as a factor in investment decisions via the price of securities will also be made.

Profit Maximization as an Incentive in Investment Decisions

It has been recognized for some time that in the large widely-held corporation with its separation of ownership and management profit maximization is not completely adequate as an explanation of economic behavior. Joel Dean points out this fact in these words:

> A corporation is not single-minded. It is composed of groups and individuals whose interests conflict. The concept of management as arbiter among employees, customers, and stockholders can lead to capital-expenditure policies and commitments that stray from the directional beam of capital productivity.[1]

The assumption of profit maximization is more valid where owner and entrepreneur are one. As one writer has said: "The *small business-man,* a term subsuming the four functions of the entrepreneur, manager, capitalist, and worker, is the protagonist featured in most of the traditional profit theories."[2] However, where owner and entrepreneur are not one, maximization of individual gain may take precedence over that of the maximization of profit for the firm. The maximization of profit for the stockholders is not necessarily in the "enlightened self-interest" of the operational managerial group. In the large corporations, especially, the desire of the officers to maintain control may supersede the desire to make maximum profits. This desire to maintain control, and possibly to maximize personal gain, may even be detrimental to firm profits.

Even where the desire for firm profits does dominate the behavior of the managerial group, the idea that this group tries to *maximize* profits needs qualification. The critics of profit maximization have offered alternative and additional motives. The doctrine of "adequate," or "satisfactory," profits has been proposed as a substitute, especially in the larger, more mature, corporation. R. A. Gordon has said: "I suspect that 'satisfactory profits,' as vague as that criterion is, is frequently a more accurate description of the primary objective than 'maximum profits.' This is particularly likely to be true of mature, successful firms."[3] As long as there are adequate profits to satisfy stockholders, the officers

1. "Measuring the Productivity of Capital," *Harvard Business Review,* January—February, 1954, p. 121.
2. Peter L. Bernstein, "Profit Theory—Where Do We Go from Here?" *The Quarterly Journal of Economics,* August, 1953, p. 409.
3. *Op. cit.,* p. 271.

of the corporation may have wide discretion as to objectives. Dean has given six reasons why corporations would want to limit profits: (1) to discourage potential competitors, (2) to woo the voting public and restrain the zeal of antitrusters, (3) to restrain wage demands of organized labor, (4) to maintain customer good will, (5) to keep control undiluted, and (6) to maintain pleasant working conditions.[4]

The desire for *secure* profits is ranked by some economists as being on a par with the desire to maximize profits. Concerning this motive one writer has said: "But there is another motive which cannot be so lightly dismissed, and which is probably of a similar order of magnitude as the desire for maximum profits: the desire for *secure* profits."[5] This desire for secure profits can be integrated with profit maximization if we set the goal as long-run profit maximization. Most of the above motives given by Dean for corporations wanting to limit profits could be construed as reasons for limiting short-run profits in order to increase long-run profits. Fritz Machlup, a staunch defender of profit maximization, argues that the desire for secure profits can be integrated with the profit maximization motive, while it is possible that the demand for "position," as advocated by some writers, cannot. He does, however, recognize that the desire for both position and security is important:

> One can deal with these considerations equally well whether they are treated under the heading of a separate security motive or as additional points under the all-inclusive profit motive. The main thing is that they are treated; under what heading they are treated is irrelevant.[6]

The market position of the firm is also a factor controlling the degree to which the profit motive can be ignored. Under noncompetitive conditions the firm may show a satisfactory profit while allowing considerable inefficiency. M. W. Reder stresses that it was the assumption of pure competition that gave profit maximization its a priori plausibility, and states that:

> If there were keen competition, the management could not depart from the principle of profit maximization—at least for long. For any excess profits would be competed away by new firms who would drive down prices and compel the entrepreneur to keep total cost down to the minimum in order to avoid losses. Therefore, any departure from the

4. *Managerial Economics,* p. 29.

5. K. W. Rothschild, "Price Theory and Oligopoly," *The Economic Journal,* September, 1947, p. 308.

6. *The Economics of Sellers' Competition,* p. 427.

principle of profit maximization would be speedily corrected by the forces of competition.[7]

The large firm operating under noncompetitive conditions may be more interested in strategy than in profit making. Maintaining or increasing the company's share of the market has received increasing attention in recent years as an objective of business operations. Dean points out that "actually in many cases money making is a secondary objective. Often the primary goal is strategic—to maintain or increase the company's share of the market, to achieve growth in sales volume or number of employees, or simply to build reputation or status."[8] Another writer has said: "The use of market-share measurement by top management has become almost universal."[9] Although this managerial group may recognize that an increase in market-share does not necessarily imply greater profit, he believes it may become a target in itself as far as middle management is concerned when it is passed on to them.

Despite the various controversies over the motive of profit maximization certain conclusions emerge: (1) There is still considerable support among writers for profit maximization as a goal of economic behavior. (2) There is an increasing tendency to broaden the profit motive even though the result is a concept (or concepts) less precisely defined than the traditional maximization of profits. (3) The so-called "non-economic" motives are now taken much more seriously than formerly in spite of the difficulties of measurement involved. (4) In the large widely-held corporation the directness of the profit motive has been blunted for the following reasons: (a) Personal ambition may be more important than profit maximization in the firm with separation of management and ownership. (b) Large profits in the large corporation have become unpopular in recent years. (c) Size, sales volume, and market-share may become the primary, short-run objectives even though profit may be the ultimate goal.

The broadening of the traditional profit motive and the recognition that it is often less direct than has been depicted, especially in the large corporation, have not only raised some doubts as to the adequacy of profit maximization in explaining economic behavior in general of entrepreneurs, but have also aroused further uncertainty as to the motives

7. "A Reconstruction of the Marginal Productivity Theory," *The Journal of Political Economy,* October, 1947, p. 453.

8. "Measuring the Productivity . . . ," p. 121.

9. Alfred R. Oxenfeldt, "How to Use Market-Share Measurement," *Harvard Business Review,* January—February, 1959, p. 68.

behind investment decisions. Some writers have questioned whether the profit motive, or at least the short-run maximization of profits, is the only determinant of the level of investment expenditures, or even the major determinant of the level of these expenditures.[10] If, in lieu of maximum profits, adequate profits is adopted as the explanation for entrepreneurial behavior, profits as a determinant of capital expenditures is blunted. If the primary immediate goal of those in charge of the daily operations of the firm is the maintenance of the company's share of the market, growth in sales volume, or the building of reputation or status, these semipecuniary motives cannot be evaluated with the same precision as profit maximization. Furthermore, a goal of "increase in market-share," "growth in sales volume," or "maximum sales volume" may become an objective in itself. Thus, even after conceding that the profit maximization assumption still has considerable validity, as an incentive for investment expenditures the relative importance of the positive component, sales, and the negative component, expenses, in the making of investment decisions should be considered. In so far as the sales component is controlling, the effect of accounting methodology on investment decisions is still further weakened since it was shown in Chapter II that it is the expense calculations and not the recording of sales or anticipated sales that are alleged to be misleading.

That the sales component is more important than expenses in determining investment decisions under noncompetitive conditions has been demonstrated a priori by Norman S. Buchanan. In the absence of technological change, under conditions of imperfect competition it is the demand curve for the product that is most unknown. While the expenses cannot be estimated with absolute accuracy, they can be estimated with more accuracy than the sales revenue, or the demand curve. According to Buchanan, "sales anticipations, both for the coming period and for several periods forward, are likely more nearly to determine output plans and investment outlays than anything else."[11] In order for expansion to take place, sales anticipations must already be so optimistic that additional facilities are needed. Unless some revenue will be sacrificed because of insufficient facilities, the added investment will not be required. However, in firms in imperfect competition, excess capacity is the rule rather than the exception. Therefore, concludes Buchanan:

10. Arthur Stone Dewing, *The Financial Policy of Corporations,* II, 816; Martin Taitel, *Profits, Productive Activities, and New Investment,* Temporary National Economic Committee Monograph No. 12, p. xix; and Dean, "Measuring the Productivity . . . ," p. 121.

11. "Anticipations and Industrial Investment Decisions," p. 145.

"In the absence of technological changes, market domination, trade position and expansion per se are essentially a function of sales volume."[12]

In pure competition, on the other hand, while the entrepreneur does not know his future prices, he does know the shape of his demand curve, and he also knows that his gross income will be proportionate to his output, and, hence, is likely to busy himself with cost and output problems. Therefore, in "the absence of technological improvements, the sensitivity of investment to price influences is a function of the degree of competition."[13] If one accepts this proposition, then the more nearly industries approach the competitive pattern, the more important do expense calculations become as a determinant of investment decisions. The more important the expense component becomes, the greater the role played by accounting methods in investment decisions.

In order to determine the motivation behind investment decisions, a number of studies using interview techniques have been made. No one of these studies has been comprehensive; each has been more in the nature of a pilot study. These studies will now be reviewed and the conclusions presented in order to see what is stressed by the businessmen who make investment decisions as being the dominant factors in these decisions.

In 1941 Ruth P. Mack published the results of an extensive study of 56 corporations covering 11 industries and including some of the nation's industrial giants. In the course of her study Mack held interviews with someone of at least vice-presidential rank and frequently with several of the minor executives as well. As a result of her study, Mack concluded:

> Except for brief periods of anticipation of perhaps a few months . . . company officials waited for sales to materialize and often for them to have materialized for some time, before risking capital investment. Insofar, then, as the companies visited were in this respect typical of business as a whole, we might conclude that for the post 1933 period the causal relation between sales and capital purchases ran from the former to the latter.[14]

In the spring of 1950 a series of interviews was conducted by Franco Modigliani and members of the staff of the Merrill Foundation Project

12. *Ibid.*, pp. 144 f.
13. *Ibid.*, p. 155.
14. *The Flow of Funds and Consumer Purchasing Power*, p. 281.

in Expectations and Business Fluctuations. These studies involved almost exclusively firms in the agricultural equipment industry and emphasized problems of capital expenditures and forward planning. These interviews were supplemented by interviews with executives in 15 manufacturing corporations in the Midwest and East in the winter and spring of 1951-1952. The firms were the largest, or among the largest, in the agricultural equipment, shoe manufacturing, beer, container (paper and cardboard), steel, and rubber industries. Individuals interviewed ranged from presidents, board chairmen, and executive vice-presidents to controllers, treasurers, production schedulers, and firm economists. Firm documents and statistics were solicited and, where obtained, were subjected to a continuing analysis. As a result of this study, Robert Eisner concluded: "The estimate of future demand is certainly the most often cited determinant of the volume of capital expenditures."[15]

In the summer of 1950 George Katona and James N. Morgan headed a personal interview study of 188 plants located in Michigan. The study was sponsored by the Research Center of the University of Michigan. When the firm had its head office in Michigan, the top executive of the firm was interviewed. If the head office was not in Michigan, then the chief executive of the plant was interviewed, with other executives often being drawn into the discussion. Public utilities, mining firms, the large automobile industries, and manufacturing plants with less than twelve employees were excluded. A large part of the sample was made up of industries prominent in Michigan: metal products, furniture, and chemicals. It was found that of the 188 respondents, 103 had expanded their plant or equipment during the last years prior to the interview, and 89 were found to have plans for contemplated expansion. The interviewees were asked the direct question as to why they had expanded or contemplated expansion. No attempt was made by the interviewers to clarify the responses since this was "deemed highly suggestive." Current demand and future demand constituted the reasons given by 69 per cent of the firms for past expansion and by 58 per cent of the firms for contemplated expansion.[16]

Michael Gort conducted interviews during the spring and summer of 1950 with officials of 25 electric utilities located in the Northeast,

15. "Interview and Other Survey Techniques and the Study of Investment," *Problems of Capital Formation,* A Report of the National Bureau of Economic Research Conference on Research in Income and Wealth, p. 577.

16. "The Quantitative Study of Factors Determining Business Decisions," *The Quarterly Journal of Economics,* February, 1952, p. 84.

East Central, and North Central regions (according to the Federal Power Commission classification of companies). Forty officials were interviewed, including presidents, chairmen of boards, vice-presidents, assistants to the president, assistant controllers, chief planning officers on the engineering level, budget officers, staff engineers, and accountants. The companies accounted for roughly two-thirds of the generating capacity of private utilities in the three regions and close to one-half of that for the whole country. Gort supplemented his interviews with an examination of documentary records. Access to unpublished records was granted in the case of 14 companies. Gort concluded that: "The most important single factor affecting decisions to spend on plant and equipment in the electric industry is the expected demand."[17]

P. W. S. Andrews and Elizabeth Brunner made a study of the capital development of the United Steel Companies, Ltd. This study consisted of a series of repeated interviews and an examination of firm documents. The authors concluded: "If one had to plump for the most important single factor in the determination of the current level of capital expenditure in individual businesses—and, therefore, the one which should predominate in any general analysis—the level of demand appears to be the one which should be selected."[18]

Irwin Friend and Jean Bronfenbrenner[19] made a study of 305 manufacturing firms whose actual expenditures on plant and equipment differed by more than 25 per cent from anticipated outlays reported by the business between mid-January and mid-March, 1949. The "sales outlook" was the principal reason given by 34.1 per cent of the firms who decided to decrease capital outlays whereas only 12.1 per cent gave "net earnings after taxes" as a reason. While only 10.4 per cent of the firms who decided to increase capital outlays gave sales as the principal reason, the proportion giving net earnings (after taxes) as a reason was still smaller, 5.2 per cent. The authors draw certain interesting conclusions: (1) "Only the smallest firms mentioned changes in the earnings outlook as a significant factor in reducing planned outlays"; (2) "It appears that when the competitive situation is an important factor, the investment response to a decline in sales is opposite in direction to that which ordinarily occurs";(3) "Movements in earnings, also, were

17. "The Planning of Investment: A Study of Capital Budgeting in the Electric-Power Industry. II," *The Journal of Business,* July, 1951, p. 181.

18. *Capital Development in Steel,* p. 359.

19. "Business Investment Programs and Their Realization," *Survey of Current Business,* December, 1950, pp. 19 ff.

found to contribute little toward the explanation of discrepancies between actual and anticipated expenditures."

In summary, Mack, together with Katona and Morgan, have found current demand to be the dominant factor in determining investment decisions. Eisner and Gort found "future demand" and "expected demand" to be the determining factor while Andrews and Brunner stressed the "level of demand." In their post-mortem study as to why planned investment expenditures were changed, Friend and Bronfenbrenner found the "sales outlook" to be the dominant factor for decreasing expenditures relative to planned expenditures. While "sales outlook" was not the most frequently mentioned reason for increasing expenditures over the estimates, it was still given twice as frequently as "net earnings after taxes." "Net earnings after taxes" was mentioned as a significant reason for reducing actual expenditures under planned expenditures only in case of the smallest firms. The conclusions reached by all these inquirers into the determinants of investment decisions are consistent in assigning present or prospective *sales* as being the primary determinant of investment decisions. Thus the empirical evidence substantiates Buchanan's postulate that expansion is a function of sales volume.

It may be true that in the mind of the businessman the amount of sales is closely associated with the amount of short-run profit. He may have in mind the breakeven chart of his business and the contribution to overhead, accompanied by a rapid rise in profits, as his firm attains a high level of sales even when emphasizing sales as the immediate determinant of investment decisions. The studies, however, do not throw any light on the extent to which the concepts of sales and profit are associated or differentiated in the thinking of the businessman when making investment expenditures.

Any generalizations relative to the determinants of investment expenditures cannot be separated from the psychological, economic, and political framework in which the expenditure decisions are made. Therefore, in interpreting the results of these interviews certain limitations should be kept in mind. The studies, made for specific companies at a given time, could not take account of any possible shifts in the relative importance of reasons for investment decisions with the passage of time. The studies were made during a period of prosperity. During this phase of the cycle the capacity of his business to keep up with increased customer demand would be uppermost in the mind of the businessman, thus accounting for "sales" or "sales outlook" being given as the chief reason for capital outlays. Increased sales as an incentive for expansion during this phase conforms to the theory that the accelerator principle works during the upswing but becomes inoperative during the downswing. During the depression phase of the cycle the desire to lower cost or to improve his product (or to develop new products) could very well take precedence over increased demand as the reason given for investment expenditures. Generalizations of motives for investment would also need to encompass the various stages of growth of individual firms.

However, if the amount of sales and profit are not closely associated in the mind of the businessman, in so far as these findings are representative of business investment behavior, profit becomes a rather roundabout determinant of investment decisions. Concerning the subtleness of the profit motive in making investment expenditures, Gort said:

> Both profit considerations and financial factors reflect themselves in a rather subtle way in a marginal area of investment decisions, consisting of optional construction, replacement and maintenance expenditures, the choice of satisfactory reserve capacity, and others. When earnings and the supply of funds decline, there is a tendency toward economy-mindedness, the planning horizon shortens, and tests for approval of capital expenditures become more rigid.[20]

Although the incentive of profit maximization is not abandoned even in the large corporation, it may be weaker than has been assumed as a determinant of investment decisions, no matter how the profits are measured—whether by accounting methods, or by "economic" criteria. In the smaller, more closely held firm, on the other hand, the non-pecuniary and the semipecuniary motives seem to be weaker than in the large firm and thus the theory of expansion in response to profit is more direct. It is easier to reconcile economic behavior, even in the large corporation, with the profit motive if the maximization of long-run profits, rather than short-run profits, is adopted as a goal. However, since the cycle is a short-run phenomenon, and since accounting is concerned with short-run profit measurement, the theory that the accountants' "misstatement" of profit accentuates the cycle is weakened when one accepts maximization of profits in the long-run as the norm of economic behavior.

Ex-Post Profits Versus Expected Profits as an Investment Factor

As shown in Chapter II, those who argue that accounting method-

20. *Op. cit.*, p. 201.

ology unduly influences business fluctuation through its effect on investment decisions support the argument by stressing *realized* income as being of a high relative importance in these investment decisions. Writers with opinions on this subject, however, are not all in agreement with this point of view. Some of them maintain that decisions to purchase plant and equipment depend upon estimates of the profitability of capital in the future. Wesley C. Mitchell emphasized *expected* profits as the motivating force behind investment decisions:

> The profits which count in determining solvency are not merely the profits or losses realized in the recent past, but also profits anticipated in the near future. Indeed, business looks forward more than it looks backward. . . . And anticipated profits play the decisive role in fixing the direction to be taken by business expansion. It is the enterprises with faith in their future which finance extensions out of their own funds or out of funds borrowed from investors.[21]

Still other writers have no decided opinion and admit that the role played by *ex-post* business income as a factor influencing investment decisions has not been agreed upon by either businessmen or economists.

What evidence is available as to the relative significance in investment decisions of *ex-post* profits versus expected profits? Heller and his colleagues at the University of Minnesota carried out a field study on investment decisions in thirteen of the leading manufacturing firms with headquarters in the Twin Cities Area. They relied chiefly on twenty-five interviews of from two to three hours each with key decision makers in exploring the anatomy of decisions to invest in plant and equipment. The companies, while the largest in the area, were medium-sized if looked at nationally, the number of employees varying from 300 to 12,000 and net worth ranging up to $93 million. In growth pattern the companies ranged all the way from two in the stagnant flour milling and grain handling business to five that were among the outstanding growth companies of the United States. The authors of *The Minneapolis Project* conclude: "As other studies, the Minneapolis Project confirms the vital importance of profits as the lubricant for private capital investment—both as a lure for taking risks and as a source of funds for managements which don't like to use outside funds."[22] One of the authors of the results of this study asks the following questions: "Does

21. *Business Cycles: The Problem and Its Setting,* p. 106; see also Abramovitz, *op. cit.,* p. 480.

22. Arthur Upgren, Frank Boddy, Carl Nelson, and Walter Heller, *The Minneapolis Project—A Pilot Study of Local Capital Formation,* p. 19.

the decision maker respond mainly to realized or to anticipated profits? Do changes in realized profits lead, or do they lag behind, changes in capital-spending programs?"[23] The following answer is given to these questions: "The impressionistic answer we got in our survey is that they lead, for forecasted profits are only slightly adjusted projections of the profits realized in the immediate past." Mordecai Ezekiel made a statistical study of the relationship between past and current profits and subsequent investment in plant and equipment based on corporate profits before income tax for the years 1921 to 1940. He concluded: "The most significant relation discovered was between corporate profits in one year and plant and equipment investment in the following year. About four-fifths of the variation in investment was explained by this simple relation."[24] Further on, the same writer stated: "When profits of both the preceding and the current year are taken into account, over nine-tenths of the variation in investment could be explained, with profits of the preceding year having a weight almost 50 per cent heavier than the profits of the current year."

Martin Taitel made an analysis of the relationship between profit and asset expansion rates of 22 leading oil producing and refining corporations. He concluded:

High profit rates, in and of themselves, have not been sufficient guaranties of high rates of asset expansion. . . . At a 5 per cent rate of return, the range has been from an average asset-contraction rate of about 1.4 per cent in 1932 to an average asset-expansion rate of 4.5 per cent in 1937 and almost 6 per cent in 1929.[25]

Albert Ralph Koch made a study of the financing of large corporations in the fields of manufacturing, trade, transportation, communications, and electric light and power from 1920 to 1939. One of Koch's findings was stated as follows:

During the depression years, corporations, even when their current sales and profit positions were relatively favorable, were unwilling to anticipate the future by modernizing and expanding their plant and equipment, although the cost of doing so was low relative to prosperous years. In tobacco, for example, although sales dropped only 13 per cent and net income before dividends actually increased 22 per cent

23. Walter W. Heller, "The Anatomy of Investment Decisions," *Harvard Business Review,* March, 1951, p. 98.

24. "Statistical Investigations of Saving, Consumption, and Investment," *The American Economic Review,* June, 1942, pp. 282 f.

25. *Op. cit.,* p. 94.

from 1929 to 1932, the fixed property/depreciation ratio dropped from 2.8 to 1.4, or 50 per cent.[26]

Katona and Morgan in connection with their survey, mentioned earlier, studied the relationship between current business conditions and expansion plans as well as that between business prospects and expansion plans. A tabulation of the results is given in Tables 14 and 15. While

TABLE 14
RELATION BETWEEN EXPANSION PLANS AND THE EVALUATION OF CURRENT BUSINESS CONDITIONS

Expansion Plans	Percentage Distribution of Firms According to Executives' Opinions of Current Business Conditions		
	Very Good	Good	Bad
To build new plants or additions to plants	45	18	22
To add new machinery	19	20	11
Uncertain or not ascertained	10	9	4
Will not expand	26	53	63
	100	100	100
Number of firms	80	77	27

Source: George Katona and James N. Morgan, "The Quantitative Study of Factors Determining Business Decisions," *The Quarterly Journal of Economics,* February, 1952, p. 87. Reprinted by permission of the publishers, Harvard University Press, Copyright, 1952, by the President and Fellows of Harvard College.

these tables show a correlation between expansion plans and both the evaluation of current conditions and business prospects, the correlations are far from perfect. Although the percentage of those who planned to expand plant and machinery and who thought business was very good, was high—64 per cent, as compared to 38 per cent who thought business was good, and 33 per cent who thought business was bad—yet the fact remains that 33 per cent of the firms who thought that business was bad still planned to expand. Table 15 shows that 60 per cent of those who expected business to be better planned to expand, yet 34 per cent of those who expected business to be better did not plan to expand. It is also worthy of note that 37 per cent of those who expected business to be worse planned to expand plant and machinery.

26. *The Financing of Large Corporations 1920-1939,* p. 30.

TABLE 15
RELATION BETWEEN EXPANSION PLANS AND THE EVALUATION OF BUSINESS PROSPECTS

Expansion Plans	Percentage Distribution of Firms According to Executives' Opinions of Business Prospects			
	Better	About the Same	Pro-con, Depends, Don't Know	Worse
To build new plants or additions to plants	49	27	25	21
To add new machinery	11	23	17	16
Uncertain or not ascertained	6	9	8	6
Will not expand	34	41	50	57
	100	100	100	100
Number of firms	35	74	60	14

Source: Katona and Morgan, *op. cit.*, p. 87.

Thus, of the studies reviewed, Taitel's indicates that there is no close relationship between profit rates and asset expansion. Koch's study indicates, that for the depression phase at least, neither a good *present* profit showing nor *present* sales showing necessarily means more investment. The Katona and Morgan study does not indicate much as to the relative importance of *realized* and *anticipated* profits. It does indicate, however, that expansion does not automatically take place as a result of favorable present business conditions as is so often implied. In fact, James Morgan has criticised Eisner's study as follows: "Most striking of all is the complete omission from the author's [Eisner] conclusions of the possibility that an actual or expected *decline* in sales and profits can be the force which induces decisions to invest."[27] The remaining two studies indicate a closer relationship between *ex-post* profits and business expansion decisions. However, one of the authors of the Minneapolis study[28] indicates that the companies surveyed did "not fit the separation-of-ownership-and-management pattern made famous by Berle and Means." There was an interwoven relationship among owners, boards of directors, and managers. Risk taking, policy making, and operating decisions often overlapped. All three functions were some-

27. "Comment," in *Problems of Capital Formation*, p. 586.
28. Heller, *op. cit.*, p. 96.

times combined in key people. It is pointed out that: "Managers who are also owners tend to keep their eyes on maximum profits rather than on internal 'empire-building' designed to build up their position as managers." When the above facts are considered, therefore, the Minneapolis Project can be reconciled with the proposition that *ex-post* profits are a more important factor in the small closely-held firm than in the large widely-held corporation—which has been the pattern emerging from this consideration of profit maximization as a factor in investment decisions.

Although past and current accounting profits are undoubtedly a factor in investment decisions, it is by no means certain from the above evidence that all, or even a substantial portion, of these decisions are made on the basis of reported profits. Not only has profit maximization itself been weakened and diffused, especially in the large corporation, but it is far from certain that accounting profits are used in lieu of *expected* profits.

An Evaluation of the Argument That Businessmen Are Misled

Even if it is conceded that profit maximization is paramount in investment decisions and that *ex-post* profits are used as a guide in lieu of prospective profits, it still remains to be considered whether businessmen are misled into overexpansion during the upswing and into underexpansion during the downswing by relying on these reported profits. Could not those who make investment decisions, if aware of the methods used in determining the profits, make allowances for this alleged misstatement? This point is admitted by even the most vociferous adherents of the doctrine that accounting methods accentuate business fluctuations.[29] Some of these writers have stated that the failure to recognize "bookkeeping" profits as fictitious has made them an important factor in business fluctuations, and that a more general recognition by industry and the accounting profession of the real nature of these profits would go a long way in stabilizing business activity. Fritz Schmidt himself recognized this possibility as shown by the following statement:

> So it shows that the application of present-day cost prices in the accounting could iron out the creases in the industrial business cycle. The climax of expansion could be avoided as soon as the entrepreneurs

29. See Butters and Niland, *op. cit.,* p. 103; Putnam, "The Role of Paper Profits . . . ," p. 136; Arundel Cotter, *op. cit.,* p. 14; and Henry B. Arthur, 'Inventory Profits . . . ," p. 33.

realize that their actual profits do not warrant the exaggerated expansion of their business concerns.[30]

Recent writers [31] on the subject of the effect of different accounting techniques on reported profits believe that there is a much better understanding of the nature of accounting profits than formerly. Brown, who has done considerable work on the effects of accounting depreciation techniques on reported profits with changing price levels, believes that in recent years a much better understanding of the meaning of business profits has taken place on the part of stockholders, management, labor groups, and the public as a result of editorials, company reports, Congressional hearings, and public addresses. Butters and Niland recently pointed out that there is better recognition of the nature of inventory profits and losses, especially:

> Inventory accounting and its relation to profit determination have been widely debated since 1939 under the combined impact of the authorization of Lifo for tax purposes, the wartime excess profits tax, and the pronounced price rises during and after the war. . . . The top management of numerous companies has had to decide whether to adopt Lifo; regardless of the decision, the consideration of the problem has brought about an increasing awareness of the nature of inventory profits. As a consequence, misinterpretation of profit figures by business executives is undoubtedly less widespread today than, say, during the 1930's.

K. Lacey, an advocate of the theory that accounting methodology accentuates cycles, has said that in recent years "the long uptrend has . . . revealed the inadequacy of depreciation provisions based on original cost, and there is now a healthy scepticism to profits as reported on conventional methods." What evidence is there to substantiate the validity of statements made by these three writers?

There was evidence in the profit hearings before the Joint Committee on the Economic Report held in December, 1948, that business leaders understood that reported profits were misstated.[32] These hearings were held in a year in which reported profits were the highest on record up to that time. Furthermore, in the preceding year, 1947, accounting profits were estimated to be misstated more than in any

30. "The Valuation of Fixed Assets . . . ," p. 17.

31. Brown, *op. cit.*, p. 84; Butters and Niland, *op. cit.*, p. 103; and Lacey, *Profit Measurement and Price Changes*, p. 29.

32. U.S. Congress, *Profits*, see statements of Charles E. Wilson, p. 57; of Robert Dunlop, p. 58; and of Eugene Holman, p. 58.

other year.[33] At these hearings Charles E. Wilson, president of General Electric, said: "In this connection, it should be noted that under present-day conditions a large percentage of the figures reported as profits are not available for distribution, since a portion of those profits must be used to offset the rise in the cost of replacing inventory and the increased cost of replacing plant and equipment." Robert Dunlop, president of Sun Oil Company, also testified: "Last year we decided that we would be less than prudent if we failed to give recognition to the inadequacy of depreciation to provide for the replacement of existing facilities at current high construction costs by setting up a replacement reserve." Eugene Holman, president of Standard Oil Company of New Jersey, also indicated his knowledge of the distorting tendency of accounting methods on profits in a period of inflation in these words: "While our profits are not appreciably inflated by inventory evaluations, they are overstated because no special depreciation reserve has been set up."

Another piece of evidence that *ex-post* profits as determined by accounting methods are not necessarily accepted at face value as the basis for policy decisions in the large corporations and thus "mislead" the policy makers in investment decisions is the fact that many of these corporations employ economists as well as accountants. A recent survey by *Fortune* revealed that twenty-five years ago there were "perhaps 100 economists employed in industry; today there are approximately 1,500."[34] Sixty-five big companies that employed only 20 economists in 1930 today have 270 on their staffs. Among 405 companies (accounting for one-fourth of all U. S. industrial assets) 141 (35 per cent) employed economists and 55 (14 per cent) used outside consultants. According to the survey, in two-thirds of the companies who use them, the economists' reports and recommendations are influential (from "moderately important" up to "crucial") in determining policy. Prominent among the companies mentioned as making use of economists are Ford Motor Company, Standard Oil of New Jersey, and Continental Can.

33. Table 7 shows corporate inventory profits to be $5,899 million for 1947 and Table 13 shows the "corporate depreciation adjustment" to be $2,677 million. The sum of the two exceeds that for any other year.

34. Charles E. Silberman and Sanford S. Parker, "The Economy's Scouts," *Fortune,* December, 1955, p. 100. For additional evidence that the use of economists by corporations is growing, see Clark S. Teitsworth, "Growing Role of the Company Economist," *Harvard Business Review,* January—February, 1959, pp. 97-104.

Would investment decisions have been any different if the method of accounting had been more "realistic"? Brown made field interviews in 22 companies after surveying their 1947 and 1948 financial statements. The group of companies selected represented about half of the large companies with a highly developed depreciation adjustment for price changes "or some such phenomenon." On the basis of this study Brown concluded:

> Under post World War II conditions replacement-cost depreciation would have constituted some change in the climate within which business decisions are made. Its influence did not seem strong enough to be emphasized by executives in firms favorable to such an adjustment.[35]

The better knowledge of the nature of accounting profits with fluctuating price levels may not always be appreciated by executives in small and medium-sized corporations. Butters and Niland state:

> The majority of business executives, especially of small and medium-size companies probably still do not fully appreciate the significance of price changes on their profit figures. This hypothesis is supported by the relatively little attention given to Lifo by small and medium-size companies.[36]

Even in the case of small companies, however, one writer points out that, though companies with relatively few stockholders may not feel that it is necessary to call the stockholders' attention to the impact of higher costs on operating policies, the problem is usually discussed at stockholders' meetings.[37]

The fact that historical costs are used in published financial statements to stockholders does not mean that they are necessarily employed for internal purposes thus resulting in the "misleading" of the managerial group. This is illustrated by a question and answer period following a talk by William Blackie, vice president of Caterpillar Tractor Company, before the Twenty-ninth Conference of the National Association of Cost Accountants, June 21, 1948. Mr. Blackie had argued very vehemently for an adaptation of accounting to changing price levels.[38]

> H. C. Todt (assistant comptroller, Bristol Laboratories, Inc.). Mr. Blackie, I would like very much to know to what extent you are using

35. *Op. cit.*, p. 49.
36. *Op. cit.*, p. 104.
37. Finley, *op. cit.*, p. 9.
38. *Op. cit.*, pp. 54 f.

the ideas which you mentioned in your speech in the preparation of your company's financial statements.

Mr. Blackie. We are not using them publicly.

In other words, the implication would appear to be that they were using the ideas internally for managerial purposes, but not in their published statements to stockholders.

There is an inconsistency in the argument that management is "misled" by accounting profits which must be "adjusted" before they can be used for managerial decisions. This inconsistency is illustrated by the following extracts from a speech made by Professor Willard J. Graham before the American Accounting Association meeting in Memphis, Tennessee, on September 9, 1948.[39]

> But where does management get the current cost and income information that it must have? Not, in most cases, from the accounting records, for they usually reflect only original cost. Special reports must be prepared, often at great expense, to secure the information that should be available from the regular cost and income reports. It is on the basis of this "adjusted" information that management appraises the effectiveness of past and current operations and plans for the future.

Later on in the same talk Professor Graham said:

> By charging unrealistic past cost against current revenue, we have constantly overstated profits in periods of rising and high prices. We have thereby artificially stimulated the continuation and expansion of business activity at high levels and have thus been partially responsible for over-expansion, inflated stock prices, and unwarranted wage demands—some of the factors that carry business "booms" to dangerously high levels.

If management makes its decisions on the basis of "this adjusted information," and if accounting information is merely the point of departure for the computations on which managerial decisions are based, it is hard to see how management can be misled by information which it does not use in its decisions.

In some of the literature on the effect of accounting methods on investment decisions, the impression appears to be left with the reader that the response to reported profits by those who make these decisions is automatic. Entrepreneurs are pictured as responding automatically to "misstated" profits in their investment decisions. A number of re-

39. *Op. cit.*, pp. 18 and 21.

searchers[40] into investment behavior have found that it is exceedingly complex and that investment expenditures are not taken lightly. They have found that there is a noticeable restraint on these expenditures and that considerable screening takes place. Concerning this cautiousness, Melvin G. de Chazeau said:

> Out of some such sense of responsibility to the firm's owners, managers have developed an exaggerated caution in the formal procedures concerning capital expenditures. Not only must the proposed expenditure run the gauntlet of an ascending series of potential vetoes, but executives who may commit the firm to other purchases and sales involving many thousands of dollars have a niggardly freedom of action in this area. Executive authorization, even for the president of a large corporation, is extremely restricted—$5,000-$10,000 was a not uncommon limit, and in one leading firm in its field, projects requiring more than $500 could not be initiated without the approval of the board of directors.

Eisner also spoke of the caution and restraint in making capital expenditures, in these words: "The formal procedures concerned with approval of capital expenditures seem characterized by a caution and restraint which suggest that management is more concerned about preventing excessive expenditure than increasing potential receipts." Heller found that the final word on investment expenditures "is usually given by some one officer who specialized in blending the technological considerations, market analyses, and financial factors which underlie investment decisions." Furthermore, this tendency for careful screening seems to be growing, as is indicated by this statement from a study of the National Industrial Conference Board: "Research leading up to this report shows that more and more companies . . . are deserting haphazard methods of appropriating capital in favor of systems of checks and balances which at least offer better hope for success than the 'hunch' or 'pet projects' approaches."[41]

Heller outlines a typical screening process in these words: "Projects up to $2,000 or $4,000 . . . can be given final approval by plant managers. Between these figures and $10,000, the production manager decides. Over $10,000, the proposal must be approved by the executive vice president and the board of directors."[42] The above procedures for

40. Melvin G. de Chazeau, "Regularization of Fixed Capital Investment by the Individual Firm," *Regularization of Business Investment,* p. 94; Eisner, *op. cit.,* p. 562; and Heller, *op. cit.,* p. 99.

41. John H. Watson III, *Controlling Capital Expenditures,* Studies in Business Policy No. 62, p. 3.

42. *Op. cit.,* p. 99.

screening capital expenditures do not fit the picture painted by many writers of the businessman recklessly rushing out during periods of rising price levels to expand his business on the basis of fictitious accounting profits. There is more reason for suspecting that during the downswing this cautiousness plus the "understated" profits during the depression phase would tend to reinforce each other.

In 1938, when Arthur wrote the following lines, few businessmen may have understood the nature of inventory profits:

> The very limited recognition accorded by business-men to the problem of inventory profits and losses is matched by an equally meager treatment by economists and statisticians. There is an almost complete absence of mention of unrealized inventory gains in the literature of business cycles.[43]

There is certainly evidence today that there is a much better understanding of these unrealized inventory profits and losses, and of the nature of accounting profits in general.

After comparing accounting to a compass which points to the magnetic pole instead of the geographic pole, and observing that science, with its exact methods, has made it possible for captains of ships to make the necessary corrections, Schmidt states:

> In business one is not yet beyond the stage of the first crude correction experiments resting on individual experience. Therefore individuals land at other points of the final success than they expected. The worst, however, is that business leaders don't think at all that scientifically constructed methods of corrections, which besides could easily be put into simple forms, could help their accounting.[44]

Are the businessmen of today, especially in the larger corporations, really misled because their income statements point to accounting profits rather than "true" profits? It is the belief of the author that, although the deviations cannot be measured as accurately as those of the magnetic compass, the fact that the deviation exists is at least generally recognized, and that leaders of large business firms have progressed much beyond the stage which Schmidt observed in his day. This is not to deny that navigation would be simpler if the compass did point to true north, and that the management of a business enterprise would be easier if the accountant reported "true" income. But this is not the point at issue.

43. "Inventory Profits . . . ," pp. 32 f.
44. Translated from "Die Industriekonjunktur-ein Rechenfehler!" p. 94.

Modification Introduced by Changes in Technology

Up to this point, technology as a factor in the investment process has been largely disregarded. In other words, the discussion has been concerned with induced investment as opposed to autonomous investment or "independent investment (more or less independent of *current* sales)" which "is opened up by inventions, new discoveries, new products, and new processes."[45] In a dynamic economy any realistic appraisal of the motives behind investment expenditures cannot ignore changing technology. One writer[46] has stated that "in capitalistic economies technological change is annually responsible for a large portion of the total volume of investment that actually occurs." Furthermore: "If technological improvements should cease or decline substantially, total private investment in highly developed capitalistic economies would probably decline to intolerably low levels." Heller concludes that satisfactory or growing markets and advanced technology provide most of the "thrust" or active stimulus for investment.[47]

When autonomous investment is considered, the importance of current profit, determined by traditional accounting techniques, as a determinant of current investment may be weakened still further. The possibility exists that changing technology may actuate investment expenditures by the firm in the absence of currently reported profits. De Chazeau has said: "The risk that rivals may approximate or better a company's own achievements can outweigh the risk of unsatisfactory current market returns," and has pointed out that the large firm is in the best position to make investment expenditures that are noncyclical.[48] It is the large firm that has the technical know-how of research, engineering, and management. Although the days of the independent inventor are not over, an increasing amount of research leading to successful inventions is being done by large industrial corporations and by government. Evidence of this fact is furnished by 125 manufacturing corporations cooperating in a survey by the National Industrial Conference Board. The Board reports: "Almost two thirds of the cooperating companies do 95% or more of their research and development work in their own laboratories. Only 15 of the 109 companies reporting on this noted that they did less than 75% of such work with their own facilities."[49] Further-

45. Alvin H. Hansen, *Business Cycles and National Income,* p. 190.
46. Buchanan, "Anticipations," pp. 149 and 155.
47. *Op. cit.,* p. 100.
48. "Can We Avoid Depression in a Dynamic Economy?" *Harvard Business Review,* July—August, 1954, p. 42.

more, Sumner Slichter[50] has pointed out that the volume of investment opportunities opened up by research does not fluctuate cyclically and may be just as large in bad years as in good ones. He states that the company's need for additional sales may be a reason for not delaying the exploiting of the results of research.

With respect to the effect of changes in technology on investment decisions Andrew and Brunner point out:

> In the case of completely new products and the introduction of processes for their manufacture, the decisions are so much a matter of broad views of trends of demand and of profit-abilities broadly estimated, together with prestige factors sometimes involved in entering new markets, that it would be misleading to think of them as at all based upon estimates of earnings, in the sense that critical minima are required before adopting a scheme. Everything is too conjectural for such rigid theoretical notions to be very helpful.[51]

Thus, with the placing of changing technology back into the institutional framework, the profit motive—whether conceived of as prospective profits or as current profits—becomes more diffused and indirect as a determinant of investment decisions.

Reported Profits, Federal Income Taxes, and Investment Decisions

The remarks concerning investment decisions to date have been based on the effect of accounting methods on income before taxes. Most of the writers dealing with the effect of accounting profits on investment decisions neglect to mention whether it is profits before, or after, income taxes about which they are speaking. However, the effect of profit after taxes on business decisions may be different from the effect of profit before taxes. Bernstein has said that "with the passage of time, the efforts of businessmen to maximize after-tax profits run more and more at variance with their traditional efforts to maximize pretax profits."[52] At least one study has been made of the relationship of aggregate investment expenditures lagged by six months and aggregate corporate profits after taxes for the period from 1919 through 1941. The following conclusion was reached: "The variations in plant and equipment outlays

49. "Research Dollars Grow with Sales," *The Conference Board Business Record,* November, 1951, p. 467.

50. "Thinking Ahead," *Harvard Business Review,* January—February, 1955, p. 158.

51. *Op. cit.,* p. 356.

52. *Op. cit.,* p. 422.

over the prewar period are fairly well described by the movements in earnings."[53]

The Lifo principle for tax purposes has not been tried as yet on any large scale, so there is actually only limited experience on which to judge how the general adoption of this method for tax purposes would modify investment decisions. In recent years, it is true that an increasing number of companies have adopted Lifo for inventories, but the Lifo principle has not been permitted with respect to fixed assets, and even those adopting it for inventory purposes are still in the minority. There has been no major drop in prices since the use of Lifo has been permitted for tax purposes, and there is no evidence as to what changes Congress would make in the tax laws in case of a severe depression.

If the Lifo principle were generally adopted with reference to both fixed assets and inventories, for tax purposes as well as for accounting purposes, the gap between the *reported profit of a firm after taxes* computed in the traditional way and computed on the Lifo principle would be narrowed. In a period of rising prices under the traditional methods, the firm would pay more taxes on its *reported* profit; whereas, if the Lifo principle were applied, the firm would pay less taxes on its *reported* profit. Therefore, the difference in reported profit after taxes between the traditional method and that reported under the Lifo principle would be less than it would be before taxes. This is illustrated by Table 16. It will be noted that the difference in reported income before taxes is $4,000 but after taxes the difference is only $2,400. The above facts can be generalized mathematically.

Let D = the difference between profits before tax reported by traditional method and that reported under the Lifo principle.
R = the reduction in after-tax profits using Lifo.
r = rate of taxation.
Then Dr = amount of tax reduction using the Lifo principle.
Therefore $R = D - Dr$ or $R = D(1 - r)$

From this formula, it can be seen that the difference between reported profit after taxes computed by using Lifo instead of Fifo will tend to vary inversely with the tax rate. In the above example, if there were no income taxes, then the difference in income would have been $4,000; whereas, if the tax rate had been 100 per cent, then in both cases there

53. U.S. Congress, Staff of the Subcommittee on Investment, Joint Committee on the Economic Report, *op. cit.*, p. 101.

would have been no profits after taxes, and the difference in after-tax profits computed by the two methods would have been zero.

TABLE 16
HYPOTHETICAL COMPARISON OF PROFITS AFTER TAXES UNDER TRADITIONAL ACCOUNTING METHODS AND THE LIFO PRINCIPLE

	Traditional Methods	Lifo Principle
Sales	$100,000	$100,000
Less cost of goods sold	60,000	62,000
Gross profit	$ 40,000	$ 38,000
Less operating expenses:		
Other than depreciation	$ 20,000	$ 20,000
Depreciation	3,000	5,000
Total operating expenses	$ 23,000	$ 25,000
Net profit before income taxes	$ 17,000	$ 13,000
Less income taxes (40%)	6,800	5,200
Net profit after income taxes	$ 10,200	$ 7,800

In the twenties and thirties with their low tax rates, the difference between after-tax profits using Lifo instead of Fifo would have been relatively large. With the high rates prevailing in the forties and fifties the difference in the spread of after-tax profits computed by Lifo rather than by Fifo would be much smaller. To the extent that investment behavior is influenced by the absolute amount of profits after taxes, high corporate income taxes represent another factor in the institutional arrangement that tends to vitiate the argument that accounting methods accentuate business fluctuations.

Although the gap between the after-tax profit of a firm computed by the two methods narrows as tax rates increase, it will not be closed short of a 100 per cent tax rate. The decrease in the size of the gap with high tax rates may be compensated for, wholly or partially, by attaching greater significance to each dollar of difference in after-tax profit than to each dollar of difference before taxes. Therefore, it may be argued, the smaller numerical "misstatement" of profit after taxes may be just as significant psychologically for investment behavior as the larger "misstatement" before taxes. If this compensation does take place, the argument that the high income tax rates of today represent an environmental factor which tends to lessen the psychological effect of "misstated" reported profits on investment decisions has, of course, been weakened.

Some of the writers on the effect of accounting methods on business fluctuations take cognizance of the smaller difference between after-tax profits versus profits before tax when Lifo rather than Fifo is used for both reporting purposes and for computing income tax liability. W. T. Baxter,[54] for example, admits that "this counter-argument should plainly make us pause." He argues, however, that the following factors weaken the effect of income taxes on the argument: (1) Tax is usually not included in cost calculations; (2) tax is not usually assessed at 100 per cent so that some profit remains to "cheer the appropriation account"; and (3) high profits convey a comfortable suggestion of high cash resources. He concludes that "tax does not appear to neutralise the error's effects. Every day observation suggests that, despite tax, high profit figures bring elation and low figures gloom."

If taxes are based on profits computed under the Lifo principle, there are other ramifications. Students of public finance advocate a federal tax policy that is countercyclical—more taxes collected in prosperity and less during the depression. By increasing tax liabilities when prices are rising and reducing them when prices are falling, traditional accounting procedures tend to place business in a tighter cash position in expanding periods and in a freer cash position in declining periods. Other things being equal, income taxes based on traditional methods of accounting would thus fit in with a countercyclical tax policy better than procedures designed to stabilize reported income before taxes. The cyclical effect of basing taxes on income computed by traditional accounting methods is not clear-cut, however. The ultimate effect of collecting more taxes during the prosperity phase will depend upon what the government does with the extra taxes collected versus what businesses would have done, if they had been allowed to keep the extra profits. If the government spends the money instead of retiring the public debt, then the result may well be as inflationary as if it had been spent by the businesses themselves, or by the stockholders if the extra profits had been declared as dividends.

There is a conflict between the "psychological effect" of leveling profits before taxes by the use of the "Lifo principle" and the "cash effect" of having more money after taxes during the boom and less during the depression, as occurs when this principle is adopted for tax purposes as well as for reporting purposes. To the extent that the leveling of profits over the cycle affects business investment decisions, the use

54. *Op. cit.*, p. 111.

of Lifo would tend to iron out fluctuations in investment expenditures. To the extent that cash position is controlling, the use of Lifo for tax purposes would tend to cause more business investment during the boom and less during the depression. Thus the "cash effect" and the "psychological effect" on investment decisions of using Lifo for both tax purposes and for financial reports tend to offset each other. Furthermore, the "cash effect" becomes stronger with higher tax rates and the "psychological effect" becomes weaker as the nature of accounting profits and losses is better understood.

If companies use financial reports based on Fifo for investment decisions during a period of rising prices, but pay income taxes on the basis of Lifo, the psychological effect of the resulting "overstated" profits and the improved cash position would tend to reinforce each other. In order to use Lifo for tax purposes, income tax regulations require its use in reports to stockholders and for credit purposes. Furthermore, the proposition that managerial decisions in the large corporation are based on historical costs is of doubtful validity, as was pointed out earlier in this chapter. It is unlikely, therefore, that the two conditions necessary for this reinforcing effect are very widespread.

Accelerated Depreciation and High Levels of Investment

The possibility that accelerated depreciation encourages a high level of investment was presented in Chapter IV. What evidence is there to substantiate or to refute this theory? The authors of the *Minneapolis Project* mention a tendency by some companies to use depreciation accruals as a guide for the allocation of investment funds. "Three companies were found to use depreciation accruals as a partial substitute for financial budgeting, either as an over-all ceiling or as a measuring rod for allocation of funds on a plant-by-plant basis."[55] Joel Dean emphasized this tendency as a depression phenomenon and says it was "fairly common during the great depression to confine each major operating unit to a capital budget that was no more than its depreciation and depletion or some fraction thereof."[56] George Terborgh cites the complaints of equipment salesmen relative to the reluctance of businessmen to replace obsolete equipment because they do not like" to take a loss" on the disposal of old equipment and states: "Resistance to remechanization from this source is of course intensified by the retarded writeoff prevailing under the present system of depreciation."[57] An inclination to

55. Arthur Upgren, *et al., op. cit.,* p. 16.
56. *Capital Budgeting,* p. 39.
57. *Op. cit.,* pp. 6 f.

use depreciation accruals as a criterion for the allocation of investment funds in combination with the reluctance of businessmen "to take a loss" on assets not fully depreciated according to accounting records indicates that acceleration of depreciation accruals would encourage a more rapid replacement of plant and equipment.

There is not general agreement among writers[58] that accelerated depreciation encourages a high level of investment, and there is evidence that depreciation accruals are not too rigidly followed for allocating investment funds as well as evidence which indicates that undepreciated assets are not a serious deterrent to replacing obsolete plant and equipment. Domar says: "It is entirely possible that accelerated depreciation will increase neither the rate of growth of investment, nor for that matter, its level. Certainly no guarantee can be given." Eisner speaks of the tendency to use depreciation allowances as a guide to investment expenditures as a "rule of thumb" that can be "changed where appropriate." He says that "despite evidence of rules of thumb which tend to allow expenditure of depreciation allowances for 'replacement,' it is not clear that high depreciation charges can be relied upon to maintain a high level of replacement expenditures. . . . The rules and formulas are changed where appropriate." Gort found no evidence that the value of undepreciated plant entered into replacement decisions: "It is an interesting fact, therefore, that in none of the companies was it observed that undepreciated value of plant and equipment entered into calculations of the desirability of capital replacement."

Thus, it may be seen that the tendency to use the depreciation allowance as a guide to investment expenditures at the firm level is far from a universal rule.

While there may well be instances in which the investment decisions of individual firms are largely controlled by their depreciation policies, there is certainly no evidence that corporate business as a whole is affected. Corporations spent $196.3 billion on plant and equipment in the ten postwar years, 1946-1955, while depreciation allowances for the same period amounted to $89.2 billion.[59] It may be argued that this is not a fair comparison since expenditures were in dollars of decreased purchasing power, but there is no close relationship between the depre-

58. Evsey D. Domar, "A Rejoinder," *The Quarterly Journal of Economics,* May, 1955, p. 301; Robert Eisner, *Determinants of Capital Expenditures,* Studies in Business Expectations and Planning, Number 2, p. 25; and Gort, *op. cit.,* p. 196.

59. Computed from *Economic Report of the President,* transmitted to the Congress, January 24, 1956, Table D, p. 227.

ciation allowances per year and expenditures on plant and equipment even when the depreciation expense is based on replacement cost. (See Table 17.) It is difficult to see how accelerated depreciation during the 1930's could have stimulated investment since allowances on either a replacement or historical cost basis already exceeded the expenditures for plant and equipment during these years. From 1939 to 1949 the total expenditures on plant and equipment, with the exception of the war years of 1942-1944, exceeded depreciation allowances on either a replacement cost or historical cost basis. In fact this has been true for twelve of the twenty-one years covered by this table.

The argument for accelerated depreciation as a stimulus to investment boils down largely to a tax argument. Domar[60] points out that accelerated depreciation affects the firm in two ways. First, with given income tax rates, income tax payments will be postponed, or even reduced. The second effect is to produce a lower profit before and after taxes on the firm's books. According to Domar, the first effect is real in the sense that the firm's position and prospects are improved. Domar refers to the second effect as an "accounting paradox" which can be corrected by formal entries on the firm's books or merely a mental note on the part of management.

Most arguments for accelerated depreciation as an inducement to invest are coupled with the assumption that the government does allow this method for tax purposes.[61] Eisner points this out as follows: "It is also important to have a clear notion that, on the one hand, depreciation allowances are, aside from tax considerations, merely a paper entry; they do not in themselves actually give the firm any funds." Goode also emphasizes the tax aspect of accelerated depreciation in these words: "Introduction of accelerated depreciation stimulates investment by lowering a tax obstacle rather than by creating entirely new incentives." He points out that investment can be stimulated in other ways, such as cutting tax rates and bringing down interest rates, but "accelerated depreciation has the advantage of being more selective in that the benefits are restricted to those who acquire new depreciable assets."

If accelerated depreciation were allowed for tax purposes, it is believed by many writers that there would be cyclical implications as well

60. "A Rejoinder," p. 300.

61. Robert Eisner, "Accelerated Depreciation: Some Further Thoughts," *The Quarterly Journal of Economics*, May, 1955, p. 293; Richard Goode, "Accelerated Depreciation Allowances as a Stimulus to Investment," *The Quarterly Journal of Economics*, May, 1955, p. 219.

TABLE 17

A COMPARISON OF CORPORATE (NONFARM) EXPENDITURES ON PLANT AND EQUIPMENT WITH DEPRECIATION ALLOWANCES

1929-1949

(Millions of Dollars)

Year	Total Durable Equipment	Nonincorporated Business Durable Equipment	Corporate Durable Equipment	Corporate Business Construction	Total Plant and Equipment	Estimated Depreciation (Original Cost)	Estimated Depreciation (Current Cost)
	(1)	(2)	(3)	(4)	(5)	(6)	(7)
1929	4,672	690	3,982	3,419	7,401	3,871	4,732
1930	3,641	535	3,106	2,812	5,918	3,986	4,530
1931	2,364	347	2,017	1,585	3,602	4,003	4,259
1932	1,330	196	1,134	750	1,884	3,693	3,578
1933	1,280	191	1,089	580	1,669	3,496	3,394
1934	1,849	276	1,573	673	2,246	3,362	3,561
1935	2,319	346	1,973	695	2,668	3,352	3,577
1936	3,181	474	2,707	1,009	3,716	3,286	3,511
1937	3,931	586	3,345	1,493	4,838	3,342	3,891
1938	2,912	433	2,479	1,106	3,585	3,352	3,800
1939	3,347	498	2,849	1,208	4,057	3,443	3,895
1940	4,514	673	3,841	1,502	5,343	3,520	4,037
1941	5,684	848	4,836	1,990	6,826	3,765	4,487
1942	3,849	575	3,274	1,265	4,539	3,914	4,868
1943	3,219	482	2,737	759	3,496	3,916	4,913
1944	4,445	665	3,780	994	4,774	3,950	4,938
1945	6,077	909	5,168	1,635	6,803	3,977	5,003
1946	9,707	1,448	8,259	3,883	12,142	4,199	5,729
1947	12,669	1,888	10,781	4,668	15,449	5,220	7,897
1948	14,326	2,130	12,196	5,376	17,572	6,150	9,418
1949	12,909	1,911	10,998	5,200	16,198	6,750	9,768

Source: Col. 1, Raymond W. Goldsmith, *A Study of Saving in the United States*, I, 877.
Col. 2, *Ibid.*, p. 891.
Col. 3, Col. 1 minus Col. 2.
Col. 4, Goldsmith, *op. cit.*, p. 620.
Col. 5, Col. 3 plus Col. 4.
Col. 6, Goldsmith, *op. cit.*, p. 955.
Col. 7, *Ibid.*

as effects on long-term growth. Many of them believe that cyclical fluctuations would be accentuated. The following statement by S. P. Dobrovolsky is typical of the reasoning behind this belief:

> It seems, therefore, that the accelerated method might become a factor accentuating cyclical fluctuations of business, if it were generally adopted by industrial firms. In periods of prosperity, when most firms are expanding, tax considerations would provide an additional incentive for a heavy new investment; in periods of depression, when most firms are contracting, the plight of private business would be further aggravated by an increase in the tax burden.[62]

According to this reasoning, the use of accelerated depreciation for tax purposes would be more effective in maintaining a high level of investment than in restoring it during a depressed period.

Before the proposition that accelerated depreciation for tax purposes accentuates cyclical fluctuations can be accepted, however, additional factors must be considered. The use made by the government of the extra taxes collected during the early years of the use life of the asset, assuming the use of traditional methods of depreciation for tax purposes, must be compared with the use made of the tax saving by the business firm, assuming accelerated depreciation is used in the computation of the income tax liability. Furthermore, even though most business investment is made during the upswing, a substantial portion of this investment may still be subject to accelerated depreciation during the depression years. Hence, the total income tax payments may be no larger during the depression years than if straight-line depreciation is used. In other words, when the total investment of the firm in fixed assets is considered, the period of increased depreciation charges may not be synchronized with the upswing and the period of decreased depreciation charges may not be synchronized with the downswing.

From such evidence as is available the author is not at all convinced that businessmen make much use of depreciation accounting as a guide in allocating investment funds, or that investment in improved facilities is deferred because of reluctance to write off undepreciated assets. Certainly, investment expenditures of the economy as a whole do not

62. "Depreciation Policies and Investment Decisions," *The American Economic Review,* December, 1951, p. 910. For expressions of similar viewpoints, see John N. Bell, "Shall We Take Heavier Depreciation in Earlier Years?" *N.A.C.A. Bulletin,* November, 1955, pp. 341 f.; Evsey D. Domar, "The Case for Accelerated Depreciation," *The Quarterly Journal of Economics,* November, 1953, pp. 509 f.; and Goode, *op. cit.*, pp. 203 f.

bear any close relationship to total depreciation allowances. In the last analysis, the argument that accelerated depreciation is stimulating to investment has validity only if coupled with the saving in income taxes. In which case, it is not accounting methodology per se that is directly influencing the inducement to invest in improved facilities, as is sometimes alleged. Accounting methods are merely the vehicle for implementing a particular governmental policy; that is, encouraging a high level of investment expenditures by bestowing special tax benefits on those who own relatively new depreciable assets.

The Use of Internal Funds as a Factor in Investment Decisions

So far, profits have been discussed primarily from the standpoint of furnishing an incentive to invest. In addition, profits as a source of funds for investment have received rather wide attention. In recent years, especially, it has been recognized that corporations (manufacturing corporations, in particular) prefer internal rather than external equity financing of investment expenditures.[63] Retained earnings and depreciation allowances are the main sources of these internal funds.

Retained earnings as a source of funds escape the erosion from income taxes which occurs when these funds are paid out as dividends and then reacquired in the capital market. Furthermore, these internal funds escape costs of flotation and may not be subjected to as rigid market tests as are external funds. Hence, it may be argued that this preference for internal financing and the relative ease of its use, coupled with the alleged overstatement of profits during periods of price rises, may constitute another reason why accounting methods stimulate investment during the upward phase of the cycle. The psychological effect of the overstated profits as an incentive to invest and the convenience of the use of these retained earnings, as compared with external sources, would tend to reinforce each other. Likewise, during the depression phase, the psychological effect of "understated" profits and the smaller amount of retained earnings reported as a result of accounting methods, viewed as a desirable source of funds, would tend to make investment expenditures less than if accounting policies were more "realistic."

In regarding profits (or retained earnings) as determined by traditional accounting methods as a source of funds for investment purposes, a distinction should be drawn between "inventory profits" (profits measured by the increase in value placed on a constant volume of

63. Evidence of this may be found in John R. Meyer and Edwin Kuh, *The Investment Decision: An Empirical Study,* pp. 137-142.

physical inventories, as in Chapter III) and the residual remaining after these profits have been removed. It has already been stressed that if the Fifo principle is also being used for tax purposes as well as for other types of reporting, the government would skim off a portion of these inventory profits in the form of corporate income taxes. If inventory investment is thought of in dollar terms, it can be said that the balance of these inventory profits after taxes is automatically invested. If inventory investment is defined in Abramovitz' terms, the turning of these profits back into the same physical volume of stock does not constitute investment. By either interpretation the role of inventory profits as a source of investment funds would be a passive one.

While there has been some attempt to attach special significance to depreciation allowances as a particular source of replacement funds and to net profits retained in the business as a source of new investment, Dean emphasizes that gross rather than net business saving should be viewed as a source of internal funds.[64] As sources of investment funds, looked at from this viewpoint, the distinction made between depreciation allowances and profits retained in the business would be irrelevant. On the other hand, profits after taxes, in addition to being a source of investment funds, are also a source of dividends, while depreciation allowances are not. Therefore, if the amount of reported profits after taxes is a factor in dividend policy, the accounting distinction between the two sources of internal funds takes on added meaning. In other words, only in so far as the amount of net profits after taxes influences the board of directors in deciding the amount to be paid out as dividends, is the total amount of internal funds available for investment materially affected by the accounting method of recording the depreciation expense.

Some writers take a more restricted view of internal funds as a source of financing investment expenditures. They believe that the cash position of a company is an important factor in its investment decisions. In times of depression it is reasoned that business will free cash from inventories and receivables as well as from fixed assets. Hence, it may be in a stronger cash position during the depression than during prosperity. In so far as investment expenditures are influenced by the cash position of the firm, this improved cash position would tend to make the investment policy of these firms countercyclical. In order to establish the validity of this argument, it is necessary to ascertain (1) if companies do have larger cash balances during depressed years than during

64. *Capital Budgeting,* p. 36.

prosperous ones, and (2) if the more liquid position is a factor in the making of investment expenditures.

Friedrich A. Lutz[65] made a study of the cash balances of 78 large (over $5 million total assets) manufacturing corporations and 73 medium-sized and small ($50 thousand to $5 million total assets) manufacturing corporations from 1914 to 1943. He found that during the thirties the large manufacturing corporations held "free" cash (cash that is not tied up by the volume of transactions) and that the movement of the inactive money showed an inverse correlation with the profit rate of these large companies. For the medium-sized and small corporations, on the other hand, the increase in free cash was small. Lutz concluded: "The phenomenon of 'inactive' or 'hoarded' corporate cash in the thirties is thus mainly one of large manufacturing corporations."

Sloan and associates published a study in 1936 of 135 leading industrial concerns covering 9 industries and with a sprinkling of corporations from other industries. It was assumed that a major cycle began in 1922 and ended in 1933 and that another major cycle began in 1934 and was still in progress at the time that the results of the study were published. One of the findings of this study is stated as follows:

> Industry's maintenance of such a strong cash position during the 1930-1933 depression phase of the cycle is truly remarkable. At the end of the cycle, despite the enormous losses which had been sustained, and despite the fact that during the three years 1931-1933 security owners received cash disbursements of over a billion dollars in excess of the net available for the common in those three years—despite these facts, our 135 corporations had 710 millions more cash in their coffers at the end of the cycle than at the beginning.[66]

In so far as availability of cash is a determining factor in investment decisions, the large corporation seems to be in the best position to take advantage of a countercyclical investment policy. Furthermore, Meyer and Kuh in their statistical study of the investment decision using data from 600 firms for the postwar years 1946 to 1950 reached the following conclusion: "Size . . . seemed to condition a firm's sensitivity to variations in liquidity inflows, small firms being more responsive to depreciation expense and profit levels than large firms. Contrarily, the large firm was much more prone to adjust investment response to tech-

65. *Corporate Cash Balances 1914-43*, pp. 5 and 7.

66. Laurence H. Sloan and Associates, *Two Cycles of Corporation Profits*, p. 40.

nical pressures on capacity."[67] Therefore, in so far as profits as a supply of internal funds (whether kept temporarily as cash or not) is an element in investment decisions, it would seem that accounting methods as an accentuating factor would be more applicable to the small firm than to the larger one.

None of the investigators[68] studying the determinants of investment decisions through interviews have rated cash position as an important factor. Concerning the supply of money available as a determinant of investment expenditures Eisner said: "On the whole, remarks by business executives suggest that questions relating to the supply of money capital do not appear to them to be crucial in capital expenditure decisions. 'We'll get the money if we need it' is a common refrain." Another pair of investigators, Andrews and Brunner, concluded: "Provided that a business is reasonably prosperous, . . . the limits imposed by the availability of financial resources have no practical significance." Gort also concluded: "Few situations were observed where specific projects were postponed because capital could not be obtained."

Thus, on the basis of the evidence, one must conclude that, although corporations, especially large corporations, do have more "free" cash during depressions and less during prosperity, cash position has not been rated a particularly important factor in investment decisions by those using the interview technique.

Accounting Profits, Security Prices, and Investment Decisions

In Chapter II evidence was presented to show that many writers think that accounting profits influence investment decisions by affecting the price of shares and, hence, the ease with which monetary capital can be raised. The relationship of accounting profits to investment via security markets has two aspects: (1) the relationship of accounting profits to security prices, and (2) the relationship of security prices to investment decisions. These two links in the chain of causation between reported profits and investment will now be separately considered.

Recent studies of the behavior of the stock market since 1929 have revealed that the market does not always mirror business conditions nor does it forecast business activity. A conclusion reached in one such study was: "An analysis of business and market trends over the past twenty-five years indicates that stock-market moves sometimes precede

67. *Op. cit.*, p. 191.

68. See Eisner, "Interview and Other Survey Techniques," p. 581; Andrews and Brunner, *op. cit.*, p. 349; and Gort, *op. cit.*, p. 200.

changes in business activity and sometimes follow them; that it is impossible to state with assurance whether the market is forecasting future conditions or reflecting existing or past conditions."[69] It was stated in this study that only for the years from 1933 to 1937 did stock market prices closely parallel business conditions. This was partly attributed to the lack of sensitivity of the market in recent years due to the increasing importance of institutional investors who can afford to overlook short-term business fluctuations. The varying of the margin requirement was also mentioned as a factor making the market less sensitive to business change.

During the early postwar years when reported profits were the highest on record up to that time, the stock market was in the doldrums. A large section of the general public during this period actually believed that accountants, rather than overstating profits as has been so frequently alleged, actually understated them. This fact was revealed by a survey made by the Opinion Research Corporation for the Controllership Foundation, Inc. Some 1,869 responded to the question: "Do you think most companies tell the truth about their profits, or do you think they actually make more than they say they do?" Forty-five per cent stated that they believed corporations made more profit than they reported.[70] Even among stockholders, 34 per cent said that corporations made more profit than they reported. In spite of the fact that they believed profits were even higher than the record-breaking profits which were being reported, there was no rush to buy equity securities during this period.

Some writers believe that the price of securities is more influenced by the pay-out policy of corporations than by reported earnings.[71] Burrel, one writer on the subject of dividends versus earnings as a market force, has said: "There has been virtually unanimous agreement that the dividend rate is an important factor and exerts an influence upon price entirely independent of the earnings factor." Some studies have even attempted to compare the relative importance of the dividend factor and the earnings factor as market forces. Graham and Dodd in referring to two of these studies have said: "Our own studies of various

69. Herbert V. Prochnow (ed.), *Determining the Business Outlook,* pp. 91 f.

70. Opinion Research Corporation, *The Public's Acceptance of the Facts and Figures of Business Accounting,* A Survey for Controllership Foundation, Inc., pp. A-25.

71. See O. K. Burrel, "Dividends vs. Retained Earnings as a Market Force," *The Commercial and Financial Chronicle,* August 21, 1952, p. 29; and Benjamin Graham and David L. Dodd, *Security Analysis,* p. 432.

industry groups during the rather stable stock market of 1947-1949 led us to a similar conclusion that the weight of $1 of distributed earnings tended to be about four times as great as that of $1 of retained earnings."

At least one writer has attributed the weak prices of stocks in the 1947 to 1949 period to the dividend policies of corporations. His statement follows:

> After all, from the investor's vantage point, distributable earnings are earnings to be paid *out* in the form of dividends. And in the valuation of securities probably one of the factors explaining the historically weak-price-earnings ratio (of 1947-1949) is that needs for capital outlays reduced dividend payout possibilities.[72]

There is an implication in this statement that investors may have decided that "profits" which could not be translated into dividends were not profits at all. If the investors do discount the reported earnings of business firms in periods of price fluctuations, the alleged relationship between these reported profits and security prices tends to break down.

Of course, it may be argued that reported earnings affect dividend policy, which, in turn, affects the prices of securities. Some writers believe that reported earnings do affect the price of shares in this way.[73] In fact, Graham and Dodd believe that earnings are important because of their bearing on present and future dividends. If this is true, the relationship between accounting profits and security prices becomes more roundabout and problematical. Burrel thinks that the dividend factor, as compared to reported earnings, has become relatively more important since 1929. To the extent that this is true, the link between reported profits and share prices has become weaker, and here is another indication that the effect of accounting methodology on business fluctuations has become weaker since Schmidt's day.

Whether the fact that security prices do not closely follow reported earnings is due to the rising importance of the institutional investor, varying margin requirements, dividend policy, the tax structure, or to a combination of these and other factors, it is at least true that there are factors operative in the short run that seem to be more influential in stock market prices than reported profits.

Even if security prices are influenced by accounting profits, it does not necessarily follow that higher security prices, in turn, are translated

72. Charles T. Horngren, "Security Analysts and the Price Level," *The Accounting Review,* October, 1955, p. 580.
73. Graham and Dodd, *op. cit.,* p. 586; and Burrel, *op. cit.,* p. 1.

into investment expenditures. The result may be a mere financial boom without any effect on output and employment. A bit of evidence bearing on this supposition was furnished by McGraw-Hill's 1950 Survey of Capital Spending Plans. The cooperating companies were asked: "Would you boost 1950 spending if you could sell new common stock for 50% more than its present market price?"[74] Only 7 per cent of the companies answered "yes" to this question.

Many writers have cited the twenties as an example of high profits, high investment, and high sales of equity securities. However, one group of writers has pointed out that in 1929 when the sale of new stock issues hit an all-time peak in September, this was not the result of increasing business and profit. Rather it was the result of inflated stock prices and the fact that business was taking advantage of these prices for refinancing.[75] Another writer has been more specific about the proportion of the proceeds of new security issues going into investment for the years 1927, 1928, and 1929. Kemper Simpson says:

> The figures . . . show that only from 7 to 12 per cent of the total proceeds of new issues were used during those years for expansion of the issuing corporations' plant and equipment, although another 8 per cent was used by them for the outright purchase of existing plants from others. In 1929 over 38 per cent went to investment trusts, holding companies, and financial companies, and nearly 16 per cent was for refunding. Even larger percentages, 30 per cent and 26 per cent, were for refunding in 1927 and 1928. In short, when one hears of the ten and eleven billion dollars of new issues for 1928 and 1929, that does not mean that issuing corporations received directly or used any such sums for expansion of productive equipment.[76]

Meyer and Kuh, while admitting that stock prices might well prove a useful variable in further investment studies, state: "It is unlikely that the relatively influential relationship between stock prices and investment is due to the fact that firms respond immediately to changes in their market share values by new security issues" and "from the data

74. "Industry's 1950 Capital Spending Plans," *Business Week,* January 21, 1950, p. 78.

75. Prochnow, *op. cit.,* p. 100.

76. "Security Markets and the Investment Process," *Papers and Proceedings of the Fiftieth Annual Meeting of the American Economic Association* in *The American Economic Review,* March, 1938, p. 42. Other students of this problem have reached similar conclusions, see e.g., Moulton, *op. cit.,* pp. 376 f.; and George A. Eddy, "Security Issues and Real Investment in 1929," *The Review of Economic Statistics,* May, 1937, pp. 79-91.

available it is very difficult to determine the casual structure, if indeed any really exists."[77]

Thus, it would appear that the two links in the chain of causation from reported profits to investment—the connection between reported profits and security prices, and between security prices and real investment—are both weak, especially in the years since the late twenties.

Summary

The thesis that business fluctuations are primarily the result of the ebb and flow in private investment expenditures has been accepted. The tentative conclusion was reached at the end of Chapter IV that, abstracting away technological change and the income tax structure, and assuming that (1) businessmen invest in such a way as to maximize expected profits, (2) prospective profits are judged by past profits as measured by accounting techniques, and (3) businessmen are misled by these accounting profits, then accounting techniques do accentuate business fluctuations.

Since the large, widely-held corporation makes such a large percentage of the aggregate investment expenditures, it follows that the motivation of investment behavior in this type of corporation is particularly important. The assumption of profit maximization has been blunted in the case of the large corporation. This blunting of the profit motive weakens the link between investment decisions and profits, no matter how the amount of profit is determined. Furthermore, while the more realistic assumptions of secure profits, or satisfactory profits, can be integrated with long-run profit maximization, the acceptance of profit maximization in the long-run as a norm of economic behavior would tend to weaken still further the link between *accounting profits* and investment decisions. To the extent that it is demand for the product that causes investment, rather than net profit alone, then the influence of accounting techniques on investment becomes even more tenuous. Here it would need to be established that the accounting methods influence the demand for the final product via the price of the product or that sales and profit are closely associated in the thinking of the businessman. Even if the profit motive in its watered down version is accepted, such evidence as is available does not lend credence to the assumption that *ex-post* profits as measured by accounting methods are used in lieu of expected profits.

77. *Op. cit.*, pp. 188 f.

Even if the first two assumptions are valid, accounting profits are a factor in accentuating business fluctuations only in so far as businessmen are misled by these reported profits. This has been recognized by may of those who insist that accounting methodology does accentuate business fluctuations via investment. However, in the large corporations, investment decisions are not made lightly but only after running the gauntlet of a screening process and after the blending of financial, technological, and market factors in which economists, engineers, and accountants, as well as other specialists, are consulted. The picture so often painted of the businessman recklessly expanding his business on the basis of "overstated" profits does not seem to fit into this pattern.

If it is accepted that a substantial part of investment in a dynamic economy is made as a result of technological advance, much investment is more or less independent of current sales and profit. Thus, the effect of accounting profit on investment is further weakened in an economy largely dominated by technological change. To the extent that investment decisions are motivated by profits after taxes, the accentuating effect of accounting methods on business fluctuations may be further weakened since the difference between profits after taxes computed on the Lifo principle and traditional methods becomes smaller the larger the tax rate. Since a large portion of the fictitious profits determined by traditional accounting methods is taxed away, or as is frequently alleged, distributed as dividends, it is difficult to see how it can be argued that they are very influential in inducing businessmen to over-invest during the upswing. The argument that accelerated depreciation would act as a stimulus to investment boils down to an argument for the use of this method for tax purposes. It is the tax saving that is largely the stimulus and not the psychological effect of the more rapid write-off of the asset. The link between accounting profits and security prices and that between security prices and investment are both weak, and the assumed pattern of investment behavior based on these two links is too simplified.

Thus the theoretical superstructure built up to support the thesis that accounting methods accentuate the cycle via its effect on investment is built on a shaky foundation since none of the assumptions can be unqualifiedly accepted. Furthermore, when the pieces of the institutional framework, which have been abstracted away, are replaced, the effect of accounting profits on investment becomes even more tenuous.

The tendency for accounting profits to accentuate business fluctuations via investment has become weaker since this theory was first propounded by Schmidt. The nature of accounting profits is now better understood, especially in the large corporation, due to the publicity attending the adoption of Lifo for tax purposes, wartime excess profits tax, and the pronounced price rise following World War II. The evidence indicates that the practice of screening investment expenditures is growing. Higher income tax rates narrow the spread between profits reported under the Lifo principle and the traditional methods.

The evidence indicates that accounting methodology as an accentuating factor is more applicable to the smaller firm than to the larger firm. In the small firm, the profit motive is more direct. Also in the small firm, the understanding of the nature of accounting profits is possibly not as good. Autonomous investment is not as likely in the small firm due to the lack of research facilities and the fact that cash may not be available. There is also an indication that the small firm is more responsive in its investment decisions to profits as a source of funds than is the large firm. The nearer an industry approaches competitive conditions, the more active the profit motive, the more important the cost calculations, and, hence, the possibility is greater that accounting methods will accentuate business fluctuations.

In the final analysis, the proposition that the businessman tends to look through rose-colored glasses during prosperity and through dark colored glasses during depression cannot be wholly vitiated. However, it would appear that on the basis of the evidence, the effect of this psychological reaction on investment decisions has been grossly exaggerated.

Chapter VI

Cyclical Effects of Accounting Methodology on Dividend Policy and on Wages

THE DISCUSSION OF ACCOUNTING METHODOLOGY as an accentuating factor in business fluctuations has so far related to the investment function. It is also alleged that accounting methods of computing costs and profits affect the consumption function. This side of the question is not unrelated to investment decisions since investment and consumption are inseparably linked through the multiplier, the accelerator principle, and their interaction.

The desire of the board of directors to use profits as a source of funds for investment purposes competes with their desire to distribute these profits as dividends. Investment expenditures through their effect on employment strengthen or weaken the bargaining position of organized labor and, in turn, affect wage rates. These expenditures by affecting the total demand for goods and services also influence the prices charged by individual firms. Thus investment expenditures, wage rates, the amount of profits paid out as dividends, and prices charged by the firm are inextricably related. In so far then as accounting methods influence investment decisions, dividend and wage policy and the pricing of the products of individual firms are indirectly affected.

Many writers have attributed to accounting methodology more direct effects upon consumption expenditures. The effect of accounting on dividend policy has been stressed during periods of prosperity although it has sometimes been applied to the depression phase of the cycle. The discussion of the relationship of accounting methodology to wage policy is largely a development of the years since World War II and has thus been confined largely to the prosperity phase of the cycle.

Depreciation accounting has also received its share of criticism with respect to adverse effects on consumption. The effect of depreciation accounting on consumption is often discussed as if it were unrelated to dividend, wage, and price policy. The argument with respect to the effect of depreciation accounting on consumption is essentially a secular stagnation argument and will be discussed before investigating the effects of accounting upon dividend and wage policy.

Effects of Depreciation Accounting on Consumption

Depreciation allowances have been endowed with much importance by some writers as having a depressing effect upon income, consumption, and employment. This theory is predicated on the belief that the provision for the depreciation allowance withholds money that should be returned to the income stream, with the result that the prevailing level of income, consumption, and employment cannot be maintained. It is argued that not all the receipts taken in by the firm through sales are counterbalanced by immediate cash outlays. While the outlays for tangible goods, direct labor, and certain overhead expenses return a portion of the firm's receipts to the income stream, the provision for depreciation does not return anything immediately. There is thus a "broken circuit" in the income stream. The authors of one publication have given their idea of the size of this "short circuit":

> During a decade when business losses were running some TWO BILLION DOLLARS a year, there was, as we have but just seen, an ANNUAL excess of depreciation charges, over and above such losses and what was paid out on replacements, amounting to from TWO and THREE-TENTHS to some THREE BILLION DOLLARS. This is a big-money gap-of-deficiency we are talking about in this connection.[1]

In a stationary economy, depreciation allowances would be offset by expenditures for the replacement of new assets, but the effect of depreciation allowances is thought to be especially adverse to consumption in an economy characterized by extremes of prosperity and depression. In a dynamic economy, the effect of depreciation allowances on consumption is thought to be particularly serious immediately following a protracted period of investment in long-lived assets. It is asked by this group of writers, if business cannot find offsets for its own depreciation allow-

1. Joseph E. Goodbar and Lorenzo U. Bergeron, *A Creative Capitalism*, p. 99.

ances, then how can it find outlets for the new saving which a wealthy community will wish to make? This viewpoint was thought by John Maynard Keynes to apply particularly to the United States during the early thirties:

> In the United States, for example, by 1929 the rapid capital expansion of the previous five years had led cumulatively to the setting up of sinking funds and depreciation allowances, in respect of plant which did not need replacement, on so huge a scale that an enormous volume of entirely new investment was required merely to absorb these financial provisions; and it became almost hopeless to find still more new investment on a sufficient scale to provide for such new savings as a wealthy community in full employment would be disposed to set aside. This factor alone was probably sufficient to cause a slump.[2]

Furthermore, the accumulated funds are sometimes thought of as hoarded, presumably in liquid form, thus interrupting the circuit of dollars. Add this alleged tendency of the corporation to hoard to the fact that accountants, according to this school of thought, are said to overdepreciate and the argument is completed. Concerning this tendency for accountants to overdepreciate, Stuart Chase has said: "It was, and is, bad form to underdepreciate. It simply isn't done. The records must gallop ahead of moth and rust—far ahead. This is sound, conservative, universal accounting practice."[3] This argument is thus the antithesis of the argument presented in Chapter V that accountants do not depreciate fast enough and, therefore, retard investment expenditures.

In evaluating the effect of depreciation on consumption, it may be well to clear up certain misconceptions that seem to have arisen concerning the form in which the recovery of the capital investment is kept as well as the size of the depreciation charge compared to the expenditure on plant and equipment. The impression is frequently left with the reader that the corporation segregates a sum of cash, at least, investments in readily marketable securities, for the purpose of replacing the asset when it is worn out—in other words, the depreciation allowance is funded. While this viewpoint is not always stated explicitly, it is difficult to see how there could be any argument that depreciation allowances create a "broken circuit" in the income stream without at least making this tacit assumption. The National Industrial Conference Board reported that only 1.4 per cent of the 572 cooperating corporations in their study funded depreciation allowances.[4] Thus the cash may be

2. *The General Theory of Employment, Interest, and Money,* p. 100.
3. *Idle Money Idle Men,* p. 108.
4. Finley, *op. cit.,* p. 11.

used immediately for the general purposes of the business, such as acquiring inventories, paying operating expenses, and acquiring fixed assets, and hence be returned to the income stream. This study, like so many others, was made during the prosperity phase. During depressions, large businesses, especially, do tend to accumulate liquid resources, as was previously shown by Lutz' study. Any relationship between the tendency to overdepreciate due to accounting methods during deflationary periods and these idle funds still remains to be considered.

During the thirties, much was made of the fact that corporations had become more self-sufficient since more and more of their needs for funds were being supplied internally. At least two researchers[5] who studied corporations for the period when this argument was most in vogue did not find an increasing tendency to rely on internal financing. In a study of a sample of 84 large manufacturing corporations and 27 large trade corporations for the period 1921 to 1939 Koch did not find clear evidence of this tendency. He says: "Much of the recent discussion of big business financing implies that total funds retained from operations (internal funds) have become more and more important during the past two decades. Our samples of manufacturing and trade corporations do not present clear evidence of this." Dobrovolsky came to a similar conclusion in his study of manufacturing corporations for the period from 1915 to 1943. According to Dobrovolsky:

> Finally, it is important to note that, although there are many individual deviations from the general pattern of relationship, no general tendency can be observed for the ratio of internal to external financing, at given rates of corporate investment, to change over the period of time examined. In other words, allowing for variations in the rate of corporate investment, manufacturing corporations seem not to have become either more or less financially self-sufficient.

In order to give an idea of the size of the discrepancy between depreciation charges to income and expenditures on plant and equipment, especially during the Great Depression, Table 18 is presented. The comparison of capital expenditures with depreciation allowances during the thirties is misleading since during some of these years earnings were not sufficient to cover expenses including depreciation; that is, depreciation allowances were not earned. Therefore, the comparison is made between "earned depreciation" and expenditures on plant and equipment, since only to the extent that profits equal or exceed the

5. See Albert Ralph Koch, *op. cit.*, p. 80; and Sergei P. Dobrovolsky, *Corporate Income Retention 1915-43*, p. 6.

TABLE 18

A COMPARISON OF "EARNED DEPRECIATION" WITH CORPORATE EXPENDITURES ON PLANT AND EQUIPMENT

1929-1949

(Millions of Dollars)

Year	Estimated Depreciation Original Cost	Profits After Tax	"Earned Depreciation"	Total Expenditures on Plant and Equipment	Excess of Expenditures over "Earned Depreciation"
	(1)	(2)	(3)	(4)	(5)
1929	3,871	8,420	3,871	7,401	3,530
1930	3,986	2,455	3,986	5,918	1,932
1931	4,003	–1,283	2,720	3,602	882
1932	3,693	–3,424	269	1,884	1,615
1933	3,496	–362	3,134	1,669	(1,465)
1934	3,362	977	3,362	2,246	(1,116)
1935	3,352	2,259	3,352	2,668	(684)
1936	3,286	4,273	3,286	3,716	430
1937	3,342	4,685	3,342	4,838	1,496
1938	3,352	2,289	3,352	3,585	233
1939	3,443	5,005	3,443	4,057	614
1940	3,520	6,447	3,520	5,343	1,823
1941	3,765	9,386	3,765	6,826	3,061
1942	3,914	9,433	3,914	4,539	625
1943	3,916	10,646	3,916	3,496	(420)
1944	3,950	10,808	3,950	4,774	824
1945	3,977	8,502	3,977	6,803	2,826
1946	4,199	13,881	4,199	12,142	7,943
1947	5,220	18,549	5,220	15,449	10,229
1948	6,150	20,734	6,150	17,572	11,422
1949	6,750	17,347	6,750	16,198	9,448

Source: Col. 1, Goldsmith, *op. cit.*, I, 955.
Col. 2, U.S. Department of Commerce, *National Income—A Supplement to the Survey of Current Business*, 1951 ed., Table I, p. 150.
Col. 3, Col. 1 plus Col. 2 when Col. 2 is negative, otherwise, Col. 1.
Col. 4, Col. 5 of Table 17.
Col. 5, Col. 4 minus Col. 3.
Note: Parentheses indicate negative.

annual depreciation expense does the full amount of the depreciation charge become a source of funds. From column 5 it can be seen that the deficiency in expenditures on plant and equipment compared with depreciation charges existed only for the years 1933 to 1935, inclusive, and for the year 1943. Throughout the remaining years, expenditures on plant and equipment exceeded earned depreciation allowances by from $233 million in 1938 to $11,422 million in 1948.

Thus, by comparing plant and equipment expenditures with depreciation allowances when earned, it may be seen that the picture is not so bleak as it is often painted. It is recognized, of course, that the usual danger of using aggregates is present in that many important differences among individual firms are concealed. However, one cannot escape the conviction that the length of the period during which there was a deficiency of expenditures on plant and equipment as compared to earned depreciation allowances, as well as the amount of this deficiency, may have been overestimated.

It can be admitted that the depreciation charge is unique in that it does not represent an expenditure at the time that it is recorded in the accounts of the firm.[6] Provided depreciation charges are earned, one can also agree with Alfred C. Neal that "accumulation of depreciation allowances without compensating replacement expenditures either in the same industry or somewhere else in the economy is likely to operate in the same direction as the maintenance of private saving; that is to say, in the face of a great fall in investment activity, it is likely to be deflationary for the economy as a whole."[7] In this respect, corporate saving is, of course, no different from any other saving.

It can be further admitted that business "rolls its own." In fact, Oscar Altman of the Investment Banking Section of the S.E.C. stressed that the tendency of business to rely on internal financing was one of the main conclusions to be drawn from the testimony before the Temporary National Economic Committee.[8] One could even go further than Altman and conclude, contrary to the findings of Koch and Dobrovolsky, that the tendency for internal financing was increasing. However, the fact that businesses do not often need to go to Wall Street to obtain money for the expansion of their plants does not mean that *total* savings will necessarily be increased by the full amount of the corporate savings. Alvin Hansen stressed in his testimony before the T.N.E.C. that in order to prevent a fall in national income "it is necessary to have an offset for all saving."[9] To the extent that an increase in gross corporate savings is even partially offset by a decrease in savings in the personal sector of the economy the resulting drop in national income will be smaller than it otherwise would.

6. Perry Mason rightly points out that this "uniqueness" is also shared by accrued expenses and the amortizable prepaid expenses. See "The Financial Aspects of Depreciation Accounting," *The Accounting Review,* September, 1935, p. 238. However, because of the relative size of these items they will not be considered further.

7. *Industrial Concentration and Price Inflexibility,* p. 149. Reprinted by permission of Public Affairs Press.

8. U.S. Congress, *Savings and Investment,* Hearings Before the Temporary National Economic Committee, Part 9, 76th Cong., 1st Sess., p. 3696.

9. *Ibid.,* p. 3539.

As alternatives to the retaining of the funds resulting from "excessive" depreciation charges during the depression of the thirties, corporations might have returned the excess to the income stream in the form of higher dividends or higher wages. During this period with the high unemployment that existed it is difficult to see how the recording of smaller depreciation charges on the books of corporations would have caused the paying of higher wages. If, as a result of more "realistic" depreciation charges, higher wages had been paid, however, then due to the high propensity to consume of the wage earners, the reduction in corporate savings would not have been offset to any great extent by an increase in personal savings, and hence total savings would have decreased. If, on the other hand, depreciation charges had been reduced and a correspondingly higher amount had been paid out as dividends, the effect on total savings would have depended on the use which dividend recipients made of their receipts. In so far as total accounting cost is a factor in the pricing of consumer goods, there is the additional possibility that smaller depreciation charges would have contributed to lower prices, thereby, depending upon the elasticity of demand, causing an increase in total consumption expenditures. Thus in the final analysis the question of whether depreciation accounting and especially "excessive" depreciation allowances are depressing to the economy depends upon whether the recording of this excess depreciation causes the corporate system to take more from outside the system in the form of sales revenue or to pay out less as dividends or wages than would occur if the depreciation charges were more "realistic." The effect of depreciation expenses upon selling prices will be evaluated in Chapter VII, and the effect of accounting methodology upon dividend policy and wages will be evaluated in the remainder of this chapter.

Cyclical Effects of Accounting Methodology on Dividend Policy

Some writers on the effect of accounting methods on business fluctuations believe that the reported profits unduly influence dividend policy.[10] Furthermore, it is believed that accounting methods influence dividend policy in such a way as to accentuate the cycle. It is argued that, since more money will be distributed as dividends from the overstated profits during prosperity, the effect must be inflationary since

10. See Lacey, *Profit Measurement and Price Changes,* p. 22; and Eldon S. Hendriksen, "The Influence of Depreciation Accounting on National Income," *The Accounting Review,* October, 1951, p. 509.

it will increase the demand for goods.[11] Schmidt, for example, argues: "If the paid-out dividends are too high because of depreciation's being too low, there will be plenty of money in the buying market for consumption goods, accompanied by a rise of prices." More recently, Walter Adams has expressed the same opinion: "The effect of these increased dividend disbursements on the economy is inflationary, since larger incomes mean greater potential demand, which means higher prices and a continuation of the inflationary merry-go-round."

Thus in evaluating this argument it is necessary, first, to determine whether dividend policy is unduly influenced by *reported* profits and, second, whether, even though dividend policy is unduly influenced by the reported profits, this would tend to accentuate the cycle.

Butters and Niland have shown that dividends are more closely related to *reported* profits than to profits adjusted for inventory profits and losses. They plot the dividends paid by all corporations from 1933 to 1948 against reported profits after taxes and such profits adjusted for inventory gains and losses. They conclude: "The closer relationship which these charts show between dividends and profits as reported (without the inventory adjustment) constitutes at least suggestive evidence that corporate directors in the aggregate look more to stated profits than to adjusted profits (which more nearly approximate disposable profits) in determining dividend policies."[12] They attribute this closer relationship to two factors. The influence of the amount of currently reported profit, which produces a feeling of overconfidence (or even carelessness) on the part of many managements, affects their decisions relative to dividends. Pressure from stockholders, who regard rising profits as an indication of the ability of the corporation to pay higher dividends, constitutes the second factor.

Before jumping to the conclusion that managements of corporations will recklessly pay out reported profits as dividends if the profits are overstated, it should be pointed out that reported profits are only one factor in the determination of the amount to be declared as dividends. The payment of a dividend is a legal as well as a financial problem. It may be said that, in general, the amount of reported profits only sets the *maximum* amount that can be paid as dividends in the long run. In the short run, dividends may be paid in many cases on the basis of accumulated earnings of the past, even if no profit is being currently earned.[13]

11. Fritz Schmidt, "The Basis of Depreciation Charges," p. 263; and Walter Adams, *op. cit.*, p. 127.

12. *Op. cit.*, p. 110.

13. Butters and Niland mention this possibility.

Furthermore, since all reported earnings do not need to be paid out as dividends, the board of directors is left with a wide margin of discretion in its dividend policy with any given reported earnings.

The amount of cash available at the time of the declaration of the dividend is also an important factor in determining the amount to be distributed as dividends. Despite the common reference to "paying dividends out of profits," in most cases the only practical asset suitable for distribution to stockholders is cash. While the presence of retained earnings and reported profits is an accounting phenomenon, profits and cash are not synonomous. In a period of rising prices profits are not usually kept in a form available for dividend distribution. The earnings may be locked up in receivables. Assuming, however, that these receivables are collectible, within a short time the earnings should be available for dividends. The earnings may have already been converted into assets that are not readily distributable as dividends. In this second case, the decision as to dividend distribution was automatically made at the time it was decided to increase the capital investment.

The problem of tying up profits in noncash assets is particularly acute when the volume of business is rising. This increased volume of business requires a bigger dollar investment in inventories as well as the carrying of larger receivables, and since the payment of dividends is considered at periodic intervals, the cash balance and current position are likely to appear more relevant than current income, or the amount of retained earnings in determining dividend policy. According to Lutz, in large corporations, particularly, the movement of "free" cash "shows an inverse correlation with the profit rate."[14] Thus, a corporation may perpetually find itself short of cash out of which to pay dividends during the upswing even though it may be earning profits.

As to the second reason given for reported profits unduly influencing dividend policy—the clamor of stockholders for larger dividends—there is far from universal agreement. Dewing thinks that boards of directors generally have not succumbed to stockholder pressure. He states that "viewing the matter broadly, it is distinctly to the credit of the majority of American businessmen who reach higher managerial positions that their natural insight enriched by a wide experience is sufficient to protect the stockholders against their own avarice in demanding larger dividends than prudence justifies."[15] Furthermore, the stock dividend is used to some extent as a device to allay the clamor by stock-

14. *Op. cit.,* p. 5.
15. *Op. cit.,* I, 754 f.

holders for greater cash dividends during periods of high profits but low cash balances.

In spite of their conclusions drawn from aggregate corporate profit and dividend data, cited above, Butters and Niland report a diversity of reaction in their field interviews toward reported profits in determining dividend policy. Executives of some companies have reported that dividend payments "are responsive to fluctuations in reported profits. Officers of other companies . . . have stated that their dividend decisions are governed by their company's need for funds as shown by projected cash budgets and that little attention is given to the level of profit as such."[16] As a result of his interviews (previously described in Chapter V) Brown states: "Our field work indicates that firms would be affected differently by a change to replacement-cost depreciation. Some indicated that it had been somewhat effective in blunting dividend demands."[17]

As shown by Table 19, dividend policy has been very conservative in the years since World War II. During this period the percentage paid out ranged from a low of 35.1 in 1948, to a high of 58.3 in 1954. These figures should be compared with 76 per cent for the prewar year of 1939, and with 90.2 per cent and 69.9 per cent for the prosperous years of 1927 and 1929, respectively. During the years 1930 to 1938, more was paid out in dividends than earned except in 1937 when they equaled profits.

In order to shed further light on the relationship of the misstatement of profits to dividend policy two questions might be raised. First, in each of the years in which profits were said to be overstated did the undistributed profits of all corporations for that year exceed the alleged overstatement of profits, thus indicating that overstated profits were not paid out as dividends? Second, in each of the years in which profits were said to be understated due to accounting methods, did all corporations pay out dividends in excess of these understated profits, thus indicating that in their dividend policy corporations were partially compensating for this understatement? Table 20 shows that in each of the seventeen years of profit overstatement from 1929 to 1949, undistributed profits exceeded the amount of overstatement of profits in all years except the five years 1933 to 1937. Hence, with the exception of the years 1933 to 1937, it was not "overstated" profits that were being paid out as dividends. In every one of the four years in which profits are shown by Table 20 to be understated, dividends were paid in an amount exceeding

16. *Op. cit.*, p. 109.

17. *Op. cit.*, p. 86.

TABLE 19

A COMPARISON OF CORPORATE PROFITS AND CORPORATE DIVIDENDS, 1919-1957

(Billions of Dollars)

Year	Profits after Taxes	Dividends	Dividends as Per Cent of Profit
	(1)	(2)	(3)
1919	5.7	2.9	50.9
1920	3.9	2.9	74.4
1921	0.5	3.0	600.0
1922	3.9	2.9	74.4
1923	5.2	3.8	73.1
1924	4.3	3.5	81.4
1925	5.5	3.9	70.9
1926	5.8	4.4	75.9
1927	5.1	4.6	90.2
1928	6.3	4.9	77.8
1929	8.3	5.8	69.9
1930	2.5	5.5	220.0
1931	–1.3	4.1	. . *
1932	–3.4	2.6	. . *
1933	–0.4	2.1	. . *
1934	0.9	2.6	288.9
1935	2.2	2.9	131.8
1936	4.3	4.5	104.7
1937	4.7	4.7	100.0
1938	2.2	3.2	145.4
1939	5.0	3.8	76.0
1940	6.5	4.0	61.5
1941	9.4	4.5	47.9
1942	9.5	4.3	45.3
1943	10.5	4.5	42.9
1944	10.4	4.7	45.2
1945	8.3	4.7	56.6
1946	13.4	5.8	43.3
1947	18.2	6.5	35.7
1948	20.5	7.2	35.1
1949	16.0	7.5	46.9
1950	22.8	9.2	40.4
1951	19.7	9.0	45.7
1952	17.2	9.0	52.3
1953	18.0	9.2	51.1
1954	16.8	9.8	58.3
1955	23.0	11.2	48.7
1956	23.0	12.0	52.2
1957	21.8	12.4	56.9

Source: 1919-1928, All columns, James A. Finley, *Handling Higher Replacement Costs,* Studies in Business Policy No. 47, p. 6.

1929-1957, Col. 1 and Col. 2, U.S. Department of Commerce, *Survey of Current Business,* July, 1958, Table I, pp. 4 f.

*Not computable.

TABLE 20

A COMPARISON OF THE MISSTATEMENT OF CORPORATE ACCOUNTING PROFITS WITH UNDISTRIBUTED PROFITS

1929-1949

(Millions of Dollars)

Year	Misstatement of Profits	Undistributed Profits
1929	389	2,597
1930	(2,716)*	(3,045)*
1931	(2,158)	(5,381)
1932	(1,162)	(5,998)
1933	2,041	(2,428)
1934	824	(1,619)
1935	452	(613)
1936	963	(284)
1937	508	(8)
1938	(515)	(906)
1939	1,166	1,209
1940	717	2,398
1941	3,193	4,921
1942	2,158	5,136
1943	1,770	6,153
1944	1,275	6,128
1945	1,590	3,803
1946	6,793	8,073
1947	8,576	11,988
1948	5,420	13,484
1949	1,162	9,795

Source: Misstatement of profits—Table 5, column 3, Undistributed profits—U.S. Department of Commerce, *National Income—A Supplement to the Survey of Current Business,* Table 1, p. 150.

*Parentheses indicates understatement of profit and negative undistributed profits.

this understatement. Therefore, it would seem that in the aggregate these understated profits resulting from accounting methods did find their way back into the income stream through dividend payments.

It is true that many individual corporations tend to pay out a relatively fixed percentage of reported profits, if positive, as dividends. Therefore, during the years when profits were overstated, individual corporations adhering to a fixed dividend policy of this sort would pay out more in dividends than they would if accounting methods had resulted in less reported profit. The data in Table 20 cannot reveal the extent to which dividend payments would have been different if accounting methods had been different. However, one writer on the subject of depreciation on replacement cost, J. Frank Gaston, with reference to the years 1931 to 1936, said: "Would such a calculation in those years of depression and early recovery have had any effect upon dividend policy, or investment by corporations? Since income was larger, would dividends be larger? It seems rather unlikely that such would be the case."[18] He points out that while decisions on dividend distribution depend partially upon income, liquidity position is also a consideration. In view of the decline of cash balances of corporations from $22.4 billion to $15.9 billion from the end of 1929 to the end of 1931, and the contraction in sales volume, Gaston doubts that the increase in corporate profits, as a result of the use of replacement costs in computing depreciation, would have had very much effect in increasing dividend disbursements.

Thus it may be seen from Tables 19 and 20 that total dividends in a given year are not tied closely to total reported corporate profits of that year and that the "misstatement" of profits by accounting methods has at least been partially compensated for by the dividend policy of the corporate system. It may well be true, as a famous writer in the field of corporate finance has stated, that directors have tended to discount reported profits as a factor in dividend policy as a result of their lack of faith in these figures.[19]

In summary, the declaration of dividends is a legal and financial problem as well as an accounting problem. Reported profits establish an upper limit in the long run for divided payments. Dividends can be paid if there are accumulated earnings of the past and are not necessarily limited by current profits. Furthermore, boards of directors need not pay out all current earnings as dividends. On the upswing the need for additional working capital limits dividends even though earnings may be high. The evidence over the years since 1929 does not indicate that the "misstatement" of accounting profit in any one year has unduly influenced boards of directors as a whole relative to dividend policy.

Even if the theory that the misstatement of accounting profits unduly influences corporate dividend policy were accepted, the question of whether the paying out of more dividends during prosperity and less during depression due to this misstatement accentuates the fluctuations of business as a whole remains to be considered.

If the corporation retains more funds in the business during prosperity as a result of more "realistic" reporting of profits, the effect is not necessarily stabilizing. The result will depend upon what the corporation does with the retained earnings versus what the stockholders would do with the increased dividends that it is alleged they do receive as a result of the overstatement of profit. If the corporation retains funds in the

18. *Op. cit.*, p. 15.

19. Dewing, *op. cit.*, p. 752.

business, it must have a purpose for doing so. Just what the corporation does with these funds will depend, among other factors, upon the phase of the cycle in which the decision is to be made.[20] During prosperity, when it is alleged that the cutting down of dividends would be deflationary, if the firm used the retained earnings to increase its outlays on inventories and fixed plant, the result is, of course, expansionary. If the firm used the funds to buy the securities of other companies or to lend for others to buy securities, the result might also be a contribution to the speculative fever. According to some writers[21] this factor contributed to the boom of 1928 and 1929. Wilbur, for example, mentions this influence:

> . . . the funds which have been withheld from the stockholders during business prosperity are apt to be drawn, by higher rates and greater liquidity offered, to open-market borrowers and call-money markets, where their presence goes to expand short-term credit and helps to bring about the very inflation which was to be so carefully avoided. This country's experience in 1928 and 1929 revealed what a tremendous force for inflation and speculation the pouring of surplus cash of corporations into the call-loan market may be.

During periods of depression, on the other hand, if we assume that the stabilization of reported profits would cause more dividends to be paid out than otherwise, the result could be stimulating to business provided the dividend recipients used the receipts for consumption expenditures. If, in lieu of retaining the larger reported profits as hoarded cash, these profits were paid out as dividends, the result would be to help in maintaining the level of consumption and therefore of investment. It has already been shown in Chapter V that, according to Lutz, during the depression of the thirties large corporations were inclined to maintain idle cash balances. The retirement of bank debt in lieu of dividend payments is also a possibility during depressions. Lutz thinks there is evidence that this may have happened in the case of medium-sized and small corporations, especially, during periods of contraction.[22]

Thus an a priori case can be made that dividend stabilization is inflationary in both boom and depression. There is no reason to suppose

20. Lawrence R. Klein also states that it depends upon the age of the firm and of the industry, see "Savings Concepts and Data: The Needs of Economic Analysis and Policy," *Savings in the Modern Economy,* ed. by Walter W. Heller, Francis M. Boddy, and Carl L. Nelson, p. 109.

21. See Donald E. Wilbur, "A Study of the Policy of Dividend Stabilization," *Harvard Business Review,* April, 1932, p. 376; Lutz also mentions this possibility, *op. cit.,* p. 1.

22. *Op. cit.,* p. 7.

that the retaining of more funds during prosperity, due to accounting methods designed to equalize profits, will be stabilizing, since the corporation will probably use the funds for investment during this phase. Since, during the depression, some of the stockholders could be expected to use the funds for consumption, there is better reason to suppose that the paying out of more dividends during this phase of the cycle would be stabilizing.

Attention will now be directed to the use of funds which are paid out as dividends by the corporation during the prosperity phase, assuming that accounting methods cause more to be paid out as dividends than would be the case if the profits were reported on an "economic" basis. It must be considered that since reported profits are higher and if these reported profits are actually paid out, the government will get a substantial slice in the form of individual income taxes which it would not have received had the corporation retained the funds. Whether the amount going to the government will be used in such a way as to contribute to inflation will depend upon the fiscal and monetary policies that happen to prevail at that particular time. If the government uses the extra tax revenue to retire debt, this would tend to be stabilizing during the prosperity phase. If the government used the additional revenue for expenditures, the results may be approximately the same as if the corporation had retained the profits in the business and used them for expansion. Thus the use of funds by the corporation versus paying dividends and the consequent sharing of these dividends by the government cannot be evaluated except in particular instances. However, in recent years, since the government has largely used income taxes for current expenditures rather than for retirement of the public debt, there is no reason to suppose that this use of the funds by the government would be any less inflationary than if the corporation had retained the funds and used them for investment.

This still leaves for consideration the use of the residual dividend funds (after income taxes) which go to the stockholders. As a first step in tracing the effect upon business fluctuations of paying out varying amounts in dividends based on alternative accounting methods, the question of the income level of the dividend recipients is pertinent. Selma F. Goldsmith,[23] in a study of the ratios of concentration of various

23. "Statistical Information on the Distribution of Income by Size in the United States," *Papers and Proceedings of the Sixty-second Annual Meeting of the American Economic Association in The American Economic Review*, May, 1950, p. 327.

sources of income, found interest and dividends to be highest in concentration. In fact, it has been pointed out that the concentration of dividend income accounts for the major part of the wide spread between the income of individuals. Martin Taitel[24] stated that "the major share of the difference between the average $50,000 income and the average $1,000,000 income is due to the difference between the average amount of dividends included in those incomes." More specifically, he gave the following rough distribution of dividends: Forty per cent of the dividends was received by less than 0.1 per cent of families and single individuals; another 20 per cent was received by less than 1 per cent of the families and single individuals; another 20 per cent was received by less than 2 per cent of the families and single individuals; and the remaining 20 per cent was received by the remaining 96 per cent of the families and single individuals, with most of them receiving no dividends.

There is additional evidence as to the income groups receiving dividends.[25] Taitel states that between 40 and 50 per cent of all dividends were received by individuals with incomes of 20,000 or more 1935-1936 dollars while another 20 to 25 per cent were received by individuals with incomes between 5,000 and 20,000 1935-1936 dollars. Thus, between 60 and 75 per cent of all dividends were received by individuals with incomes of $5,000 or more. Another writer, Raymond W. Goldsmith, found that in 1937 probably fewer than 10 per cent of all individuals with incomes under $1,000 owned stock; 70 per cent of those with incomes of $10,000 and over and 94 per cent of those with incomes of $50,000 owned stock. Furthermore, this pattern of distribution was of long standing.[26] Taitel concludes that "there has been no marked change in the relative distribution of dividends according to income level of recipients during the past two decades." Selma Goldsmith showed that a movement toward equality of incomes did take place from 1935-1936 to 1944 and attributed this to the declining importance of interest and dividends during those years, but stated that this movement was arrested in 1945. In the years since World War II much has been written and spoken concerning "People's Capitalism." One of the chief ingredients of this concept is the contention of more widely dispersed stockholdings

24. *Op. cit.*, pp. 50-52.

25. See Taitel, *op. cit.*, p. 56; and Raymond W. Goldsmith, *The Distribution of Ownership in the 200 Largest Nonfinancial Corporations,* Temporary National Economic Committee Monograph No. 29, p. 10.

26. See Taitel, *op. cit.*, p. 56; and Selma F. Goldsmith, *op. cit.*, pp. 335 and 337.

among the population. As a result of a recent study, one writer has concluded that this claim of more widespread stock-ownership is without foundation.[27]

Thus, if the amount of dividends going to stockholders is modified by accounting methods, it effects the amounts going to the highest income groups since stock ownership in the major corporations is highly concentrated and, hence, dividend receipts are highly concentrated. In view of the low propensity to consume of these dividend recipients, it is difficult to believe that, as a result of accounting methods, the paying out of more dividends during the depression phase, and less during the prosperity phase, would greatly modify consumers' expenditures.

Accounting Profits, Dividend Policy, and Business Fluctuations

The evidence does not support the supposition that reported profits have unduly influenced dividend policy. On the contrary, boards of directors—consciously or unconsciously—in their dividend policies have gone a long way toward neutralizing the effects of accountants' "misstatement" of net profits. Neither is it a foregone conclusion that, even if more funds have been dispensed as dividends during prosperity or less during depression, the cycle has thereby been accentuated. The evidence shows that a large proportion of dividend recipients would probably not use the extra dividends for consumption anyway. During the depression, if we could assume that more dividends would be distributed if profits were reported on a so-called economic basis—which is very problematical—it still does not necessarily follow that consumption expenditures would thereby be materially stimulated.

Since dividends are considered by many writers to constitute one of the main factors determining the price of securities, and since it has been shown that there is no close association between accounting profits per year and the payments of dividends in that year, it follows that the casual links between accounting profits, dividend policy, security prices, the ease or difficulty of raising monetary capital, and decisions to invest in plant and equipment are so weak that no one can say with assurance that accounting methods accentuate business fluctuations through this chain.

In the discussion of the adverse effects of "excessive" depreciation allowances on consumption expenditures during depression, it was concluded (earlier in this chapter) that one way in which this could occur

27. Victor Perlo, "'Peoples Capitalism' and Stock-Ownership," *The American Economic Review,* June, 1958, p. 335.

was through its influence on dividend policy. If dividend distribution per year is not tied closely to accounting profits, it is difficult to see how excessive depreciation allowances during the thirties prevented the returning of money as dividends to the income stream that otherwise would have been returned.

It is far from a settled fact that the effect on consumption caused by the stabilization of dividend policy based on reported corporate earnings, determined by more "realistic" accounting methods, would materially affect the level of national income.

The Cyclical Effect of Accounting Methodology on Wage Policy

Many of the writers who believe that accounting methods accentuate the cycle by affecting consumption state that wage policy as well as dividend policy is modified by these methods.[28] One of the earlier writers on the subject, George E. Putnam, said: "Increased wages and extraordinary dividend payments, both of which grow out of the misinterpretation of 'profits,' enhance the demands of consumers for the products of industry all along the line." A later writer, Walter Adams, has expressed a similar point of view: "The existence of large money profits during a period of rising prices prompts the entrepreneur not only to increase dividend disbursements but also to grant often substantial wage increases, particularly in industries where strong trade-union organizations can make their pressure felt." Thus it may be seen that the connection between accounting methods, wages, and business fluctuations has been stressed during periods of prosperity. Since this argument reached a crescendo in the early postwar years, the labor-management controversy of those years, as well as the relationship of accounting methods thereto, will now be reviewed.

In the years immediately following World War II, the leaders of organized labor argued that prices and wages were out of balance since prices had risen faster than wages. As a result of the lag of wages behind prices, profits had also risen faster than wages. They argued that wage increases could have been taken out of the high profit margins and still leave industry a profit that was reasonable. In fact, profits were

28. See Putnam, "The Role of Paper Profits . . . ," p. 135; Adams, *op. cit.*, p. 127; Fritz Schmidt, "Is Appreciation Profit?" p. 289; Henry B. Arthur, "Something Business Can Do About Depressions," *The Journal of Accountancy*, January, 1939, p. 10; H. T. McAnly, "Curbing the Effect of Our Erratic Dollar in Pricing Inventories and Providing for Depreciation," *The New York Certified Public Accountant*, August, 1948, p. 576; Graham, *op. cit.*, p. 20; and Hendriksen, *op. cit.*, p. 510.

reaped at the expense of wages. Therefore, the purchasing power of labor was being destroyed. This thought was expressed by one labor spokesman as follows: "We believe present profits are far too high. We believe this because we are convinced that present profits will destroy the purchasing power base which is essential to maintenance of prosperity and full employment."[29] Since labor leaders did not expect prices to be reduced voluntarily, they thought wages must be increased. Labor leaders thus supported an underconsumption theory of the cycle.

According to the viewpoint of management, profits should have had no bearing on the wage bargaining. Wages should have been determined on the basis of productivity. Even if profits were a factor, business executives insisted that actual profits were lower than *reported* profits because of fictitious inventory gains and inadequate depreciation allowances. Furthermore, it was contended that a good share of the profits was needed in the business to provide for further expansion and improvements, thus benefiting workers as well as stockholders in the long run. In this contention corporate executives had the support of many economists. Joel Dean, for example, states: "From the standpoint of labor, capital expenditures are the basic economic source of future wage advances since they embody the creative forward strides of advancing technology."[30] Since labor is a cost that must be incorporated in the price of the final product, if wages were raised, prices must be increased to cover the increased labor cost.

This divergence in points of view between labor leaders and the managers of corporations as to the role of profits may now be summarized. The businessman regarded profits as earnings available for stockholders or to be reinvested in the business. Leaders of organized labor regarded profits as a residue to be shared as higher wages.

Accounting methods were injected into the controversy through the use by organized labor of the "ability-to-pay" criterion. In fact, if the "ability-to-pay" were eliminated in wage disputes, the profits made by an industry or firm would be irrelevant as a direct argument for a wage increase. This criterion, of course, enters indirectly into every wage negotiation. Although the recognition of the ability-to-pay argument is not new,[31] it was popularized by Walter Reuther in 1945. Moreover, in

29. Testimony of Donald Montgomery, UAW-CIO, Chief, Washington Office United Automobile Workers, U.S. Congress, *Profits,* p. 30.

30. "Measuring the Productivity . . . ," p. 120.

31. Z. Clark Dickinson gives an example of the use of financial reports in wage negotiations in the printing industry as early as 1919; see *Cellective Wage Determination,* p. 206.

the postwar profit-price-wage controversy, labor leaders made it plain that by "ability-to-pay" they were referring to *reported* profits. Stanley H. Ruttenberg, for example, stated: "In the judgment of the CIO, profits are profits regardless of the source from which they are derived. Inventory profits are money and the money can be used by the corporation for whatever purpose they see fit."[32] It may thus be argued that accounting methodology contributed to the postwar wage-price spiral since the overstated profits may have influenced labor leaders to seek larger wage increases than they otherwise would. On the other hand, if profits had been reported on a more "realistic" basis, this would have allayed the demands of organized labor. Before it can be said that accounting methods did contribute to the early postwar wage-price spiral, however, it is necessary to show that (1) the granting of the wage increases caused the higher prices, (2) ability-to-pay was a significant factor in the granting of the pay increases, and (3) if profits had been more "realistically" reported, wage demands would have been blunted.

The relationship of wages to prices is both a cost-price and a demand-price relationship. Sumner Slichter[33] believes that the wage increases immediately following World War II affected prices through increased demand rather than as costs. This is based on the absence of a close relationship between the wage increases granted and the advances in the prices of the final product. Furthermore, he attributed less than half of the increase in the demand for consumer goods during the last two years of the period studied to higher wages in private industry. Personal consumption expenditure between 1945 and 1947 rose by $20.7 billion; wage and salary payments rose by $14.8 billion, of which $5.3 billion resulted from the growth in the labor force, and $9.5 billion arose from higher wages. Therefore, Slichter concludes that only about 45 per cent of the increased demand during this period can be attributed to higher wages, which indicated the importance of other expansionary forces. He mentions as other forces: (1) the tendency for individuals to save a declining portion of their rising incomes, and (2) holdings of cash and demand deposits were high relative to prices and expenditures. Another writer[34] has given the following summary of the forces contributing to the early postwar inflation: "Forces other than labor also contributing to the inflation were the higher incomes and expenditures

32. Testimony of Stanley H. Ruttenberg, U.S. Congress, *Profits*, p. 41.

33. "Wages and Prices," *Proceedings of the Academy of Political Science*, XXIII (1948-1950), 50 f.

34. Walter A. Morton, "Trade Unionism, Full Employment, and Inflation," *The American Economic Review*, March, 1950, p. 17.

of farmers, proprietors and other high-income groups, the eagerness to procure goods, dishoarding, reduction in the proportion of savings, the growth of consumer credit, expenditures for new plant and equipment, the growth in mortgage debt on urban real estate, and large federal and local expenditures for domestic and international purposes." This same writer concludes: "The wage-price spiral was, therefore, a cause of inflation but not the sole cause nor even a sufficient cause to bring about the degree or price change that has taken place."

Attention is next directed to the relationship of the ability-to-pay criterion to the granting of the wage increases. First, it should be pointed out that ability-to-pay is only one of a number of criteria used in requesting and granting wage increases.[35] Jules Backman mentions five criteria that have emerged from wage negotiations. George W. Taylor states that "there is no one criterion of wage determination which is universally applicable. The criteria differ with the industry, the phase of the business cycle and the business problems that have to be faced at certain times." One writer on labor-management relations, Ernest Dale, points out that a good many unions do not even make use of the ability-to-pay criterion in wage negotiations. Furthermore, according to Wilbur F. Pillsbury, the ability-to-pay is usually coupled with other criteria such as, the cost of living, or a comparison with wages in other firms in the same industry and with other industries. Even in the General Motors negotiations in 1945, when ability-to-pay had its greatest publicity, Slichter states that the ability-to-pay was not the real issue.

Recent discussions of ability-to-pay have led many people to expect unions to argue that the ability of an employer to pay a wage increase proves that he should pay it. Even in the General Motors negotiations in the fall of 1945, however, the union did not use the ability-to-pay argument in this way. In fact, ability-to-pay was not the positive basis for the union's demand on General Motors. It was used merely as anticipatory rebuttal. The union's argument for a wage increase was that higher wages were needed to avert a catastrophic drop in postwar markets.[36]

How does the ability-to-pay criterion rank with the other criteria

35. See Jules Backman, *Economics of a Fourth Round Wage Increase,* Testimony on Behalf of Steel Companies Before the Presidential Steel Board, August, 1949, pp. 1 f.; George W. Taylor, "Criteria for Wage Determination," *Management Record,* June, 1949, p. 242; Ernest Dale, *Sources of Economic Information for Collective Bargaining,* Research Report No. 17, p. 118; and Wilbur F. Pillsbury, *The Use of Corporate Financial Statements and Related Data by Organized Labor,* Indiana Business Report Number 18, p. 13.

36. *Basic Criteria Used in Wage Negotiations,* pp. 30 f.

used in wage negotiations? A study that throws light on this question was made by Woytinsky and Associates in the summer of 1948. The report of this study gives the views of over a hundred of those most concerned with collective bargaining—chief officers of the largest labor unions and those officials in leading business concerns most concerned with labor relations. The persons interviewed were encouraged to give their candid views in their own words with the promise of anonymity. No conclusions were drawn but the report was presented for factual information. Representatives of all but one union having a membership of more than 200,000 members were interviewed. In all, 52 interviews with labor leaders representing 11,500,000 members and 88 interviews with management leaders were arranged. Emphasis was placed on the thinking of the leaders rather than on arguments that they had used at the negotiation table or before the public. A tabulation of the results of the survey of labor leaders is given in Table 21. It is worthy of note that during a period when reported profits were high, and during a time when the ability-to-pay argument was in its heyday, the amount of profits was ranked fifth in the factors considered by labor leaders in their wage aims. Only three unions, 9.9 per cent of the total membership represented, named it among the most important factors. In only 25 unions, accounting for 45.6 per cent of the union members represented in the survey, was it even mentioned as a factor. Table 22 reveals that Management respondents also ranked the earnings position of the company fifth as a factor in their wage proposals.

Labor leaders are not willing to use the ability-to-pay as a universal criterion. Backman states that this criterion is "one which cannot be and will not be widely applied by labor as a criterion of wage adjustment."[37] This position is substantiated by statements of labor leaders themselves as shown by the following editorial in the *New York Times*:

> Now Mr. Reuther has publicly announced that the demand made upon the corporation to open its books in order to determine its ability to pay "was just a maneuver to win public support and to get the company over a barrel." At the same time, UAW President Thomas admitted that the ability-to-pay theory had "got us into quite serious difficulties with other unions." He went on to point out that "Ford, for example, offered to show us their books if we would consider ability to pay the principle. We'd certainly have been in a jam on that. They were losing $30,000,000 a year, so instead of getting an increase we'd have got a decrease."[38]

37. *Op. cit.*, p. 60. 38. March 26, 1946, p. 28.

TABLE 21

FACTORS CONSIDERED BY UNION LEADERS IN WAGE AIMS OF 1947 AND 1948

Response	Named Among All Factors			Named Among Most Important Factor		
		Union Members			Union Members	
	Number of Unions	Number (Thousands)	Per Cent of Total	Number of Unions	Number (Thousands)	Per Cent of Total
Number of respondents	52	11,523	100.00	52	11,523	100.0
Factors considered in setting wage goals:						
Cost-of-living changes	50	11,408	99.0	43	9,704	84.2
Comparison with other localities	34	8,112	70.4	1	200	1.7
Comparison with other occupations or industries	29	6,056	52.6	4	560	4.9
Comparison with other unions	26	5,061	43.9	.	. .	. .
Profits	25	5,253	45.6	3	1,137	9.9
Productivity	18	4,367	37.9	5	2,340	20.3
Standard of living	14	1,919	16.7	13	1,847	16.0
Other	3	950	8.2	2	640	5.6

Source: W. S. Woytinsky and Associates, *Labor and Management Look at Collective Bargaining*, p. 73.

TABLE 22

MAJOR FACTORS CONSIDERED IN MANAGEMENT'S WAGE PROPOSALS, 1947 AND 1948

Response	Total	Manufacturing Companies	Nonmanufacturing Companies
Number of respondents	88	47	41
Factors considered in developing proposals:			
Changing in cost of living	80	44	36
Wages, etc., of other firms in the industry	40	21	19
Wages, etc., of other firms in the area	39	23	16
Increases won by certain big unions	28	16	12
Earnings position of the company	25	11	14
Effect on price of product	20	12	8
Strength of union or a strike threat	12	4	8
Changes in productivity	6	4	2

Source: Woytinsky and Associates, *op. cit.*, p. 84.

The argument is used also by management in the form of "inability-to-pay." The business decline of 1949 brought about an increasing emphasis by management on this inability-to-pay. Evidence of this may be found in articles concerning wage negotiations in the *New York Times* during June, 1949.[39] The Ford Motor Company of Canada, for example, pleaded inability to meet a $100 pension plan for men of sixty-five with twenty-five years of service. The company estimated that it would take $13 million per year and insisted they had never earned anything like this much profit in any year. According to the *Times*, the textile companies and the Ford Motor Company of Detroit also used the same plea in refusing to grant pay increases. In fact, Slichter has stated that the argument in this form has been more frequently used by employers than by unions. He states that in these cases "unions have usually argued that the employer's ability or inability to pay is irrevelant, that employers should be required to pay a wage that is 'fair,' and that employers who cannot do so should go out of business."[40] Thus ability-to-pay emerges as a highly opportunistic argument that is used by management representatives when the situation is adverse but is held by them to be irrelevant in times of prosperity, while unions argue in just the other way. In fact, one writer on labor-management relations has stated

39. June 4, 1949, p. 7; June 17, 1949, p. 4; and June 19, 1949, p. 34.
40. *Basic Criteria* . . . , p. 25.

that the appeal for public sympathy was the main purpose of the presentation of financial data.[41]

Even if it is admitted that the granting of higher wages caused higher prices, and that the "ability-to-pay" was a significant factor in the granting of pay increases, the question of whether wage demands would have been blunted, if profits had been more "realistically" reported, remains to be considered. Students of the subject of the use of financial information by unions stress that financial statements are not the principal factor in wage negotiations. One such writer has said: "Financial statements will never be the principal factor in labor disputes. Labor relations although centering on wages, dollars and cents, extend far beyond that basic issue."[42] In evaluating the effect of reported profit figures in wage negotiations, it should be appreciated that organized labor has distrusted financial statements. Furthermore, the leaders of organized labor have not approved of more "realistic" accounting methods. Union leaders have been especially unsympathetic toward the use of Lifo for inventory purposes. Solomon Barkin,[43] director of research, Textile Workers Union of America, CIO, has said: "The 'Lifo' procedure is unacceptable to the trade unionist, even though it has been approved in recent years by the Bureau of Internal Revenue for tax purposes." Barkin also stated the union viewpoint relative to depreciation: "The trade union attitude is basically unsympathetic to the maintenance of accounts on any basis other than the actual original cost of the tangible property."

When the union's attitude toward Lifo principle is coupled with the basic distrust of accounting statements, it is difficult to see how the use of this principle would have toned down wage demands. Evidence of this was a statement made by Donald Montgomery of the United Automobile Workers: "We have occasion to examine hundreds of financial reports each year in connection with negotiations. Far from exaggerating profits, there is hardly a device developed by accounting ingenuity to minimize profits which does not appear in the reports we see."[44]

Certainly, any argument based on the assumption that a change in accounting techniques would have allayed the wage demands of or-

41. Ernest Dale, "The Accountant's Part in Labor-Management Relations," *The Journal of Accountancy,* July, 1950, p. 14.

42. J. B. C. Woods, "The Accountant's Role in Labor-Management Relations," *The New York Certified Public Accountant,* August, 1954, p. 504.

43. "A Trade Unionist Views Net Income Determination," *N.A.C.A. Bulletin,* June, 1951, pp. 1203 and 1205.

44. U.S. Congress, *Profits,* p. 43.

ganized labor would be too naive. It is agreed by writers in this field that, in many cases, the unions go to the bargaining table armed with as much financial information as management representatives. Pillsbury states: "In reviewing the methods and sources used in obtaining data, it is safe to say most union research departments do everything possible in order to obtain corporate financial data for use in collective bargaining."[45] As to the sources used Barkin states:

> Unions for their part have usually prepared themselves for these conferences with extensive information of an economic, industrial and financial nature. For the last category, its staffs would have assembled data from various sources such as public financial reports, the statements filed with the Securities and Exchange Commission and the Stock Exchange. Where the above are unrewarding, they will resort to financial services, investment houses, credit information agencies, summaries of industry-wide financial experience, and reports by the Bureau of Internal Revenue, the Securities and Exchange Commission and the Department of Commerce.[46]

Barkin has further stated that "labor people can reconstruct financial statements as easily as management accountants."[47]

Nat Goldfinger, economist, Department of Research, American Federation of Labor and Congress of Industrial Organizations, has given the following opinion of the effect of a change in accounting procedures upon collective bargaining demands:

> In unions like the United Automobile Workers and United Steelworkers, whose collective bargaining demands and settlement set the tone for much collective bargaining nationally, changes in accounting procedures would not have had an effect upon collective bargaining demands. The research departments of these two unions, among others, regularly analyze corporate financial reports in great detail and present their own interpretation of these reports to the union officers and the bargaining committees. . . . Had inventory profits been eliminated from net profit reports by different accounting techniques, for example, I am confident that the research departments of most unions would have sought them out.[48]

While the wage demands of organized labor as a cause of the in-

45. *Op. cit.,* p. 25.
46. "Financial Statements in Collective Bargaining," *The New York Certified Public Accountant,* July, 1953, p. 439.
47. In a letter to the writer, December 2, 1955.
48. In a letter to the writer, January 4, 1956.

flation following World War II may have been unduly emphasized in many cases, there is more reason to believe that wage increases played a larger role in the 1956 and 1957 inflation.[49] Because of escalator clauses in many wage contracts, wages went up as the cost of living advanced. These higher wages, in turn, were translated into higher prices which increased the cost of living which increased wages again. In this "cost push" type of inflation the question as to whether the higher wages caused the increased cost of living, or vice versa, involves the same difficulties as solving the old riddle of whether the chicken or the egg came first. This period of inflation was milder than those following World War II and the Korean Conflict and, hence, the "distorting" effect of accounting techniques in the computation of profits was much less. Furthermore, in wage negotiations the ability-to-pay criterion was not stressed so heavily as formerly by leaders of organized labor. Therefore, accounting methodology was not as directly involved as in the wage-price spiral following World World II. Only in so far as the representatives of the companies, hoodwinked by the "overstated" profits, agreed more readily to the terms of the labor contracts could it be said that accounting methodology was one of the culprits.

Conclusions on the Cyclical Effect of Accounting on Wages

It is admitted that increased wages added to the early postwar inflationary spiral. However, this factor has often been overstressed since there were many influences in additon to wage increases that contributed to inflation during this period.

Since accounting statements are used in determining the ability-to-pay, the influence of accounting methods as a factor in wage determination is only as strong as the ability-to-pay criterion. Surveys have shown that neither corporate executives nor union representatives rank this criterion very high in wage negotiations. When it is used, it is usually coupled with other factors and does not stand alone. Furthermore, accounting statements are only one factor used by labor leaders in determining the ability-to-pay. Ability-to-pay has emerged as an opportunistic argument that is used by both management representatives and union leaders with an eye to winning public support.

Even if it is admitted that the granting of higher wages did contribute

49. See conclusions of Otto Eckstein, "Inflation, The Wage-Price Spiral and Economic Growth," in *The Relationship of Prices to Economic Stability and Growth,* Compendium of Papers Submitted by Panelists Appearing Before the Joint Economic Committee, p. 374; also John P. Lewis, "Pricing for Stability and Growth," *ibid.,* p. 392.

to the inflationary spiral and that ability-to-pay was an important criterion used in wage negotiations in the early postwar years, it by no means follows that, if accounting procedures relative to inventories and to depreciation had been changed, the leaders of organized labor would have reduced wage demands. There is reason to believe that labor leaders would have taken these accounting changes as just another device to "hide" excessive profits and, in interpreting the statements for ability-to-pay, would have taken the change in techniques into consideration.

Any inherent assumption that union leaders would have been fooled by changes in accounting techniques designed to make the profits more "realistic" should be heavily discounted. The links between "overstated" profits, the ability-to-pay criterion, and the consequent wage increases contain naive assumptions as to the behavior of labor leaders similar to those already encountered relative to the relationship between accounting profit and the investment decisions of businessmen.

It is possible that the high *reported* profits in the early postwar years may have affected the atmosphere in which collective bargaining took place. Just how much the bargaining for wage increases was affected it is impossible to say. The adoption of accounting techniques which would have reduced reported profits would have avoided the embarrassing paradox of many accountants stating publicly that profits reported in financial statements, even though certified by public accountants, were really not profits at all. In the more recent inflation of 1956 and 1957, reported profits, as computed by accounting techniques, played an even less important role than in the wage contracts of these earlier years.

Chapter VII

Implications of the Use of Accounting Data in Pricing Decisions

In addition to the influence of accounting methods on consumption through its effects on the dividend and wage policies of business firms, one other possible effect on consumption should be considered. It is believed by some writers that accounting methodology influences the level of national income by affecting consumption expenditures through its effects on the pricing decisions of business firms.[1] It is the aim of the businessman to sell at prices that will cover costs and leave a margin of profit. Furthermore, it is argued that in the minds of businessmen the costs which prices are to cover are those computed by accounting methods. Since accounting costs based on the Fifo principle tend to be rigid, in years of decreasing production accounting methods are said to contribute to the reluctance of businesses to lower prices. It is contended that if the accounting concept of cost more nearly approached that of replacement cost, there would be encouragement to sell at lower prices when the cost of replacement falls. During an inflationary period, on the other hand, since costs based on traditional accounting methods tend to lag behind replacement costs, prices based on these original costs would tend to be lower. This type of pricing, by failure to perform its rationing function, would tend to encourage the boom.

1. For example, see James Arthur Estey, *Business Cycles,* pp. 503-505; Edwin G. Nourse, *Price Making in a Democracy,* pp. 374 f.; and Norman S. Buchanan, *The Economics of Corporate Enterprise,* pp. 289 f.

Inherent in the above argument are the assumptions that prices are largely cost-oriented rather than demand-oriented and that cost-oriented prices are not as flexible cyclically as demand-oriented prices. The argument as it has emerged has been applied with very few exceptions to the depression phase. Since the three postwar recessions have been relatively mild most literature on the subject has stemmed from the depressed thirties, and arguments used are closely allied to the stagnation effects of depreciation accounting discussed in Chapter VI.

While the relationship of accounting costs and pricing decisions has been emphasized from the standpoint of consumption, investment decisions may also be said to be indirectly affected by the relationship. It may be said that accounting costs affect pricing policies, which influence demand. Demand, in turn, affects investment expenditures through the accelerator principle. Concerning the intricate relationship of pricing decisions and investment decisions, Robert F. Lanzillotti has said: "The investment decision presupposes a price (and usually a market-share) assumption, which in turn, determines short-run price decisions thereafter. Thus, investment decisions in effect are themselves a form of pricing decision, and over time become an inherent part of price policy."[2]

Before attempting an evaluation of the argument that accounting contributes to business fluctuations by its influence on pricing policy, a more detailed inquiry into the relationship of accounting costs and price-making policy will be made.

Alleged Relationship of Accounting Methodology to Price Rigidity

In order that price-making on the basis of cost take place, it must be assumed that the producer has some control over the total amount of the product supplied, and, hence, this method of price-making is incompatible with pure competition. In other words, when writers speak of the cyclical effect of accounting techniques on prices, they are speaking of what is often referred to as "administered prices." Edwin G. Nourse and Horace B. Drury have defined "administered prices" as "prices established by the decision of executives who have power to decide in advance the price at which goods shall be sold and to back up that decision by expanding or contracting operations in volume large enough to have a significant effect on the market."[3] Gardiner C. Means stresses

2. "Pricing Objectives in Large Companies," *The American Economic Review*, December, 1958, p. 940.

3. *Industrial Price Policies and Economic Progress*, p. 9.

infrequency of change as a characteristic of administered prices. An administered price, according to Means, is "a price which is set by administrative action and held constant for a period of time."[4]

Writers on the subject of the relationship of accounting to pricing decisions rely heavily on the assumption that prices are set on the basis of average costs plus a percentage markup. R. A. Gordon, however, points out that "average-cost pricing" may mean setting price at average variable cost plus a conventional percentage markup, or total unit cost plus a markup.[5] Writers who stress accounting costs as a factor in pricing emphasize the use of "full cost" in pricing decisions.[6] Nourse and Drury state this concept of the accounting-made price as follows:

> But a great deal of industrial price-making simply looks at a commodity in the market as a cumulation of cost items for materials, labor, machine service, and various overhead costs. When these have been added together and a "proper" loading for profit added, you have your price Q. E. D. The cost accountant produces the records of the past to show that those are the costs the business has incurred and which it must recover or quit.

Hall and Hitch also give a similar view of price making on the basis of the "full cost" principle: "The formula used by the different firms in computing 'full cost' differs in detail . . . but the procedure can be not unfairly generalized as follows: prime (or 'direct') cost per unit is taken as the base, a percentage addition is made to cover overheads (or 'oncost', or 'indirect' cost) and a further conventional addition (frequently 10 per cent) is made for profit."

Furthermore, it is stated by many writers that cost-plus pricing and administered prices are the prevalent ones in modern business.[7] Means states that administered prices seem to be inherent in modern technology. Backman points out that selling prices are determined in most

4. *Industrial Prices and Their Relative Inflexibility,* Senate Document No. 13, 74th Cong., 1st Sess., p. 1.

5. *Op. cit.,* p. 284.

6. See Nourse and Drury, *op. cit.,* p. 256; and R. L. Hall and C. J. Hitch, "Price Theory and Business Behavior," *Oxford Studies in the Price Mechanism,* p. 113.

7. For evidence of viewpoints expressed in this paragraph, see Alfred R. Oxenfeldt, *Industrial Pricing and Market Practices,* p. 162; J. K. Galbraith, "Monopoly Power and Price Rigidities," *The Quarterly Journal of Economics,* May, 1936, p. 460; Gardiner C. Means, "Notes on Inflexible Prices," *Papers and Proceedings of the Forty-eighth Annual Meeting of the American Economic Association,* in *The American Economic Review,* March, 1936, p. 35; Jules Backman, *op. cit.,* p. 87; and Edwin G. Nourse, "Cost Finding and Price Determination," *National Association of Cost Accountants Year Book,* 1945, p. 28.

industries by using percentage markups over cost. Nourse speaks of the influence of corporate executives on price policy in these words: "Over a large and strategically important area of modern industrial business, prices are not made by the broad and impersonal forces of the general market. They are strongly influenced by the managerial policy of corporate executives." Since the average total cost of the accountant is based largely on historical costs instead of replacement costs, accounting costs are prevented from falling at the beginning of the depression phase. Furthermore, if average total costs are being used to determine pricing policies, when the demand for the product recedes, this decrease in demand is met with a reduction in output rather than a downward adjustment in price. Galbraith has stated the effect of accounting-cost pricing as follows:

> If average costs are being used to determine price policy and the producer's demand recedes then output at the ruling price, of course, falls off. The new unit or average costs are higher than before unless cost rates have undergone a marked decline. The producer may and probably will realize the futility of increasing prices. But on the other hand, he is powerfully restrained from reducing prices, for to do so is to run directly counter to the advice of the accounting system.[8]

According to some writers this is what did happen in the thirties.[9] An accountant, Samuel J. Broad, writing of the contribution of accounting techniques to the reluctance of businessmen to reduce prices, states:

> The depression of the early 1930's was deepened by an unwillingness to reflect the inventory losses which would have to be taken under the historical cost method if selling prices were drastically reduced. When prices decline, to avoid showing the loss we put off selling at prices sufficiently low to create demand, and we put off buying for lack of markets. Lower selling prices based on lower replacement costs should promote more sales.

Another writer, E. D. Kennedy, states that the preference of manufacturers for reducing output instead of prices was a factor in the 1937-1938 recession.

There are tendencies at work that extend the rigidities of prices at the firm level to the industry and to the whole economy. An important

8. *Op. cit.*, p. 471.

9. See Samuel J. Broad, *op. cit.*, p. 25; and E. D. Kennedy, "Steel Man's Story," *The New Republic*, March 11, 1940, pp. 338 f.

factor influencing a change of price in an oligopolistic market is the anticipated or observed behavior of competitors. Any arrangement, therefore, that would tend to promote uniform cost calculations among rival producers would tend to "stabilize" prices based on average costs of all the producers and thus would make for inflexible prices within the industry. Fritz Machlup points out that "the general adoption of an average cost rule is in effect a price agreement among the members of the particular industry."[10] The trade association is said to be an arrangement which facilitates price maintenance. C. Clive Saxton, for example, states: "The aim of all Trade Associations (however defined by the promoters) seems to be the elimination of that form of competition which draws most attention to the reduction of price of the product of a particular firm below that of others making the same or a similar product."[11]

One of the means of establishing price stability among the association members is by the use of uniform methods of accounting.[12] One writer, Charles Albert Pearce, has said: "When an association is actively striving to stabilize prices through its accounting program, the promotion of uniform accounting and the dissemination of average-cost information provide a logical avenue to personal contact between the association staff and the individual members." In fact, it is pointed out by this writer that two objectives of uniform accounting programs of trade associations overshadow all others: "(1) the maintenance of profitable and stable prices and (2) the stimulation of economies." Finally, the rigid prices in one firm or industry are rigid costs to another. Galbraith points this out in these words:

A whole complex of such costs is thus established with the aid of modern techniques of price and production control. So far as they in turn are of importance in determining price policy they act to "shore up" the structure of industrial prices.[13]

In summary, it is argued that prices in much of modern-day business are "administered" prices and that "administered" prices are cost-plus prices with cost considered to be average total cost as derived from the accounting records. This method of pricing makes prices inflexible, especially in a downward direction and, hence, any drop in demand is

10. "Marginal Analysis and Empirical Research," *The American Economic Review*, September, 1946, p. 543.

11. *The Economics of Price Determination*, p. 15.

12. See Arthur Robert Burns, *The Decline of Competition*, pp. 49-55; Simon N. Whitney, *Trade Associations and Industrial Control*, pp. 42 f.; and Charles Albert Pearce, *Trade Association Survey*, Temporary National Economic Committee Monograph No. 18, pp. 295-297.

13. *Op. cit.*, p. 472.

accentuated by the firm's resistance to the lowering of prices. Finally, forces are at work that tend to translate this price rigidity at the firm level to other firms and industries. Many writers believe that this price inflexibility tends to accentuate the downward swing of the cycle.

An Evaluation of Cost-Plus Pricing as a Factor in Price Rigidity

Before evaluating the relationship of cost-plus pricing to price rigidities, it should be appreciated that those who stress this relationship are assuming that the list price, or publicly announced price, is the one ultimately paid by the consumer. In fact, the observance that this price remains unchanged for relatively long periods of time becomes the main evidence that rigid prices exist. Writers have stated that these recorded prices, however, may not be the prices actually paid by the customers.[14] Burns pointed out this fact in these words: "The prices may be list prices which are subject to large and fluctuating discounts with the result that the series is no guide to actual prices." Nourse and Drury use the steel industry to illustrate this situation.

> The published base prices stay at the same levels for long periods of time. But every day individual bargains are struck that nullify these prices. Two buyers may buy the same amount of the same kind of steel from the same mill at widely different prices, and no one except the seller will be any the wiser.

In addition to discounts, there are various other means of making actual changes in price while leaving the publicly announced one unchanged. A change in quality at the same list price, for example, is the equivalent of a price change. Likewise, a change in quantity at the same price is another way of changing real price without changing the list price. Varying the allowances for trade-ins and the terms of guarantee for service and performance are also the equivalent of price changes. A change in terms of delivery and even product differentiation to create a new price class are other ways of changing the real price without changing quoted prices. Thus the basic assumption of price rigidity itself may be more apparent than real. It is conceded, however, that these hidden price changes are only a partial explanation of the observed price rigidities.

In order to place the arguments relative to accounting costs as a factor in price rigidity into their proper perspective the various causes that have

14. See Arthur Robert Burns, "The Organization of Industry and the Theory of Prices," *The Journal of Political Economy,* October, 1937, p. 677; and Nourse and Drury, *op. cit.,* p. 303.

been advanced for price rigidity will now be reviewed.[15] Neal states that most explanations of price inflexibility fall into two classes: (1) monopoly power and (2) product characteristics, market, cost demand conditions, and the like. Galbraith attributes price rigidity jointly to monopoly power and the *nature* of administration. Backman emphasizes the latter cause of price rigidity: "The actions taken by those in control, rather than the fact of concentration, will be the decisive factor." Dean has classified the main reasons for price rigidity into four groups: (1) the nature of demand, (2) the degree of competition, (3) rigid costs, and (4) custom, tradition, idea of just price, etc. The nature of demand also influences the frequency of price change. As to the nature of the demand for the product, Tucker has stated: "We may say then that the elasticity of demand for a product determines whether a reduction in the intensity of demand, i.e., a shift of the demand curve to the left, must result in a great change in the amount sold or the price obtained, or only a small change." This elasticity of demand is, in turn, dependent on such factors as the durability of the product and the availability of substitutes. Since many industrialists believe that the demand for their product is inelastic,[16] this makes for rigidity of prices.

Since much industrial pricing is done under conditions of oligopoly, the reaction of competitors must be considered in the firm's pricing policy. It has been assumed that producers under these market conditions fear that if they cut prices, then competitors will also cut them, and if they raise prices, competitors either will not raise them at all, or as much. Under these assumptions, maintaining the status quo as far as prices are concerned is rational behavior. Gordon, for example, states that under conditions of oligopoly: "Before the price is changed, strong efforts will be made to adjust to the new situation in the other ways that are available—through varying output, selling expense, product specifications, production techniques, and the like."[17]

Dean has pointed out that "the role of custom and tradition in setting prices in many areas must not be underestimated."[18] The practice of furnishing price lists in advance to salesmen, dealers, and the public adds

15. For a very comprehensive and detailed list of the reasons for price inflexibility, see Jules Backman, "The Causes of Price Inflexibility," *The Quarterly Journal of Economics,* May, 1940, pp. 474-476; Neal, *op. cit.,* p. 47; Galbraith, *op. cit.,* p. 463, n. 8; Joel Dean, *Managerial Economics,* pp. 458-460; and Rufus S. Tucker, "The Reasons for Price Rigidity," *The American Economic Review,* March, 1938, pp. 52 f.

16. See Dean, *op. cit.,* p. 458; and Hall and Hitch, *op. cit.,* p. 116.

17. Gordon, *op. cit.,* p. 283.

18. Dean, *op. cit.,* p. 460.

to rigidity of prices. Hall and Hitch have stressed this aspect of price rigidity: "Changes in price are frequently very costly, a nuisance to salesmen, and are disliked by merchants and consumers."[19] There is also a fear that if prices are once reduced, they will be difficult to raise again. Buyers may protest less against a stable price than against a 10 per cent reduction which is later restored.[20] Thus while a rigid cost structure is a factor, it is only one out of many factors contributing to rigid prices.

A strict adherence to price-making on the basis of costs would seem to imply that the demand for the product is ignored. However, there is evidence that cost-plus pricing serves only as a guide to price-setting and is not blindly followed. Homer B. Vanderblue, in his study of the pricing policies of the automobile industry, states that the price once set must stand the test of the market place. Merely having a cost analysis as a guide will not return the costs no matter how carefully the cost analysis is made.[21] Differential margins over costs in the case of multiproduct firms incorporate the demand influences in the pricing formulas themselves.[22] In introducing new products a judgment of the price at which the article will sell is frequently made, and after allowing for markups, the amount available for manufacturing the product is determined.[23] This practice, plus the accounting method of allocating overhead to the various finished products of multiproduct firms on the basis of the relative selling prices, raises the question as to whether selling price is based on full cost or whether full cost is itself determined by selling price. This resurrects the age-old problem of whether costs are price-determined or price-determining. In actual price-making decisions, therefore, it may well be questioned as to whether cost-plus pricing in its pristine simplicity is often encountered.

What evidence is there that cost-plus pricing is actually used? There is indirect evidence to sustain the belief that it is not voluntarily used at the crucial times when demand and supply are out of balance at the prevailing price. Machlup points out that the existence of cartels, fair-

19. Hall and Hitch, *op. cit.*, p. 116.

20. See Saul Nelson, *Price Behavior and Business Policy*, Temporary National Economic Committee Monograph No. 1, p. 35.

21. "Pricing Policies in the Automobile Industry," *Harvard Business Review*, Summer, 1939, p. 396.

22. See Richard B. Heflebower, "Full Costs, Cost Changes, and Prices," *Business Concentration and Price Policy*, p. 364.

23. See Wroe Alderson, "Business Price Policies and Economic Stability," *The Relationship of Prices to Economic Stability and Growth*, p. 404; also Robert F. Lanzillotti, "Some Characteristics and Economic Effects of Pricing Objectives in Large Corporations," *ibid.*, p. 446.

trade laws, minimum price laws, and bans against selling below cost are conclusive evidence of the incentive to sell more cheaply than average cost plus a "fair" profit. The existence of maximum prices enforced by legislative fiat, on the other hand, is evidence of the temptation to charge more than the average cost plus a "fair" profit. Machlup asks: "What other testimony is needed to demonstrate that there must indeed be millions of pricing decisions every year that are not based on the average-cost rule?"[24]

One of the best known studies showing the use of full cost pricing is that of Hall and Hitch. The evidence considered was based on interviews with 38 firms—33 manufacturers of a wide variety of products, 3 retailers, and 2 builders. Table 23 shows the degree of adherence to the "full cost" principle. It is worthy of note that even in this study, which

TABLE 23

DEGREE OF ADHERENCE TO FULL COST PRINCIPLE

Not adhering	8
Adhering rigidly	12
Adhering normally	15
Adhering in principle	3
	38

Source: R. L. Hall and C. J. Hitch, "Price Theory and Business Behavior," *Oxford Studies in the Price Mechanism,* eds. T. Wilson and P. W. S. Andrews, p. 119.

has been heralded as demonstrating the use of the full cost principle, less than one-half the firms adhered "rigidly" to this principle, although an additional 15 firms stated they adhered "normally." A study of the reasons, given in Table 24, for a departure from the full cost principle is even more revealing. These reasons do not show the ignoring of demand and the blind pricing on the basis of cost so often implied by the critics of full cost pricing. Furthermore, the authors themselves point out certain limitations of the evidence, especially, the biased character of the sample.[25]

In Saxton's study of 50 firms by questionnaire he found 36 who said that they fixed prices on the basis of standard costs or estimated costs.[26] Answers as to how demand affected prices were so varied, however, that they were not tabulated.

24. *The Economics of Sellers' Competition,* p. 73.
25. *Op. cit.,* p. 108.
26. *Op. cit.,* p. 181, question 19.

TABLE 24

OCCASIONS ON WHICH A DEPARTURE FROM THE FULL COST PRINCIPLE IN A DOWNWARD DIRECTION MIGHT BE MADE

Depressed trade	6
Cyclically on competitive lines	2
When necessary to "keep going"	4
Necessity to follow a competitive price	8
If competitor broke agreement	1
Loss leaders	2
Attempt to capture new markets	2
To obtain a large contract	3
Seasonally to stimulate sales	2
To clear old stock	1
Cases where demand was elastic	2

Source: Hall and Hitch, *op. cit.*, p. 121.

Maybelle Kohl made a study of price-making procedures in 1953 that consisted of 40 personal interviews with either price-making executives or representatives well informed on their company's pricing procedures. The firms represented were large, nationally known manufacturing firms located in northern Illinois, southern Wisconsin, and the New York City area. The pricing factors mentioned by those interviewed are shown in Table 25. Cost alone as a factor is mentioned by only three interviewees.

TABLE 25

FACTORS USED IN PRICING

Cost, competition	15
Competition, cost	12
Cost, competition, demand	4
Cost	3
Competition, demand	2
Cost, demand, competition	1
Demand, competition, cost	1
Cost, demand, competition, investment	1
Competition, cost, investment	1
	40

Source: Maybelle Kohl, *The Role of Accounting in Pricing*, p. 132.

Cost was frequently mentioned as a factor in pricing during the Congressional hearings on the size of profits, which were held in December, 1947.[27] Even here, however, the cost to the producer was only one factor

27. See, for example, testimony of Hiland G. Bacheller, president of Allegheny-Ludlum Steel Corporation, U.S. Congress, *Profits*, p. 115; and Clarence Francis, chairman of the board, General Foods Corporation, *ibid.*, pp. 124 f.

mentioned in setting prices. Clarence Francis, chairman of the board, General Foods Corporation, for example, made the following statement relative to the factors considered by his company in setting prices: "On the basis of all known or probable costs and on more or less reasonable assumptions about the decisions which competitors will make on their prices or their promotion or their new products, the general economic picture, our own market research into distribution possibilities, everything that we may want to do for specific products or that we can estimate about Government policies, the vagaries of nature, the labor situation, etc., must be taken into account in setting a price."

Vanderblue,[28] in his study of the pricing policies of General Motors Corporation, admitted that prices were "administered" and "are not jiggled with the seasons or as the phase of the business cycle changes." However, earlier he had stated that the setting of price on a particular design and make depended upon three considerations: "what the product will cost; what the market will pay for it; and in what quantity it can be sold."

In summary, it is far from certain that cost-plus pricing is as widely used as is so often stated. There is considerable evidence that even when it is used, it is modified for demand influences and to meet competition. Furthermore, cost computed by any method is only one factor in the pricing of the product. If there is oligopoly with collusion, tacit or otherwise, cost becomes a much stronger factor in the setting of price. The evidence that prices, even though set on a cost-plus basis, are adhered to is even less clear. Thus, even though administered prices may be characteristic of a large segment of the economy, it does not necessarily follow that these prices are cost-plus prices rigidly adhered to under changing conditions of demand.

Even if it is conceded that (1) administered prices are characteristic of the economy, and (2) administered prices are cost-plus prices rigidly adhered to, one question still remains: are the actual historical costs of the accountant the ones typically used for price-making purposes even when they differ greatly from replacement costs? Table 26 shows that 25 per cent of the 559 cooperating companies surveyed by the National Industrial Conference Board took higher replacement costs into account when pricing the product.

Maybelle Kohl found that total product cost estimates were usually

28. "Pricing Policies in the Automobile Industry: Incidence of Demand," *Harvard Business Review,* Autumn, 1939, p. 79; and "Pricing Policies . . . ," *Harvard Business Review,* Summer, 1939, p. 400.

TABLE 26
COMPANIES CONSIDERING CURRENT REPLACEMENT COSTS IN PRODUCT PRICING

Assets (Millions of Dollars)	Companies Reporting	Number	Per Cent of Total
0 - 4.9	175	46	26
5 - 24.9	221	50	23
25 - 99.9	115	32	28
100 and over	48	14	29
	559	142	25

Source: James A. Finley, *Handling Higher Replacement Costs,* Studies in Business Policy No. 47, p. 8.

in terms of current costs except for some elements of overhead.[29] In a research study of costs for pricing purposes made by the National Association of Cost Accountants,[30] 36 out of the 55 companies participating in the survey used current market, or the anticipated replacement cost of materials, in computing product costs for pricing. It was also found that where standard costs were used, the standard costs were revised when a general change in labor rates took place. On the other hand, only a few companies adjusted the depreciation element because of changing price levels. Some of the reasons given in this study for the failure to adjust depreciation were: (1) depreciation is only a small portion of total product cost; (2) most depreciable assets have been acquired at recent price levels and hence the problem is not important; and (3) some companies have concluded that there is no practical way to ascertain depreciation in terms of the current price level.

Kohl found that only two firms attempted to incorporate a charge for depreciation based upon either current or future replacement costs of fixed assets in pricing estimates.[31] However, allowances for future replacement of fixed assets at higher prices were usually made through a flexible net profit figure.

Even if historical rather than replacement costs are used for price-making purposes, it does not necessarily follow that the unit costs used for this purpose are arrived at by adding all the actual historical accounting costs and dividing this sum by the quantity produced. A recent study of the pricing policies of large industrial corporations made for the Brookings Institution revealed that even in companies in which the accounting departments compiled the most detailed cost data, actual

29. *The Role of Accounting in Pricing,* p. 138.

30. "Product Costs for Pricing Purposes," Research Series No. 24, *N.A.C.A. Bulletin,* August, 1953, pp. 1686-1689.

31. *Op. cit.,* p. 140.

per unit cost of production had very little influence on the structure of prices, but the costs used for price-making purposes were based on a "normal" rate of output (e.g., 75-80 per cent of rated capacity).[32] Assuming the use of straight-line depreciation, fixed overhead (including depreciation) would not be absorbed into inventory during depressed periods when the firm is operating at less than this rated capacity, and unit standard costs would be lower than actual unit costs. On the other hand, during periods of prosperity when the plant is running nearer to capacity than "normal," fixed overhead (including depreciation) would be overabsorbed and standard unit costs would be higher than actual unit costs. Therefore, if the company is pricing by using a fixed percentage of markup based on standard costs, prices would tend to be lower during depression and higher during prosperity than those based on actual "full" historical costs. Even by the use of this method prices will be less flexible over the cycle than if depreciation is based on replacement cost rather than historical costs.

While these studies of the relationship of accounting costs and pricing were made during a period of high prices and not during a depression, when the argument that accounting methods contributed to price rigidity has been used most often, the results are at least presumptive evidence that costs used for pricing purposes are not always "actual" historical accounting costs. For the severe depression of the thirties the writer did not find any evidence to indicate the kind of costs actually used for price-making. For this period there is only the indirect evidence of the existence of informal price maintenance agreements and of legal restrictions against pricing below costs, referred to earlier by Machlup, to indicate that there was a tendency for pricing below "full costs."

An Evaluation of Price Inflexibility as an Accentuating Factor

Even if it is accepted that (1) price-making on the basis of cost is prevalent, (2) the costs used for price-making purposes are the actual historical costs of the accountant, and (3) rigid costs are a material factor causing rigid prices, it is not a foregone conclusion that cyclical fluctuations are thereby accentuated. Those who have argued that price-making on the basis of accounting costs contribute to cyclical instability have taken as a basic premise that inflexible prices accentuate business fluctuations. An evaluation of this assumption will now be made.

32. Lanzillotti, *op. cit.*, p. 466; see also Alfred R. Oxenfeldt, "Cyclical Implications of Private Pricing Policies," *The Relationship of Prices . . .* , p. 446, for a similar statement.

Alvin H. Hansen differentiates between structural and cyclical price flexibility.[33] He states that structural price flexibility "implies an adjustment of prices to changes in unit costs springing from unequal rates of technological progress in different industries or from shifts in the pattern of wants." Structural price rigidity is usually decried for retarding the secular advance in living standards rather than for contributing to cyclical movements. Hansen states: "There is, as far as I am aware, no disagreement among economists with respect to the desirability of structural price flexibility." Cyclical price flexibility, according to Hansen, "has to do with the sensitivity of prices to fluctuations of the business cycles." Accounting has been largely associated with the lack of this latter type of price flexibility.

While the knowledge that certain prices are "sticky" while others are sensitive had been recognized at least since the days of Adam Smith, the basic source of the emphasis on this factor in the last half of the thirties is found in the studies of Gardiner C. Means.[34] According to Means, there are two essentially different types of markets in operation —the traditional market in which supply and demand are equated by a flexible price and the administered market in which production and demand are equated at an inflexible administered price. In the first type of market, economic adjustments are brought about principally by fluctuations in price. In the second type of market, economic adjustments are brought about primarily by changes in volume of production, with price changes being secondary in producing adjustments. When the businessman has the power to choose between lowering prices or lowering production, he may decide to maintain prices and curtail production even though this means idle men and idle machines. According to Means, the net effect of business control over industrial policy is "to aggravate any fluctuations in economic activity and prevent any necessary adjustments." In fact, Means states that "the whole depression might be described as a general dropping of prices at the flexible end of the price scale and a dropping of production at the rigid end with intermediate effects between." Depression sensitivity of prices has been associated with raw materials, agricultural products, market-dominated prices, nondurable goods, and standard commodities.[35] Depression in-

33. "Price Flexibility and Full Employment of Resources," *The Structure of the American Economy,* Part II, National Resources Planning Board, p. 27.

34. See *Industrial Prices . . .* , pp. 11 and 8.

35. National Resources Committee, *The Structure of the American Economy,* Part I, A Report Prepared by the Industrial Section under the Direction of Gardiner C. Means, p. 139.

sensitivity of prices has been associated with fabricated products, manufactured goods, administration-dominated prices, durable products. and differentiated products.

On the role of price dispersion in economic fluctuations there is far from wholehearted agreement, however. While admitting that price dispersion is correlated with fluctuations in output and employment, many economists have raised the issue: Which is cause and which effect? Hansen[36] states that "a mere artificial rectification of the price dispersion may get at the root causes of the decline in income and employment no more than a tampering with the thermometer can change the temperature." While admitting that a balanced cost-price structure is favorable to the proper functioning of an economy, he states: "It does not necessarily follow that, once forces are at work deranging a balanced cost-price structure, an effort at correction of such price maladjustment per se can be relied upon to improve the rate of business activity." Price dispersion is thus viewed as the result and not the cause of the decline in national income and in employment.

Moreover, Means' findings have been challenged by other economists. Backman studied the price changes of 264 commodities from 1929 to 1933. The data were plotted so that a trend downward from left to right would confirm Means' conclusions that inflexible prices are accompanied by sharp curtailment in production while more flexible prices were associated with greater stability in production. Backman concluded: "The data tend slightly downward to the right but within such broad limits as to negate the conclusion that there is a close inverse relationship between price inflexibility and stability of production."[37] He also found that commodities which remained unchanged in price from 1929 to 1933 had declined in production ranging from less than 1 per cent to 93 per cent.

An effective argument that has been presented against lowering prices as a method of lessening the amplitude and duration of the depression phase is that a reduction in price engenders an expectation of further price drops. Albert Gailord Hart[38] has stated that in interpreting current experience there are three basic patterns: (1) to expect things to stay as they are, (2) to expect things to go on changing as they have recently been changing, or (3) to expect things to return to a condition

36. *Op. cit.*, p. 28.

37. "Price Inflexibility and Changes in Production," *The American Economic Review*, September, 1939, pp. 484 and 485.

38. "Failure and Fulfillment of Expectations in Business Fluctuations," *The Review of Economic Statistics*, May, 1937, p. 77, n. 2.

regarded as more nearly "normal" than the recent past. When prices are stable, the first pattern seems natural. When they are changing, the second applies to short-range forecasts, but the third always remains in the background and rules long-range forecasts. If price stability is associated with things remaining as they are, then it would seem that a stable price level, instead of accentuating swings in production and employment, would tend to stabilize them. Speaking of the Great Depression, Richard M. Bissell, Jr., states: "Perhaps, if the behavior of prices and costs had been more stable, . . . our heroic public spending would have initiated a sustaining revival."[39]

It has been pointed out by one writer that the implication that demand, and hence production and employment, would be maintained merely by reducing price during a period of depression is not substantiated if factors other than the price of the product are the primary influence upon demand.[40] It has been shown that items for which production declined the most from 1929 to 1933 were those whose purchase could be postponed.[41] Income diverted from this postponement of purchases could have been used to maintain consumption and, hence, production, of those items that were nondurable and whose prices were flexible. The items designed to satisfy postponable wants may have declined because those wants were postponable and not because prices were maintained. Therefore, it may be concluded that in some cases the characteristics of the products rather than the inflexible prices, may account for the greater fluctuation in the production of certain goods.

If the view is taken that business fluctuations are primarily the result of the rise and fall of investment expenditures, then for a fall in price to be effective in stemming deflation, there must be a stimulating effect upon investment. In line with the third basic pattern of Hart above, if price changes are to stimulate investment, then *present* prices must be low relative to *expected* future prices which are considered to be "normal." It is in this sense that a drastic price cut, which is expected to be final, is thought by some writers to be stimulating to consumption and through the accelerator principle also to investment. However, not all economists believe that even drastic price cuts at the beginning of a depression will have any effect on arresting the fall in national income but believe that price cuts in capital goods toward the end of the depres-

39. "Prices, Costs, and Investment," *Papers and Proceedings of the Fifty-third Annual Meeting of the American Economic Association* in *The American Economic Review,* February, 1941, p. 227.

40. Backman, "Price Inflexibility . . . ," p. 481.

41. Nelson, *op. cit.,* p. 40.

sion phase may be stimulating to investment.[42] Price cuts at the beginning of the downswing, on the other hand, may cause purchasing decisions to be postponed, aggregate demand to fall off, and the amount of unemployment to be increased still further. Many entrepreneurs and consumers will be more inclined to increase cash balances than to increase expenditures.

In discussing price and production relationships it is often assumed that national income remains constant. On this assumption, a reduction in prices could be expected to lead to an increase in aggregate demand and hence to increased output. Prices, however, not only represent costs to those with incomes to spend but they also represent income to those who have commodities or services to sell. The effect that a given price cut will have on the total expenditure for a product will depend upon the elasticity of demand for the product. However, products for which demand is subject to the widest cyclical fluctuations also have a relatively inelastic demand schedule and thus the opportunity for stabilizing output by destabilizing prices is greatly diminished.[43]

For some years following the outbreak of World War II, the controversy over price flexibility and its relationship to cyclical fluctuations remained dormant. In fact, during the late forties stable prices were regarded with some esteem while flexible prices were often viewed with alarm and there was a "tendency to regard the cyclically inflexible prices as a stabilizing influence in the cycle."[44] More recently the discussion of the role of price flexibility has been revived, but the emphasis has been changed. Much more attention has been given in these recent discussions to the relationship of price changes to long-term economic growth. Complete price stability and a desirable rate of economic growth have been viewed by many writers as being incompatible. According to a rather widely held view, for example, a gradually rising price level is a penalty that must be incurred in order to stimulate economic growth. Furthermore, it is recognized that the questions of the relationship of price changes to stability and of price changes to long-term growth are inseparable. This whole problem of the effect of price movements on economic stability and growth is one on which there is as yet no general agreement.

In summary, while economists have generally agreed on the de-

42. Hansen, *op. cit.,* p. 30.

43. Burns, *The Decline of Competition,* p. 245.

44. J. K. Galbraith, "Monopoly and the Concentration of Economic Power," *A Survey of Contemporary Economics,* p. 114.

sirability of structural price flexibility, there has been no such general agreement on cyclical price flexibility. The findings of Means have been questioned by other economists who have made additional statistical studies. Means' study did not answer the crucial question of whether the decline in output of the inflexibly priced products would have been less during the Great Depression if the prices of these products had been more flexible. While it is recognized that no study could have been expected to furnish an answer to this question, some later writers seemed to have assigned greater weight to the results than was merited. In general, the products whose demand has varied widely cyclically are those with inelastic demand schedules. In recent years there seems to be a tendency to regard stable prices with more favor than formerly. It is recognized that these years cover a period of prosperity and, hence, stable prices might be regarded with much less favor during a future period of severe business decline.

Summary and Conclusions

The theory that accounting methods accentuate business fluctuations by influencing price-making decisions of businessmen is based on three main postulates: (1) that certain prices are relatively stable throughout the cycle; (2) these prices are largely based on accounting costs which are cyclically inflexible; and (3) inflexible prices accentuate the business cycle. The degree of price rigidity itself is a debatable question. The real price paid by the buyer may differ considerably from the list price. However, this is only a partial explanation of *observed* price rigidity. Price-making on the basis of costs is most applicable to oligopolistic markets. Even under conditions of oligopoly, however, cost is only one factor in price-making. Cost-plus formulas are modified for changing conditions of demand and for competition. Even though it is admitted that traditional accounting costs are cyclically inflexible, there is evidence that in recent years the costs used for price-making purposes are not always actual accounting costs but are often replacement costs, or cost computed on the basis of a "normal" rate of output. During the depression years of the thirties no studies were found as to the nature of costs used for price-making purposes.

Even if it is admitted that (1) price rigidity is a fact; (2) prices under conditions of oligopoly are cost-plus prices; (3) costs used for price-making purposes are typically average total historical costs as computed by accounting methods; and (4) rigid costs are one of the principal explanations of price inflexibility, the role of price inflexibility itself as an accentuating factor in business fluctuation is still an unsettled one. It has been shown that the first and third propositions are of doubtful validity. While there may be more justification for acceptance of the second and fourth propositions, the relative importance of cost in both has been overemphasized. Considering the unsettled role of price inflexibility and the tenuous relationship of accounting techniques to pricing, the thesis that accounting methodology accentuates business fluctuations by influencing price-making decisions cannot, at present, be accepted by the author.

Chapter VIII

Summary of the Principal Findings and Conclusions

In the first chapter the primary purpose of this study and a corollary to the main purpose were set forth. A restatement of this purpose with a summary of the principal findings relative to it and a restatement of the corollary with a statement of related findings will now be made.

The primary object was to try *to determine if accounting, as generally practiced, is capable—given certain assumptions—of affecting business decisions relative to investment, dividend policy, wages, and prices in such a way as to accentuate business fluctuations on both the upswing and the downswing, as is rather frequently alleged, and to determine if the underlying assumptions seem realistic, given the institutional framework within which modern business operates.*

Aside from net foreign investment and governmental expenditures, any discussion of an accentuating factor must be in terms of its effect upon business investment expenditures and consumers' expenditures. The thesis that business fluctuations are *primarily* the result of the changes in business expenditures is accepted.

If the income tax structure and technological changes are ignored, then accounting methodology accentuates business fluctuations if it is assumed: (1) businessmen attempt to invest in such a way as to maximize expected profits; (2) past profits as measured by accounting techniques are accepted in lieu of expected profits; and (3) businessmen misinterpret profits as reported by the accountant in such a way that they are inclined to overinvest during the upswing and underinvest during the downswing.

The first assumption is considered valid from a long-run point of view but only partially true in the short run in the large, widely-held corporation. Studies on investment behavior, especially in the larger corporation, have shown that current sales and prospective sales are given far more frequently than profit as a basis for investment decisions. However, it is likely that sales may be associated with profit in the thinking of the businessman.

While *ex-post* profits, as determined by accounting methods, appear to be taken into consideration in the making of investment decisions, the evidence indicates that expected profits are not merely the projection of these past profits, as is so often implied. It is not possible, at present, to judge the relative weight assigned by the businessman to past profits, expected profits, and any other factors which he takes into consideration in making investment decisions.

The assumption that businessmen, especially in the large corporations, are misled by the "misstatement" of profit due to accounting methods is unwarranted. It is agreed by most writers that accounting methodology as an accentuating factor via investment decisions depends largely on the validity of this third assumption. Hence, even after abstracting away technological improvements and the corporate income tax structure, the proposition that accounting methods accentuate business fluctuations by unduly influencing investment decisions cannot be wholeheartedly accepted.

In a dynamic economy, much investment takes place as a result of technological change. Much of this investment is said to be autonomous. To the extent that this is true, short-run profits as measured by accounting methods would not be a factor in investment decisions.

Assuming that the same accounting methods are used for general reporting purposes and for income tax purposes, the spread between after-tax profits as computed by traditional accounting methods and methods proposed for stabilizing profits cyclically, is narrowed considerably. Furthermore, the higher the tax rate, the more nearly equal the after-tax profits become. Therefore, even assuming accounting profits are a factor in investment decisions, to the extent that it is profits after tax that are considered in making investment decisions, the variance between the amount of investment made as a result of the alternative accounting methods will not be as great as at first supposed.

Thus in a dynamic economy, with high corporate income tax rates, *ex-post* profits as a factor in making investment decisions should be assigned even less weight than in a static economy without corporate income taxes.

The propositions that accounting profits unduly influence security prices and that security prices, in turn, influence investment decisions, may be true at times. However, the evidence indicates that these links between reported profits and investment expenditures are not as strong as are often supposed.

The reluctance of the businessman to "take a loss" by writing off the larger undepreciated balance of an old asset resulting from the use of the straight-line method is often used as an argument for accelerated depreciation. The argument is thus a negative one: Straight-line depreciation is a deterrent to investment. When accelerated depreciation is used for income tax purposes, the argument becomes a positive one: The saving in income tax is stimulating to investment. The positive argument appears to be the valid one. It is not the psychological effect of the more rapid write-off of assets per se that is the stimulant to investment. The stimulating effect stems from the larger amount of funds available for investment as a result of the income tax savings, and the incentive to keep these funds invested in relatively new assets in order to continue to reap these tax savings.

Thus, while the theory that accounting methodology accentuates business fluctuations by influencing business investment expenditures cannot be completely invalidated, this aspect of accounting methodology as an accentuating factor has been unduly emphasized.

Accounting methods are alleged to affect consumption expenditures as well as investment expenditures. It is reasoned that depreciation expense is included in sales price and this expense may not have an immediate offsetting expenditure. This argument has been emphasized during severe depressions. The validity of this contention depends on whether the recording of this excessive depreciation causes the corporate system to take more revenue from outside the system, or to pay out less as dividends and wages, than would be done if the amount of this expense were more "realistic." Since this "excessive" depreciation would be unlikely to affect wage policy, the soundness of the argument depends largely upon its effects on dividend disbursements. It has been shown that dividends per year have not closely followed reported profits per year. Even if dividend policy is guided by reported profits, the conclusion that the cycle is thereby accentuated due to the effect on consumption does not necessarily follow. Since the recipients of dividends are, in general, the large savers, the effect on consumption of varying amounts of dividend payments is probably negligible.

It is admitted that higher wages have been a factor which has added to inflation since World War II. In so far as accounting methods contributed to the ease of securing these wage increases by organized labor, it can be said that accounting methods accentuated the upswing. However, it was found that the "ability-to-pay" criterion, which links the increased wages with accounting methodology, was not taken very seriously by organized labor. It is possible that high reported profits may have affected the atmosphere in which postwar collective bargaining took place, but it is not possible from this study to say to what extent. Due to the traditional distrust of accounting statements by the leaders of organized labor, it is likely that any accounting techniques that would have resulted in smaller reported profits would have been acclaimed by them as just another device for hiding "excessive" profits. Therefore, it is unlikely that wage demands would have been reduced by a change in accounting methods designed to stabilize profits cyclically.

The theory that accounting methodology accentuates business fluctuations by influencing business pricing policies depends on three postulates: (1) certain prices are not cyclically flexible; (2) these prices are largely based on accounting costs which are inflexible cyclically; and (3) inflexible prices accentuate the cycle. It has been found that the degree of price flexibility is itself a debatable question. Price-making on the basis of cost is most applicable to oligopolistic markets, but even here, cost is only one factor which is considered in setting price. Furthermore, when cost-plus pricing is used, there is evidence that it is not usually average cost determined by taking total historical costs from accounting records and dividing by the number of units produced, as is often implied. For the depression phase, no evidence was found to substantiate or refute the claim that accounting costs are those widely used in price setting. It may be possible that the use of accounting costs may be one factor contributing to the reluctance of businessmen to lower prices, especially in oligopolistic markets during depression. However, the role of price flexibility itself as a factor in business fluctuations is an unsettled one. If price inflexibility does accentuate business fluctuations, the possibility exists that accounting methodology may have been one of the contributing factors during the depressed thirties.

An attempt was also made *to determine if there have been changes in the institutional arrangement, or in accounting techniques, since*

Schmidt's day that would tend to modify the significance of accounting methodology as an accentuating factor in business fluctuations.

Since Schmidt wrote his treatise in 1927, there have been changes in both the institutional arrangement within which business operates, and in accounting techniques, that would tend to weaken accounting methodology as an accentuating factor in making investment decisions.

Assuming that the same accounting methods are used for computing profits, both for profit reporting and for income tax purposes, it was mentioned earlier that the higher the tax rate, the smaller the spread between profits, after tax, when computed by traditional methods, and methods which partially iron out cyclical fluctuations in profits. Income tax rates have increased enormously since the time of Schmidt's writings. Therefore, it is possible that this increase in tax rates decreases the importance of accounting methodology as an accentuating factor. Since governmental expenditures are largely independent of the methods of accounting used by business firms, it follows that an increase in the proportion of total expenditures made by governmental units constitutes an institutional arrangement which tends to weaken accounting methodology as an accentuating factor.

The increasing use of Lifo by business firms as the method of inventory valuation for financial reporting represents a change in accounting techniques which would tend to weaken accounting methodology as an accentuating factor. Furthermore, the use of this method is concentrated in the larger corporations, especially those in which the value of inventories is sizable, which gives to this factor a significance not indicated by reference to the number of companies using it. Moreover, the nature of accounting profits is now better understood by businessmen than at the time of Schmidt's writings. This fact has decreased any tendency of the businessman to overinvest during the upswing and to underinvest during the downswing as a result of the "misstatement" of profits by accounting methods.

Both the degree of competition and the size of the business unit are factors which have a bearing on the proposition that accounting methodology accentuates business fluctuations. It is the assumption of competition which gives profit maximization its a priori plausibility. The nearer a firm approaches the competitive pattern, the stronger the profit motive; the stronger the profit motive, the closer the tie between accounting methods and business investment decisions. Since the demand curve is known under pure competition, the entrepreneur tends to focus his attention on output and cost calculations. Since it is accounting cost calculations which are said to be misleading, it follows that the more crucial these calculations become, the greater the weight which should be assigned to accounting methodology as a factor in making business investment decisions. However, under oligopoly, the possibility exists that, even in the short run, accounting costs affect selling prices. Selling prices may affect the volume of sales which, in turn, affects investment.

The possibility that accounting methodology influences business investment decisions is, in general, more remote in the larger corporation than in the smaller one. Students of investment decisions have found that in the large corporations they tend to be group decisions in which engineers, economists, and accountants, as well as others, participate. Hence no one method of calculation nor one pattern of thinking is likely to prevail. It has also been shown that large corporations have most of the research facilities. As a result, it is the large firm from which autonomous investment can be expected. In the larger corporation, the profit motive, especially in the short run, tends to be less direct than in the smaller firm. The fact that the larger corporations will, in general, be less competitive than the smaller firms also makes the profit motive, in the short run, less direct in the larger corporation.

At present, very little is actually known as to what factors are considered by the businessman in making investment decisions. Even less is known as to the relative weights assigned by him to the factors which he does consider in making these decisions. So far, the studies on investment behavior have been only pilot studies. Furthermore, most of this investigation has been done since 1940, and is, therefore, largely applicable to the prosperity phase of the cycle. The controversy over price flexibility as a factor in business fluctuations is also an unsettled one. Until more light is shed on these three problems, the possibility that, on balance, accounting methodology may accentuate business fluctuations should not be completely brushed aside. However, despite the fact that the majority of writers who have touched on the subject believe that accounting methodology does accentuate business fluctuations, the evidence, at present, does not support the theory.

In conclusion, by disavowing his belief in certain of the dire consequences of "wrong" accounting, it is conceivable that the author may be identified in some readers' minds with the staunch advocates of traditional accounting methods. It is reiterated, however, that his intent was neither to defend nor to condemn these conventional methods, but rather to evaluate the results that have been attributed to them.

Bibliography

BOOKS

ABRAMOVITZ, MOSES. *Inventories and Business Cycles.* New York: National Bureau of Economic Research, Inc., 1950.

ANDREWS, P. W. S., and BRUNNER, ELIZABETH. *Capital Development in Steel.* Oxford: The Alden Press, 1951.

BONBRIGHT, JAMES C. *The Valuation of Property.* Vol. 1. New York: McGraw-Hill Book Company, Inc., 1937.

BOULDING, KENNETH. *Economic Analysis.* Rev. ed. New York: Harper & Brothers, Publishers, 1948.

BROWN, E. CARY. *Depreciation Adjustments for Price Changes.* Cambridge: The Riverside Press, 1952.

BUCHANAN, NORMAN S. *The Economics of Corporate Enterprise.* New York: Henry Holt and Company, 1940.

BURNS, ARTHUR ROBERT. *The Decline of Competition.* New York: McGraw-Hill Book Company, Inc., 1936.

BUTTERS, J. KEITH, and NILAND, POWELL. *Effects of Taxation—Inventory Accounting and Policies.* Cambridge: The Riverside Press, 1949.

CHASE, STUART. *Idle Money Idle Men.* New York: Harcourt, Brace and Company, 1940.

CLARK, JOHN MAURICE. *Studies in the Economics of Overhead Costs.* Chicago: The University of Chicago Press, 1923.

COTTER, ARUNDEL. *Fool's Profits.* New York: Barron's Publishing Company, Inc., 1940.

COWLES, ALFRED, 3RD, and ASSOCIATES. *Common Stock Indexes 1871-1937.* Bloomington, Indiana: Principia Press, Inc., 1938.

DEAN, JOEL. *Capital Budgeting.* New York: Columbia University Press, 1951.

———. *Managerial Economics.* New York: Prentice-Hall, Inc., 1951.

DEWING, ARTHUR STONE. *The Financial Policy of Corporations.* 2 vols. 5th ed. New York: The Ronald Press Company, 1953.

DICKINSON, Z. CLARK. *Collective Wage Determination.* New York: The Ronald Press Company, 1941.

DOBB, MAURICE. *Capitalist Enterprise and Social Progress.* London: George Routledge and Sons, Ltd., 1925.

DOBROVOLSKY, SERGEI P. *Corporate Income Retention 1915-43.* New York: National Bureau of Economic Research, 1951.

EISNER, ROBERT. "Interview and Other Survey Techniques and the Study of Investment," *Problems of Capital Formation.* A Report of the National Bureau of Economic Research. Conference on Research in Income and Wealth. Princeton: Princeton University Press, 1957.

ESTEY, JAMES ARTHUR. *Business Cycles.* New York: Prentice-Hall, Inc., 1946.

FABRICANT, SOLOMON. *Capital Consumption and Adjustment.* New York: National Bureau of Economic Research, 1938.

———. "On the Treatment of Corporate Savings in the Measurement of National Income," *Studies in Income and Wealth.* Vol. I. New York: National Bureau of Economic Research, 1937.

FINNEY, H. A., AND MILLER, HERBERT E. *Principles of Accounting—Intermediate,* 5th ed. New York: Prentice-Hall, Inc., 1958.

FRIEND, IRWIN, AND NATRELLA, VITO. *Individuals' Saving.* New York: John Wiley and Sons, Inc., 1954.

GALBRAITH, J. K. "Monopoly and the Concentration of Economic Power," *A Survey of Contemporary Economics.* Edited by Howard S. Ellis. Philadelphia: The Blakiston Company, 1948.

GOLDSMITH, RAYMOND W. *A Study of Saving in the United States.* Vols. I and II. Princeton: Princeton University Press, 1955.

GOODBAR, JOSEPH E., AND BERGERON, LORENZO U. *A Creative Capitalism.* Boston: Boston University Press, 1948.

GRAHAM, BENJAMIN, AND DODD, DAVID L. *Security Analysis.* 3rd ed. New York: McGraw-Hill Book Company, Inc., 1951.

GRANT, EUGENE L., AND NORTON, PAUL T., JR. *Depreciation.* New York: The Ronald Press Company, 1949.

HALL, R. L., AND HITCH, C. J. "Price Theory and Business Behavior," *Oxford Studies in the Price Mechanism.* Edited by T. Wilson and P. W. S. Andrews. Oxford: At the Clarendon Press, 1951.

HANSEN, ALVIN H. *Business Cycles and National Income.* New York: W. W. Norton and Company, Inc., 1951.

———. *Fiscal Policy and Business Cycles.* New York: W. W. Norton and Company, Inc., 1941.

HAROLD, GILBERT. *Bond Ratings as an Investment Guide.* New York: The Ronald Press Company, 1938.

HEFLEBOWER, RICHARD B. "Full Costs, Cost Changes, and Prices," *Business Concentration and Price Policy.* Princeton: Princeton University Press, 1955.

HICKS, J. R. *Value and Capital.* 2nd ed. Oxford: At the Clarendon Press, 1950.

KATONA, GEORGE. *Psychological Analysis of Economic Behavior.* New York: McGraw-Hill Book Company, Inc., 1951.

KEYNES, JOHN MAYNARD. *The General Theory of Employment, Interest, and Money.* New York: Harcourt, Brace and Company, 1935.

KLEIN, LAWRENCE R. "Savings Concepts and Data: The Needs of Economic Analysis and Policy," *Savings in the Modern Economy.* Edited by Walter W. Heller, Francis M. Boddy, and Carl L. Nelson. Minneapolis: University of Minnesota Press, 1953.

KOCH, ALBERT RALPH. *The Financing of Large Corporations 1920-39.* New York: National Bureau of Economic Research, 1943.

KUZNETS, SIMON. "Changing Inventory Valuations and Their Effect on Business Savings and on National Income Produced," *Studies in Income and Wealth.* Vol. I. New York: National Bureau of Economic Research, 1937.

LACEY, K. *Profit Measurement and Price Changes.* London: Sir Isaac Pitman and Sons, Ltd., 1952.

LAVINGTON, F. *The Trade Cycle.* P. S. King and Son, Ltd., 1922.

LUTZ, FRIEDRICH A. *Corporate Cash Balances 1914-43.* New York: National Bureau of Economic Research, 1945.

MACHLUP, FRITZ. *The Economics of Sellers' Competition.* Baltimore: The Johns Hopkins Press, 1952.

MACK, RUTH P. *The Flow of Funds and Consumer Purchasing Power.* New York: Columbia University Press, 1941.

MEYER, JOHN R., AND KUH, EDWIN. *The Investment Decision: An Empirical Study.* Cambridge: Harvard University Press, 1957.

MITCHELL, WESLEY C. *Business Cycles: The Problem and Its Setting.* New York: National Bureau of Economic Research, Inc., 1927.

MORGAN, JAMES. "Comment," *Problems of Capital Formation.* A Report of the National Bureau of Economic Research. Conference on Research in Income and Wealth. Princeton: Princeton University Press, 1957.

MOULTON, HAROLD G. *Controlling Factors in Economic Development.* Washington: The Brookings Institution, 1949.

NEAL, ALFRED C. *Industrial Concentration and Price Inflexibility.* Washington: American Council on Public Affairs (Public Affairs Press), 1942.

NOURSE, EDWIN G. *Price Making in a Democracy.* Washington: The Brookings Institution, 1944.

———, AND DRURY, HORACE B. *Industrial Price Policies and Economic Progress.* Washington: The Brookings Institution, 1938.

OXENFELDT, ALFRED R. *Industrial Pricing and Market Practices.* New York: Prentice-Hall, Inc., 1951.

PATON, WILLIAM A. *Advanced Accounting.* New York: The Macmillan Company, 1947.

PIGOU, A. C. *Industrial Fluctuations.* London: Macmillan and Co., Limited, 1929.

PROCHNOW, HERBERT V. (ed.). *Determining the Business Outlook.* New York: Harper & Brothers, 1954.

SAXTON, C. CLIVE. *The Economics of Price Determination.* London: Oxford University Press, 1942.

SCHMIDT, CARL T. *German Business Cycles 1914-1933.* New York: National Bureau of Economic Research, 1934.

SLOAN, LAURENCE H., AND ASSOCIATES. *Two Cycles of Corporation Profits.* New York: Harper & Brothers, 1936.

TERBORGH, GEORGE. *Realistic Depreciation Policy.* Chicago: Machinery and Allied Products Institute, 1954.

TINBERGEN, JAN, AND POLAK, J. J. *The Dynamics of Business Cycles.* Chicago: The University of Chicago Press, 1950.

TURGOT, ANNE ROBERT JACQUES. *Reflections on the Formation and the Distribution of Riches.* New York: The Macmillan Company, 1898.

VEBLEN, THORSTEIN. *The Theory of Business Enterprise.* New York: Charles Scribner's Sons, 1904.

WHITNEY, SIMON N. *Trade Associations and Industrial Control.* New York: Central Book Company, 1934.

GOVERNMENTAL PUBLICATIONS

ALTMAN, OSCAR L. *Saving, Investment, and National Income.* Temporary National Economic Committee Monograph No. 37. Washington: U.S. Government Printing Office, 1941.

Economic Report of the President. Transmitted to the Congress, January 24, 1956. Washington: U.S. Government Printing Office, 1956.

FRIEND, IRWIN, AND BRONFENBRENNER, JEAN. "Business Investment Programs and Their Realization," *Survey of Current Business,* December, 1950, pp. 11-22.

GOLDSMITH, RAYMOND W. *The Distribution of Ownership in the 200 Largest Nonfinancial Corporations.* Temporary National Economic Committee Monograph No. 29. Washington: U.S. Government Printing Office, 1940.

HANSEN, ALVIN H. "Price Flexibility and Full Employment of Resources," *The Structure of the American Economy,* Part II. National Resources Planning Board. Washington: U.S. Government Printing Office, June, 1940.

MEANS, GARDINER C. *Industrial Prices and Their Relative Inflexibility.* Senate Document No. 13. 74th Cong., 1st Sess. Washington: U.S. Government Printing Office, 1935.

NATIONAL RESOURCES COMMITTEE. *The Structure of the American Economy,* Part I. A Report Prepared by the Industrial Section under the Direction of Gardiner C. Means. Washington: U.S. Government Printing Office, June, 1939.

NELSON, SAUL. *Price Behavior and Business Policy.* Temporary National Economic Committee Monograph No. 1. Washington: U.S. Government Printing Office, 1940.

PEARCE, CHARLES ALBERT. *Trade Association Survey.* Temporary National Economic Committee Monograph No. 18. Washington: U.S. Government Printing Office, 1941.

The Relationship of Prices to Economic Stability and Growth. Compendium of Papers Submitted by Panelists Appearing Before the Joint Economic Committee. 85th Cong. 2d Sess. Washington: U.S. Government Printing Office, March 31, 1958.

TAITEL, MARTIN. *Profits, Productive Activities, and New Investment.* Temporary National Economic Committee Monograph No. 12. Washington: U.S. Government Printing Office, 1941.

U.S. CONGRESS. *Corporate Profits.* Hearings Before the Joint Committee on the Economic Report. 80th Cong., 2d Sess. Washington: U.S. Government Printing Office, 1949.

———. *Profits.* A Report of a Subcommittee of the Joint Committee on the Economic Report on Profit Hearings. 80th Cong., 2d Sess. Washington: U.S. Government Printing Office, 1949.

———. *Saving and Investment.* Hearings Before the Temporary National Economic Committee, Part 9. 76th Cong., 1st Sess. Washington: U.S. Government Printing Office, May, 1939.

———, Staff of the Subcommittee on Investment, Joint Committee on the Economic Report. *Factors Affecting Volume and Stability of Private Investment.* Senate Document No. 232, 81st Cong., 2d Sess. Washington: U.S. Government Printing Office, 1950.

U.S. DEPARTMENT OF COMMERCE. *Survey of Current Business,* May, 1953, and July, 1958.

———, Office of Business Economics. *National Income—A Supplement to the Survey of Current Business.* Washington: U.S. Government Printing Office, 1951.

———, Office of Business Economics. *National Income—A Supplement to the Survey of Current Business.* Washington: U.S. Government Printing Office, 1954.

BULLETINS, MONOGRAPHS, AND REPORTS

AMERICAN ACCOUNTING ASSOCIATION, Committee on Concepts and Standards Underlying Corporate Financial Statements. "Price Level Changes and Financial Statements," *The Accounting Review,* October, 1951, pp. 468-474.

———, Executive Committee. "Accounting Concepts and Standards Underlying Corporate Financial Statements," *The Accounting Review,* October, 1948, pp. 339-344.

American Economic Association. "The Problem of Economic Instability." A Report Prepared by a Subcommittee of the Committee on Public Issues, *The American Economic Review,* XL (1950), 505-538.

American Institute of Accountants. *Accounting Trends and Techniques.* Annual Cumulative Surveys Prepared by the Research Department. New York: American Institute of Accountants, 1950, 1953, and 1957.

———. *Changing Concepts of Business Income.* Report of Study Group on Business Income. New York: The Macmillan Company, 1952.

———, Committee on Accounting Procedure. *Accounting Research Bulletins No. 5, No. 8, No. 16, No. 22, No. 29, and No. 33.*

———, Research Department. "Inventories," *The Journal of Accountancy,* October, 1940, pp. 324-335.

Backman, Jules. *Economics of a Fourth Round Wage Increase.* Testimony on Behalf of Steel Companies Before the Presidential Steel Board, August, 1949.

Bissell, Richard M., Jr. "Prices, Costs, and Investment," *Papers and Proceedings of the Fifty-third Annual Meeting of the American Economic Association. The American Economic Review,* February, 1941, pp. 200-227.

Blackie, William. "What is Accounting Accounting For—Now?" *National Association of Cost Accountants Conference Proceedings,* 1948, pp. 26-54.

Blough, Carman G. "The Accountants' View." *Replacement Costs and Depreciation Policy.* Studies in Business Policy No. 27. New York: National Industrial Conference Board, January, 1948, pp. 9-11.

Broad, Samuel J. "The Effects of Price Level Changes on Financial Statements." *National Association of Cost Accountants Conference Proceedings,* 1948, pp. 7-25.

Buchanan, Norman S. "Anticipations and Industrial Investment Decisions," *Papers and Proceedings of the Fifty-fourth Annual Meeting of the American Economic Association. The American Economic Review Supplement No. 1,* March, 1942, pp. 141-155.

Dale, Ernest. *Sources of Economic Information for Collective Bargaining.* Research Report No. 17. New York: American Management Association, 1950.

de Chazeau, Melvin G. "Regularization of Fixed Capital Investment by the Individual Firm," *Regularization of Business Investment.* A Report of the National Bureau of Economic Research. Special Conference Series No. 4. Princeton: Princeton University Press, 1954, pp. 75-109.

Eisner, Robert. *Determinants of Capital Expenditures.* Studies in Business Expectations and Planning, Number 2. Urbana: University of Illinois Press, 1956.

Fabricant, Solomon. *Measures of Capital Consumption, 1919-1933.* National Bureau of Economic Research Bulletin No. 60, June 30, 1936.

———. *Revaluations of Fixed Assets, 1925-1934.* National Bureau of Economic Research Bulletin No. 62, December 7, 1936.

Farmer, N. D. "The Argument in Favor of Depreciation on Replacement Values," *National Association of Cost Accountants Yearbook,* 1923, pp. 191-197.

Finley, James A. *Handling Higher Replacement Costs.* Studies in Business Policy No. 47. New York: National Industrial Conference Board, 1950.

Gaston, J. Frank. *Effects of Depreciation Policy.* Studies in Business Economics No. 22. New York: National Industrial Conference Board, 1950.

Goldsmith, Selma F. "Statistical Information on the Distribution of Income by Size in the United States," *Papers and Proceedings of the Sixty-second Annual Meeting of the American Economic Association. The American Economic Review,* May, 1950, pp. 321-341.

HESSE, FRANK M. "Management's Viewpoint," *Replacement Costs and Depreciation Policy.* Studies in Business Policy No. 27. New York: National Industrial Conference Board, January, 1948, pp. 12-14.

LITTLETON, A. C. "The Relation of Accounting to the Business Cycle," *Papers and Proceedings of the Ninth Annual Meeting of the American Association of University Instructors in Accounting.* Chicago: The Association, 1924, pp. 108-116.

MEANS, GARDINER C. "Notes on Inflexible Prices," *Papers and Proceedings of the Forty-eighth Annual Meeting of the American Economic Association. The American Economic Review,* March, 1936, pp. 23-35.

MILLS, FREDERICK C. *Changes in Physical Production, Industrial Productivity and Manufacturing Costs, 1927-1932.* National Bureau of Economic Research Bulletin No. 45, February 20, 1933.

NATIONAL ASSOCIATION OF COST ACCOUNTANTS. "Product Costs for Pricing Purposes." Research Series No. 24. *N. A. C. A. Bulletin,* August, 1953.

NATIONAL BUREAU OF ECONOMIC RESEARCH. *Cost Behavior and Price Policy.* A Study Prepared by the Committee on Price Determination for the Conference on Price Research. New York: National Bureau of Economic Research, 1943.

NOURSE, EDWIN G. "Cost Finding and Price Determination," *National Association of Cost Accountants Year Book,* 1945, pp. 27-39.

OPINION RESEARCH CORPORATION. *The Public's Acceptance of the Facts and Figures of Business Accounting.* A Survey for Controllership Foundation, Inc. Princeton: Opinion Research Corporation, March 19, 1947.

PATON, W. A., AND LITTLETON, A. C. *An Introduction to Corporate Accounting Standards.* American Accounting Association, 1940.

PILLSBURY, WILBUR F. *The Use of Corporate Financial Statements and Related Data by Organized Labor.* Indiana Business Report No. 18. Bloomington: Bureau of Business Research, Indiana University, November, 1954.

SCHMIDT, FRITZ. "The Valuation of Fixed Assets in Financial Statements," *Proceedings of the International Congress on Accounting,* 1929.

———. "Die Industriekonjunktur—ein Rechenfehler!" *Zeitschrift für Betriebswirtschaft,* 2. Sonderheft, 1927.

SIMPSON, KEMPER. "Security Markets and the Investment Process," *Papers and Proceedings of the Fiftieth Annual Meeting of the American Economic Association. The American Economic Review,* March, 1938, pp. 41-55.

SLICHTER, SUMNER H. *Basic Criteria Used in Wage Negotiations.* Chicago: The Chicago Association of Commerce and Industry, 1947.

———. "Wages and Prices," *Proceedings of the Academy of Political Science,* XXIII (1948-1950), 47-63.

SWIFT AND COMPANY, *50th Anniversary Year Book,* 1935.

TERBORGH, GEORGE W. *Depreciation Policy and the Postwar Price Level.* Chicago: Machinery and Allied Products Institute, 1949.

———. "Economic Aspects of Underdepreciation," *Replacement Costs and Depreciation Policy.* Studies in Business Policy No. 27. New York: National Industrial Conference Board, Inc., January, 1948, pp. 5-7.

UPGREN, ARTHUR; BODDY, FRANK; NELSON, CARL; AND HELLER, WALTER. *The Minneapolis Project—A Pilot Study of Local Capital Formation.* Minneapolis: Investors' Diversified Services, Inc., 1950.

WATSON, JOHN H., III. *Controlling Capital Expenditures.* Studies in Business

Policy No. 62. New York: National Industrial Conference Board, April, 1953.
WOYTINSKY, W. S., AND ASSOCIATES. *Labor and Management Look at Collective Bargaining.* New York: The Twentieth Century Fund, 1949.

ARTICLES

ADAMS, WALTER. "Accounting Practices and the Business Cycle," *The Journal of Business,* April, 1949, pp. 119-133.

ARTHUR, HENRY B. "Inventory Profits in the Business Cycle," *The American Economic Review,* March, 1938, pp. 27-40.

———. "Something Business Can Do About Depressions," *The Journal of Accountancy,* January, 1939, pp. 7-14.

BACKMAN, JULES. "The Causes of Price Inflexibility," *The Quarterly Journal of Economics,* May, 1940, pp. 474-489.

———. "Price Inflexibility and Changes in Production," *The American Economic Review,* September, 1939, pp. 480-486.

BARKIN, SOLOMON. "Financial Statements in Collective Bargaining," *The New York Certified Public Accountant,* July, 1953, pp. 439-446.

———. "A Trade Unionist Views Net Income Determination," *N. A. C. A. Bulletin,* June, 1951, pp. 1193-1206.

BAUER, JOHN. "Renewal Costs and Business Profits in Relation to Rising Prices," *The Journal of Accountancy,* December, 1919, pp. 413-419.

BAXTER, W. T. "The Accountant's Contribution to the Trade Cycle," *Economica,* May, 1955, pp. 99-112.

BELL, JOHN N. "Shall We Take Heavier Depreciation in Earlier Years?" *N. A. C. A. Bulletin,* November, 1955, pp. 335-342.

BERNSTEIN, PETER L. "Profit Theory—Where Do We Go from Here?" *The Quarterly Journal of Economics,* August, 1953, pp. 407-422.

BLOUGH, CARMAN G. "Changing Accounting and Economic Concepts Affect Methods of Inventory Pricing," *The Journal of Accountancy,* September, 1948, pp. 204-212.

"Box Score of Business Bigness," *Fortune,* July, 1955, pp. 96-97.

BRAY, F. SEWELL. "Accounting Dynamics—III," *Accounting Research,* July, 1955, pp. 267-280.

BUCHANAN, NORMAN S. "Toward a Theory of Fluctuations in Business Profits," *The American Economic Review,* December, 1941, pp. 731-753.

BURNS, ARTHUR ROBERT. "The Organization of Industry and the Theory of Prices," *The Journal of Political Economy,* October, 1937, pp. 662-680.

BURREL, O. K. "Dividends vs. Retained Earnings as a Market Force," *The Commercial and Financial Chronicle,* August 21, 1952, pp. 1, 29, 30.

CANNING, JOHN B. "A Certain Erratic Tendency in Accountants' Income Procedure," *Econometrica,* I (1933), 52-62.

COX, GARFIELD V. "The Relation of Stock Prices to Earnings," *The Journal of Business,* October, 1929, pp. 383-395.

DALE, ERNEST. "The Accountant's Part in Labor-Management Relations," *The Journal of Accountancy,* July, 1950, pp. 12-25.

DEAN, JOEL. "Measurement of Profits for Executive Decisions," *The Accounting Review,* April, 1951, pp. 185-196.

———. "Measuring the Productivity of Capital," *Harvard Business Review,* January-February, 1954, pp. 120-130.

DE CHAZEAU, MELVIN G. "Can We Avoid Depression in a Dynamic Economy?" *Harvard Business Review,* July-August, 1954, pp. 37-44.

DEVINE, CARL THOMAS. "Depreciation and Income Measurement," *The Accounting Review,* January, 1944, pp. 39-47.

DOBROVOLSKY, S. P. "Depreciation Policies and Investment Decisions," *The American Economic Review,* December, 1951, pp. 906-914.

DOMAR, EVSEY D. "The Case for Accelerated Depreciation," *The Quarterly Journal of Economics,* November, 1953, pp. 493-519.

———. "A Rejoinder," *The Quarterly Journal of Economics,* May, 1955, pp. 299-304.

EDDY, GEORGE A. "Security Issues and Real Investment in 1929," *The Review of Economic Statistics,* May, 1937, pp. 79-91.

EISNER, ROBERT. "Accelerated Depreciation: Some Further Thoughts," *The Quarterly Journal of Economics,* May, 1955, pp. 285-296.

EZEKIEL, MORDECAI. "Statistical Investigations of Saving, Consumption, and Investment," *The American Economic Rievew,* June, 1942, pp. 272-307.

FETTER, FRANK A. "Reformulation of the Concepts of Capital and Income in Economics and Accounting," *The Accounting Review,* March, 1937, pp. 3-12.

FROEHLICH, WALTER. "The Role of Income Determination in Reinvestment and Investment," *The American Economic Review,* March, 1948, pp. 78-91.

GALBRAITH, J. K. "Monopoly Power and Price Rigidities," *The Quarterly Journal of Economics,* May, 1936, pp. 456-475.

GOODE, RICHARD. "Accelerated Depreciation Allowances as a Stimulus to Investment," *The Quarterly Journal of Economics,* May, 1955, pp. 191-220.

GORDON, R. A. "Short-Period Price Determination in Theory and Practice," *The American Economic Review,* June, 1948, pp. 265-288.

GORT, MICHAEL. "The Planning of Investment: A Study of Capital Budgeting in the Electric-Power Industry. II," *The Journal of Business,* July, 1951, pp. 181-202.

GRADY, PAUL. "Accounting for Fixed Assets and Their Amortization," *The Accounting Review,* January, 1950, pp. 3-19.

GRAHAM, WILLARD J. "The Effect of Changing Price Levels upon the Determination, Reporting, and Interpretation of Income," *The Accounting Review,* January, 1949, pp. 15-26.

HART, ALBERT GAILORD. "Failure and Fulfillment of Expectations in Business Fluctuations," *The Review of Economic Statistics,* May, 1937, pp. 69-78.

HASBROUCK, H. C. "Cost vs. Value in Depreciation Accounting for Public Utilities," *The Journal of Accountancy,* October, 1923, pp. 276-280.

HATFIELD, HENRY RAND. "Replacement and Book Value," *The Accounting Review,* January, 1944, pp. 66-67.

HEILMAN, E. A. "Realized Income," *The Accounting Review,* June, 1929, pp. 80-87.

HELLER, WALTER W. "The Anatomy of Investment Decisions," *Harvard Business Review,* March, 1951, pp. 95-103.

HENDRIKSEN, ELDON S. "The Influence of Depreciation Accounting on National Income," *The Accounting Review,* October, 1951, pp. 507-515.

HEPWORTH, SAMUEL R. "Smoothing Periodic Income," *The Accounting Review,* January, 1953, pp. 32-39.

HORNGREN, CHARLES T. "Security Analysts and the Price Level," *The Accounting Review,* October, 1955, pp. 575-581.

"Industry's 1950 Capital Spending Plans," *Business Week,* January 21, 1950, pp. 73-80.

JONES, RALPH C. "Effect of Inflation on Capital and Profits: The Record of Nine Steel Companies," *The Journal of Accountancy,* January, 1949, pp. 9-27.

KATONA, GEORGE, AND MORGAN, JAMES N. "The Quantitative Study of Factors Determining Business Decisions," *The Quarterly Journal of Economics,* February, 1952, pp. 67-90.

KENNEDY, E. D. "Steel Man's Story," *The New Republic,* March 11, 1940, pp. 336-339.

KNIGHT, FRANK H. "Profit," *Encyclopaedia of the Social Sciences,* Vol. XII, 1933.

LACEY, K. "Profit Measurement and the Trade Cycle," *The Economic Journal,* December, 1947, pp. 456-474.

LACHMANN, L. M. "Investment and Costs of Production," *The American Economic Review,* September, 1938, pp. 469-481.

LANZILLOTTI, ROBERT F. "Pricing Objectives in Large Companies," *American Economic Review,* December, 1958, pp. 921-940.

LITTLETON, A. C. "What is Profit?" *The Accounting Review,* September, 1928, pp. 278-288.

MACHLUP, FRITZ. "Marginal Analysis and Empirical Research," *The American Economic Review,* September, 1946, pp. 519-554.

MARPLE, R. P. "Depreciation Policy in Manufacturing Industries," *N. A. C. A. Bulletin,* May 1, 1936, pp. 1053-1061.

MASON, PERRY. "The Financial Aspects of Depreciation Accounting," *The Accounting Review,* September, 1935, pp. 238-246.

MCANLY, H. T. "Curbing the Effect of Our Erratic Dollar in Pricing Inventories and Providing for Depreciation," *The New York Certified Public Accountant,* August, 1948, pp. 573-582.

METZLER, LLOYD A. "Factors Governing the Length of Inventory Cycles," *The Review of Economic Statistics,* February, 1947, pp. 1-15.

MIDDLEDITCH, LIVINGSTON, JR. "Should Accounts Reflect the Changing Value of the Dollar?" *The Journal of Accountancy,* February, 1918, pp. 114-120.

MITCHELL, WESLEY C. "Accountants and Economics with Reference to the Business Cycle," *The Journal of Accountancy,* March, 1923, pp. 161-171.

MORTON, WALTER A. "Trade Unionism, Full Employment, and Inflation," *The American Economic Review,* March, 1950, pp. 13-39.

NERLOVE, S. H. "Recent Writings on Profits," *The Journal of Business,* October, 1929, pp. 361-382.

OXENFELDT, ALFRED R. "How to Use Market-Share Measurement," *Harvard Business Review,* January-February, 1959, pp. 59-69.

PATON, W. A. "Depreciation, Appreciation and Productive Capacity," *The Journal of Accountancy,* July, 1920, pp. 1-11.

———. "Measuring Profits Under Inflation Conditions: A Serious Problem for Accountants," *The Journal of Accountancy,* January, 1950, pp. 16-27.

PERLO, VICTOR. " 'People's Capitalism' and Stock-Ownership," *The American Economic Review,* June, 1958, pp. 333-347.

PIGOU, A. C. "Net Income and Capital Depletion," *The Economic Journal,* June, 1935, pp. 235-241.

PREST, A. R. "Replacement Cost Depreciation," *Accounting Research,* I (November, 1948-July, 1950), 385-402.

PUTNAM, GEORGE E. "The Role of Paper Profits in Industry," *Harvard Business Review,* January, 1926, pp. 129-137.

———. "What Shall We Do About Depressions?" *The Journal of Business,* April, 1938, pp. 130-147.

REDER, M. W. "A Reconstruction of the Marginal Productivity Theory," *The Journal of Political Economy,* October, 1947, pp. 450-458.

"Research Dollars Grow with Sales," *The Conference Board Business Record,* November, 1951, pp. 465-467.

ROTHSCHILD, K. W. "Price Theory and Oligopoly," *The Economic Journal,* September, 1947, pp. 299-320.

SCHMIDT, FRITZ. "The Basis of Depreciation Charges," *Harvard Business Review,* April, 1930, pp. 257-264.

———. "The Importance of Replacement Value," *The Accounting Review,* September, 1930, pp. 235-242.

———. "Is Appreciation Profit?" *The Accounting Review,* December, 1931, pp. 289-293.

SHOVE, G. F. "The Place of Marshall's *Principles* in the Development of Economic Theory," *The Economic Journal,* December, 1942, pp. 294-329.

SILBERMAN, CHARLES E., AND PARKER, SANFORD S. "The Economy's Scouts," *Fortune,* December, 1955, pp. 100-103, 242, 244, 247, 248.

SINGER, H. W. "Profit Measurement and the Trade Cycle," *The Economic Journal,* December, 1948, pp. 594-596.

SLICHTER, SUMNER H. "Must We Have Another Boom?" *The Atlantic Monthly,* May, 1937, pp. 600-607.

———. "Thinking Ahead," *Harvard Business Review,* January-February, 1955, pp. 19, 22, 25, 26, 28, 30, 152, 154, 158, 160, 162.

SWEENEY, HENRY W. "Effects of Inflation on German Accounting," *The Journal of Accountancy,* March, 1927, pp. 180-191.

———. "Maintenance of Capital," *The Accounting Review,* December, 1930, pp. 277-287.

SWEET, HOMER N. "The Case for a 'Cost or Market' Basis," *N. A. C. A. Bulletin,* December 1, 1937, pp. 400-409.

TAUSSIG, F. W. "The Employer's Place in Distribution," *The Quarterly Journal of Economics,* October, 1895, pp. 67-94.

TAYLOR, GEORGE W. "Criteria for Wage Determination." *Management Record,* June, 1949, pp. 241-242.

TEITSWORTH, CLARK S. "Growing Role of the Company Economist," *Harvard Business Review,* January-February, 1959, pp. 97-104.

TINBERGEN, J. "The Dynamics of Share-Price Formation," *The Review of Economic Statistics,* November, 1939, pp. 153-160.

TUCKER, RUFUS S. "The Reasons for Price Rigidity," *The American Economic Review,* March, 1938, pp. 41-54.

VANDERBLUE, HOMER B. "Pricing Policies in the Automobile Industry," *Harvard Business Review,* Summer, 1939, pp. 385-401.

———. "Pricing Policies in the Automobile Industry: Incidence of Demand," *Harvard Business Review,* Autumn, 1939, pp. 64-81.

VATTER, WILLIAM J. "Depreciation Methods of American Industrial Corporations 1927-1935," *The Journal of Business,* April, 1937, pp. 126-146.

WILBUR, DONALD E. "A Study of the Policy of Dividend Stabilization," *Harvard Business Review,* April, 1932, pp. 373-381.

WOODS, J. B. C. "The Accountant's Role in Labor-Management Relations," *The New York Certified Public Accountant,* August, 1954, pp. 499-506.

NEWSPAPERS

The New York Times. March 26, 1946; June 4, 1949; June 17, 1949; June 19, 1949.

MICROFILMS

KOHL, MAYBELLE. *The Role of Accounting in Pricing.* Ann Arbor, Michigan: University Microfilms, 1954.

UNPUBLISHED MATERIAL

BARKIN, SOLOMON. Letter to the writer, December 2, 1955.

GOLDFINGER, NAT. Letter to the writer, January 4, 1956.

Index